WHITE TONGUE, BROWN SKIN

WHITE TONGUE, BROWN SKIN

THE COLONIZED WOMAN AND LANGUAGE

MAYA BOUTAGHOU

UNIVERSITY OF VIRGINIA PRESS
Charlottesville and London

The University of Virginia Press is situated on the traditional lands of the Monacan Nation, and the Commonwealth of Virginia was and is home to many other Indigenous people. We pay our respect to all of them, past and present. We also honor the enslaved African and African American people who built the University of Virginia, and we recognize their descendants. We commit to fostering voices from these communities through our publications and to deepening our collective understanding of their histories and contributions.

University of Virginia Press
© 2024 by the Rector and Visitors of the University of Virginia
All rights reserved
Printed in the United States of America on acid-free paper

First published 2024

9 8 7 6 5 4 3 2 1

LIBRARY OF CONGRESS CATALOGING-IN-PUBLICATION DATA
Names: Boutaghou, Maya, author.
Title: White tongue, brown skin : the colonized woman and language / Maya Boutaghou.
Description: Charlottesville : University of Virginia Press, 2024. | Includes bibliographical references and index.
Identifiers: LCCN 2024010104 (print) | LCCN 2024010105 (ebook) |
  ISBN 9780813952208 (hardcover ; acid-free paper) |
  ISBN 9780813952215 (paperback ; acid-free paper) |
  ISBN 9780813952222 (ebook)
Subjects: LCSH: Dutt, Toru, 1856–1877—Criticism and interpretation. | Ziyādah, Mayy—Criticism and interpretation. | Djebar, Assia, 1936–2015—Criticism and interpretation. | Devi, Ananda—Criticism and interpretation. | Language and languages in literature. | Multilingualism and literature. | Postcolonialism in literature. | Women in literature. |
  BISAC: LITERARY CRITICISM / Feminist | SOCIAL SCIENCE / Ethnic Studies / Asian Studies | LCGFT: Literary criticism.
Classification: LCC PR9499.2.D88 Z58 2024 (print) | LCC PR9499.2.D88 (ebook) | DDC 809/.9334—dc23/eng/20240511
LC record available at https://lccn.loc.gov/2024010104
LC ebook record available at https://lccn.loc.gov/2024010105

The publication of this volume has been supported by *New Literary History*.

Cover art: MaryliaDesign/istock.com
Cover design: Cecilia Sorochin

For Didier Coste and Françoise Lionnet
For their loyal love of literature

To those who see with one eye, speak with one tongue and see things as either black or white, either Eastern or Western.
—TAYEB SALIH, *Season of Migration to the North*

CONTENTS

Acknowledgments	xi
Note on Translations	xii
Introduction	1
1. Who Is the Subject in Translation?	15
2. Being Cosmopolitan in Nineteenth-Century Calcutta: Toru Dutt (1856–1877)	37
3. Being Cosmopolitan in Nineteenth-Century Cairo: Mayy Ziyadah (1886–1941)	66
4. The Maghrebi Bard: Assia Djebar (1935–2015)	85
5. The Mauritian Bard: Ananda Devi (1957–)	117
6. Being a Subject in Translation	142
Conclusion	151
Notes	159
Bibliography	193
Index	209

ACKNOWLEDGMENTS

In academia, writing a book is a life journey with many encounters. With this book too I experienced many, and each conversation guided the process. I would like to start by thanking warmly colleagues and friends who were part of the first steps in this journey: my Andrew Mellon Fellows at UCLA who read the early babbling of the project during our monthly seminar, Sze-Wei Ang, Joseph Bauerkemper, Greg Cohen, Marcela Fuentes, Jeannine Murray-Román, Sonali Pahwa, Sarah Valentine, Travis Workman, and our admired mentors, Françoise Lionnet and Shu-mei Shih. Parts of the project received comments from several colleagues, some of whom are dear friends: Steven Blevins, Caroline Faria, Olivia Harrison, Vrushali Patil, Jean Muteba Rahier, Jahan Ramazani, Janell Rothenberg, Adelaide Russo, Laurie Shrage, and Laetitia Zecchini. A book cannot come into being without important bibliographical work, and I spent time in libraries in different parts of the world. I would like to thank the librarians whose work made this possible in the following libraries: the Librairie Sainte Geneviève (which holds the unique copy of *Fleurs de rêve* by Mayy Ziyadah); the Bibliothèque nationale de France (which holds one of the very few available copies in French of *Le Journal de Mlle d'Arvers*); the Jawaharlal Nehru University library in New Delhi; the Jadavpur University library in Calcutta; the University of California, Los Angeles, library; and the University of Virginia library. I am also grateful for the support of the University of Virginia's Office of the Dean of the College of Arts and Sciences and of *New Literary History*.

NOTE ON TRANSLATIONS

All translations from French and Arabic are mine unless indicated otherwise. Words and texts in Arabic are transliterated using the simplest method.

WHITE TONGUE, BROWN SKIN

INTRODUCTION

Contexts: Place and Time

White Tongue, Brown Skin considers colonialism a disease that introduced symptomatic multilingualism and cultural pluralism in former colonized regions: India, Egypt, Algeria, and Mauritius. *White Tongue, Brown Skin* explores multilingual writings in two periods (the end of the nineteenth century and the second half of twentieth century) and four different colonial contexts while addressing a long-term history of connections between India and Mauritius, as well as between Egypt and Algeria. A synchronic perspective justifies the link between India and Egypt, on the one hand—they both witnessed similar Renaissance movements—and, on the other hand, Algeria and Mauritius as both young, plurilingual, decolonized nations arising in the second half of the twentieth century after gaining their independence in 1962 and 1968, respectively.

The first period discussed in this book will be end-of-the-nineteenth-century India and Egypt. The question here is not about tracing back the history of multilingual writing, but about the constitution of a multilingual, colonial, and postcolonial *self* in nineteenth-century India and Egypt and twentieth-century Algeria and Mauritius, mainly perceived through the paradigmatic literary production of the women writers of these regions. Historically, Egypt and India constituted the models of cultural development for Algeria and Mauritius. At the turn of the century, India and Egypt shared some structural and historical similarities, which permits this comparison between them. My approach therefore sheds light on what is still not commonly recognized in postcolonial studies: a sense of cultural continuity despite colonial intervention.

Moreover, there is a horizontal connection between Egypt and Algeria in terms of cultural and political models of national identity construction. Indeed, both were parts of the collapsing Ottoman Empire, both were under French influence during the nineteenth century, and both exemplify the Pan-Arab/Pan-Islamist affirmation in the early phase of the twentieth century during the rise of nationalism. Finally, India and Mauritius are highly connected in terms of migratory flows; in Mauritius, the most important diasporic population came from India. Mauritius was also colonized by the French and the British.

The writers whose texts I present and analyze are Toru Dutt (1856–1877) from India, Mayy Ziyadah (1886–1941) from Egypt;[1] Assia Djebar (1935–2015) from Algeria, and Ananda Devi (1957–) from Mauritius.[2] For each author, a rich intellectual and historical context will be provided, showing their agency in the cultural life of their time. Regarding Toru Dutt, one cannot ignore the conversation about the modernization of Hinduism (around the Brahmo Samaj movement), nor the impact of nationalist writers such as Bankim Chandra Chatterjee (1838–1894); Rabindranath Tagore (1861–1941); Henry Louis Vivian Derozio (1809–1831), a leading Bengali poet during the Bengali Renaissance; or Dutt's uncle, Romesh Chandra Dutt (1848–1909), who is considered the father of modern Indian history. Between 1913 and 1936, during the Nahda (Arab renaissance), Mayy Ziyadah organized a very successful *salon littéraire* in her house in Cairo. Famous intellectuals were part of the weekly gathering, including Ahmad Lutfi al-Sayyid (1872–1963); the Egyptian politician, judge, and poet 'Abd al-'Aziz Fahmi (1870–1951); the Syrian poet Sulayman al-Bustani (1856–1925); Ahmad Shawqi (1868–1932); and Khalil Mutran (1872–1949). Assia Djebar, the author and filmmaker, celebrated in the 1950s as the new Françoise Sagan, was by the same token an anticolonial fighter and a member of the National Liberation Front (Front de Libération Nationale), whose friendship with Frantz and Josie Fanon, Alice Cherki, and others in her midst are important to understanding her impact as both an engaged intellectual and one of the most internationally acclaimed Francophone Algerian writers. Finally, Ananda Devi, one of the most visible Mauritian authors, is the uncontested leader of contemporary writing in the Indian Ocean, a region that counts among its luminaries such creatives as Marie-Thérèse Humbert, Shenaz Patel, Nathacha Appanah, Sydley Richard Assonne, Yussuf Kadel, Khal Torabully, and Barlen Pyamootoo. Even though the focus of *White*

Tongue, Brown Skin is on these specific figures, the project extends beyond their work to include a large, modern, postcolonial, cultural, and intellectual history in cosmopolitan contexts. My goal is to elaborate a broader understanding of the local histories specific to the emergence of a multilingual *subject*. I shed light on colonized subjectivity by focusing on reading, speaking, translating, and hearing the colonial language, while also bringing into conversation and comparison diverse histories of emerging subjectivity.[3] Postcolonialism from *below*, or from localized histories, starts with an approach grounded (linguistically) in textual analysis in historical contexts—such is the perspective I have developed in my previous books: *Occidentalismes, romans historiques postcoloniaux et identités nationales au dix-neuvième siècle* (Occidentalisms, postcolonial historical novels, and national identity in the nineteenth century, 2016) and *Ernest Renan: "Qu'est-ce qu'une nation?"* (Ernest Renan, 2020). Though the object of this book is philosophical, it is also deeply rooted in history and semiotics to address the specificity of each region and to escape the risk of overlooking cultural differences.

Born to Translate

White Tongue, Brown Skin is the result of a long, inherited struggle against the mainstream discussion around the guilt involved in speaking and writing in the colonial language—here mainly French and English—in formerly colonized regions. This book originates in the following question: What does it mean to be the heir, as a woman writer, of a colonial and postcolonial culture where the use of a European language is perceived as a colonial legacy?

It took some time to appreciate how the argument of this book was more than my own remix of mainstream discourses on the linguistic violence of colonialism established, among others, by Frantz Fanon (1925–1961), Ngugi wa Thiong'o (1938–), and Louis-Jean Calvet (1940–). With this book, I intend to shed light on writers who endorsed the double nature of the colonial experience taking place from the second half of the nineteenth century onward: the birth of a *female subjectivity* in the alluring yet ambiguous moment where the colonized learns the colonizer's language: the birth of a *me* that leads to an *I*.[4] The ontological naissance of the writers analyzed in this book will offer a structure that is applicable to myriad users of colonial languages, including those beyond the gender divide.

First, I must describe and define this "ontological subject"—*sujet*, as in the French, whose meaning is closer to "agent," rather than the English, which is closer to "topic" or "subject matter." In fact, the dynamic of this subject is to be prone to perpetual translation. The Babelic existence of this subject finds its origin in a collectively traumatic experience, grounded in the global history of colonialism. The condition of the colonized subject is rooted in a violently imposed multilingualism embedded in the mind of the individual as the burden of a permanent *self-translation* between two or more languages with unequal political and emotional power. Multilingual by definition, the colonized subject who endures a plural perception of the self, in the psychological sense, must also endure the restless movement of self-translation to maintain a form of sanity, a form of continuous communication between their disparate *selves*. Even after the twentieth-century decolonization movements and subsequent declarations of independence, this ongoing burden of a permanent self-translation has yet to end. The process of a hidden self-translation is addressed in depth here, confirming the actual translation, linguistic, and poetic turn in postcolonial studies, comparative literature, and Francophone studies.[5] In the timeline of intellectual history, the first wave of postcolonial theory was based in an English-speaking context. *White Tongue, Brown Skin* aims to acknowledge the work of theoreticians who initiated the difficult task of addressing the enunciator behind translingual texts. Lise Gauvin's immense contribution to the field of translation is one such, and her concept of *surconscience linguistique* (linguistic overconsciousness) is central to the understanding of the subject in translation.[6] While it is crucial to pay tribute to that first generation of cultural theorists who had the courage to move between two or more languages of empires (French and English), I am both using their legacy and trying to push further that which they have cultivated in the first decades of postcolonial studies. My recognition goes to the work of Françoise Lionnet, who has positioned herself at the intersection between literary criticism, philosophy, and gender studies, putting in dialogue voices twice minoritized: in the realm of literature in general, and in postcolonial Anglophone studies in particular.

The newness of this book is to view colonial experience as an essentially *multicultural and multilingual reality* that transformed, in depth, any language reflected in literary and cultural forms: its goal is to induce multilingual processes of reading and interpreting in postcolonial era.[7] The previous statement echoes Mary Louise Pratt, who has urged scholars to think linguistically: "It is impossible to think seriously about intercultural dialogues without coming to grips with *the linguistic dimension of today's planetary social, ecological, political and imaginary realignments.*"[8] The ambitious project of a new generation of scholars is to return to a literature that functions as a tool for decolonizing discourses and their episteme, in general. Simona Bertacco, in her edited volume *Language and Translation in Postcolonial Literatures* (2014), announced this need to dig deeper in textual analysis using a linguistic approach:[9]

> This volume addresses the issue of language and translation in postcolonial literatures. [. . .] (i) It insists on a return to a closer attention to the formal—and linguistic *in primis*—features of the postcolonial literary text in order to address its multilingual concerns; (ii) it aims at showcasing a critical praxis able to relate those aesthetic features to real-world issues, and it does so by focusing on language, the most pervasive, yet invisible, element in our lives. [. . . .] Working on textuality implies working on how the text is composed, the way in which words are selected and put together, the lines arranged, and this is rarely found in current studies of postcolonial literatures. (21–25)

The linguistic dimension that Bertacco evokes is essential in reading those writers who write under situations of Western colonial domination. Such is the primary topic of this book: the birth of a subject whose experience of the world is rooted in a dynamic, multilingual, urban, colonial situation. This special kind of multilingualism reshaped regions known for their ancient pluralism (mainly in terms of languages, ethnicities, and religions).[10] It is also the birth of a subject whose self emerges in the experience of *translation*. In a way, I am distinguishing against, and developing on, Georges Herbert Mead's theory of intersubjectivity in colonial contexts,[11] using the process of translation as a form of relation to the other represented by the dominant language.[12] This permanent self-translation has deep implications for interpretation and language: it calls for new ways of reading.

From a New Semiosis to a New Semiotics

Another related question guiding this project is: How do multilingual aesthetic experiences define the emergence of this ambiguous subjectivity in those colonial contexts where encounters between different languages are inextricably connected to coercions of colonial domination? The forced imposition of a colonial language implies a hidden *new semiosis*, one that is rooted in a process of translation that transforms the act of interpreting any artifact, be it literary, musical, visual, or spatial. The immediate consequence is the emergence of a new system of signification, or what I call a "new semiotics," a postcolonial semiotics, specific to the context of linguistic colonization. In this book, I am unfolding this new semiotics at work.

In "Bilingualism and Literature," Abdelkebir Khatibi (1938–2009) defines the notion of "bi-langue" (translated as "bi-language").[13] First, it describes the linguistic reality of Francophone Maghrebi writers, meaning that the context of Francophone literature is informed by a multiplicity of languages. Khatibi elaborates a fundamental statement that readers from other cultural backgrounds, especially monolingual ones, should consider carefully when speaking, thinking, or writing about Francophone writers—indeed, about any writer who evolved in a system of linguistic domination: "As long as the theory of translation, of bi-language and pluri-language has not advanced, certain Maghrebian texts will remain impregnable through a formal and functional approach. The 'mother' tongue is at work in the foreign language. From one to the other takes place a constant translation and a conversation *en abyme*, extremely difficult to bring to light" (*Plural Maghreb* 117).[14]

In *White Tongue, Brown Skin*, I provide a methodology to achieve the difficult task of making the presence of the native hidden language visible by focusing on a variety of Francophone writers from Bengal, Egypt, North Africa, and Mauritius. Although it originated in the Maghreb, "bi-language" is applicable to all Francophone regions, where it becomes a systematic response to colonialism whose major consequences are a cultural and linguistic destruction of the native episteme. The agency of the writers as subjects of colonialism is rooted in their experience as listeners and readers of multiple languages, in their decision to write in a *hidden* multilingualism, and in reconciling their plural, ambiguous lives. Their multilingualism is hidden because of the original guilt of an illicit tie to the colonial language and the vital need to perform a whitened tongue.

White Tongue, Brown Skin interprets some lesser-known texts with multilingual linguistic, stylistic, poetic, and symbolic tools. In a way, I am constructing an analytical approach, making possible the encounter between two or more semiotic systems, keeping in mind that the text is the privileged site that performs the encounter. In doing so, I am questioning the ambiguous relation to the colonial language and how it transforms the link to the other languages in the region and to the "body," to quote Khatibi again.[15] I am also developing the idea of an unexplored enunciator of the text, a being that is *in relation to a changing world* and *in a hidden translation to make this new world familiar*. It is time to see the dilemma of colonial domination from the perspective of the colonized, who is not simply a submissive receptacle of cultural and linguistic domination, but is also an active agent of this domination. It is not just the French language that transformed the colonized, but the colonized who transformed the French language, making it their own.

The *relation* between all the internalized—not always expressed—languages of the colonized woman writers in this book forms the core of the study, as the relation that is at the starting point of the transformative colonial presence in the colonized landscape. This argument makes my approach slightly different from Steven Kellman's in The Translingual Imagination (2000), among other such approaches to translingualism, in that it tries to provide the poetic and linguistic tools to read multilingual authors whose *other* language, due to colonial domination, is not a choice. *White Tongue, Brown Skin* positions itself at the heart of these linguistic and semiotic processes mainly because of my knowledge of both forms of Arabic (دارجة/*darija* and فصحى/*fusha*), English, and as a result of my exposure to Bengali during fieldwork in India and to Creole through my proximity to an important Mauritian community in France and the United States. My claim works toward truly reading and seeing these postcolonial writers, with all their languages and cultural and literary heritage, without reducing their existence to the languages that we, in our mainstream assumptions, tend to see and read in them naturally. Their being is both translingual and multilingual, and I call on the reader to adapt their modalities of readings instead of reducing these writers to the familiar. Writers are still colonized, as they are read in a monolingual lens dominated by Western languages; thus, developing a multilingual way of reading and interpreting is now an urgent task to improve our globalized modalities of communicating. Scholars from the previous generation did not have a wide range of linguistic tools to develop multilingual modalities of reading and interpreting—the new generation does. It is up to us to use them for good.

As a follow-up to my initial question, we can ask: How is multilingualism in colonial and postindependence situations negotiated through literary writing as a site of *repair*?[16] In this argument, I acknowledge the colonial experience as a *relation* whose site of repair is deeply textual because colonialism is, first and foremost, a system internalized through those discourses communicated in texts, in schools.[17] Consequently, postcolonial literary texts are *epiphenomena*, revealing the losses of the native tongue and decolonial strategies of repair.[18] Embedded in this project—and driving its development—is the assumption of a strong link between being a reader, being a writer, and being a translator. This connection is obvious when it comes to canonic European writers, but it is rarely a way to analyze writers in postcolonial contexts. Critics often forget that postcolonial writers were *readers* of the canon of classic, colonial literature, that they were embedded in a profoundly colonial and white culture, though they knew that it was a culture of domination and injustice. Is that a reason for these postcolonial women writers to reject the part of their being that was influenced by the canon of Western literature and its languages? While they are readers of multiple languages and products of a dynamic, creolized imaginary, they were pushed to write for monolingual readers, resulting in a hidden multilingual text. In postcolonial studies and other disciplines, their political agency has been studied, but not their existence as always-translators, in between languages, and, moreover, *in-between worlds*. Their fundamentally ambiguous status has been condemned but not analyzed enough in the flesh of the text. I aim to capture this multilingual poetics at work.

Of course, critics like Gauvin might object to my argument about postcolonial intersubjectivity and language, saying that any writer is writing in a foreign language, that any writing is a translation in a way, and, to quote Sartre, "on parle dans sa propre langue, on écrit dans une langue étrangère" (*Les Mots* 140; we speak in our own language, we write in a foreign language), which is fair enough. But, for the first generation of colonized writers, this language is twice foreign: foreign as it is for any writer, and foreign as it is imposed to erase the sounds of the mother tongue. Questioning the complexity of the *signifier* (primarily as an acoustic image) is at the heart of this new semiosis.

A Chutnified Theory of the Subject

Long before the development of network theory and theories of fluid identities, the writers studied here illustrate models of self-proclaimed plastic subjectivities (Malabou, *L'Avenir de Hegel*). They peel back the different layers of their lived experience of multicultural, urban colonial histories, which are reinforced by their unique journeys as *readers* of texts. This subject claims and performs a relation to the world through texts, reading it as such. Well before current conceptualizations of diversity, colonization imposed a de facto multiculturalism, which these writers performed, producing texts that celebrate plurality, in stark opposition to the hegemonic self, prescribed in successive waves by colonialism, anticolonialism, and nationalism. I address multilingualism as the urgent task of new theories of the subject that emphasize the linguistic and acoustic experience as fundamental to subject formation.[19] This expands on Khatibi's work by addressing the particularly complex legacy of colonization, the aesthetic of the bi-language in a global context. My goal is to establish a conceptual frame that articulates the postcolonial subject as a multilingual reader whose transformative process is performed within the text; this subject is the one who builds bridges to repair and to survive the destruction of colonialism. Languages in texts are bridges between scattered parts of the self. As discussed by Nita Kumar in *Women as Subject* (1994), referring to Foucault and Derrida, the notion of "subject" can be contested; at the same time, the poetics of it in specific regions of the world are different. *White Tongue, Brown Skin* approaches subject formation as a response to the historical context of colonial trauma, which no general discourse about the subject can express.

Sometimes, theory is a way to oversimplify or transcend what is rooted in place and time, which is enough to be specific. The argument herein situates the subject's ontological birth in this historical trauma. Therefore, regarding the concept of "the subject," I address the hegemony of the Western tradition over a tradition that has not yet been spoken into existence in academia. Important theories about the subject often overlap, although not emerging from the same object of study, as the concept itself seems outdated. But, as Rosi Braidotti puts it, "in order to announce the death of the subject one must first have gained the right to speak as one" (*Nomadic Subjects* 141). My aim in this book is to go back to the writings by women who are emerging as subjects in their own colonized/postindependent culture. Putting their histories of coming to subjectivity into dialogue allows me to elaborate on broader reflections about the multilingual subject and its visions of the world. The history I want to locate and to look at is the specific constitution of the subject as a being *in relation with languages,* a being of plural encounters expressed in the experience and praxis of multiple languages, each as a manifestation of a repressed reality. I am, in a sense, stubbornly convinced that there is an important insight behind the emergence of a multilingual subject whose existence as a writer is the product of a specifically *colonial* traumatic experience. It is time to observe the existence of these subjectivities without the political guilt of postcolonial discourse and to see anew the complex fabric of their languages as masked translations. The contours of this subject emanate from a poetic experience full of sounds and words without referentiality, those very words carried by conflicting sounds embedded in their multilingual soundscapes. The "I" is the result of antagonist tensions and attempts at repair. The affirmation of a "self" through writing is not a new concept in the history of women's literature, but, with Toru Dutt, Mayy Ziyadah, Assia Djebar, and Ananda Devi, their affirmation comes through the experience of a plurality of languages and the creation of a self that can accommodate such diversity. Writing can then be at the same time the door to the outside and the way to reveal their internal enemy.

The arguments in this book intend to establish a more complex understanding of multilingual subjectivities in colonial/postindependence situations through weaving together a textual, aesthetic approach and examinations of power structures (patriarchal, colonial, national). Indeed, the multilingual colonized subject's primary differentiating factor from any other Western subject has its roots in the trauma of a forced historical encounter visible within the structure of the texts, through their complex use of the colonial and native languages, and the guilt expressed—or not—by their writers. Therefore, I establish a logical connection here between "subjectivity" and "text." This subjectivity emerges through the poetics of the combined languages and the performance of the plurality in the text as an emanation of *joy*, instead of the usual postcolonial guilt and melancholia. The difference is a performance of what Paul Valéry describes in (*Rhumbs* 122): "Le poème—cette hésitation prolongée entre le son et le sens" (The poem—this prolonged hesitation between sound and meaning) that *induces* instead of *deduces* interpretation.

More precisely, I will explore the constitutions of Dutt, Ziyadah, Djebar, and Devi as subjects in translation—that is, subjects emerging through comparison and analogy, embedded in any act of translation. The analogical process and comparison will shed light on their contested plurality.[20] Indeed, I express that strong modernist assumption of the poetic power of literary language over other embodied praxes like theater, dance, or music. This assumption has its limits that will be partly explored at the end of two chapters in the narratives of city-walking within the urban and cosmopolitan spaces, which typify large parts of the novels and movies of the aforementioned writers. Another dimension that is often ignored in the critical discourse on postcolonial writers is the importance of their inherent cosmopolitanism as a result of their specific positions within the capitals of erstwhile empires: Calcutta, Cairo, Algiers, and Port Louis are capitals with a cosmopolitan ethos in their foundations. All writers are rooted in the world, in their capitals and waterscapes, facing the rest of the empire: the Mediterranean, the Indian Ocean, the Bengal Sea, the River Nile.

Multilingual Urban Cosmopolitan Subjects

The parallel between multilingual subjectivity and the city is also at the core of my analysis. It is both the transformation of the city and its plurality that the self-in-translation represents. The analogy between the multilingual self and the diversity of colonial cities allows for a series of reflections about the essence of plurality inscribed in the architecture of the city and the divide imposed on colonized people and their culture. The works of our plural writers are projections of a dreamt circulation between worlds. They are the projections of the plasticity of poetry, repairing the fixedness of city walls. In Algiers, Calcutta, and, certainly, Port Louis and Cairo, the languages spoken change from neighborhood to neighborhood. As an Algerian woman writer, I grew up recognizing differences between some more popular neighborhoods where dialectal Arabic was spoken with specific metaphors, words, puns, and so on; each spatial boundary had its own sounds. How can we read any Francophone production without considering its diversity of languages, in the way of Victor Hugo's argotic Parisian French, described as a language of its own?[21]

The ambiguous feeling of subjecthood, as coming to awareness as a being, starts with the experience of the sounds of languages spoken in colonial capitals—new sounds from the colonial language not sung by mothers in Calcutta, Cairo, Algiers, Port Louis. The sounds are multiple: Bengali, Arabic, Tamazight, English, French, Creole, Hindi, and others. For the writers discussed in this book, childhood experience is mirrored by how the cityscape was shaped with sounds, smells, and architectural forms imposed by the colonial establishment. The writing becomes, at some point, the retrospective bridge of this essential experience between the self and the surroundings, sounds and architectures—walls that uniquely define the native culture on the one hand, and the powerful, colonial rewriting of the city on the other. Languages are contaminated by this relation of power, but little girls from bourgeois families had access to the Western knowledge that shaped their ambiguous attitudes vis-à-vis the colonial power and its languages. Colonial languages became the alluring mermaid voices. My multiple Ulysses have all accepted colonial languages as part of their being, from which entails their specific experience of plurality. The gift of the language is also the gift of the cityscape. It gives the tools to read colonial space and adapt to it. Architecture is another language imposed on the colonized bodies in colonial spaces, as beautifully expressed by Fanon in *A Dying Colonialism* (1965).[22]

Language, like the space these women live(d) in, can also be divisive. Sacred languages, for example, have always been used to exclude or to include: Sanskrit, Quranic Arabic, Latin, biblical Hebrew. Colonial languages are resurgent tools of spatial exclusion, and the colonial city will mirror the divisiveness of the language; each space has its own language, dictated by its architecture and the dance of the bodies within (e.g., the casbah in Algiers opposed to the European district, Old Delhi and New Delhi). Colonialism is not often described as a multilingual aesthetic experience, though it was. And, as in other times and places, writing and translating became the source of a sense of self-repair that was openly plural, accepting multilingualism as a part of the native landscape. This skeptical attitude toward the colonial language, though rejected, criticized, and attributed as guilt, is also at the core of the creolization of the self. These writers do not passively adopt the language of the colonizer, the dominant language; they actively translate the self in between languages, and, in doing so, they transform *both* sides of the self. The plasticity of poetry, and of literature in general, is what allows for the circulation of symbols, images, and sounds to subvert the principle of colonization as a space and time of segregation. Against walls, the joyful multilingual praxis of literature dismantles the spatial and symbolic islands necessary to the propagation of colonial domination. The literature produced by multilingual writers bridges the disparate parts of the city and, consequently, grants them representation. These authors thus establish a cityscape that is a plural space of encounters and contaminations of shapes from different architectural traditions. "I feel the languages in the city, therefore I am" could be the motto of this modern colonial subjectivity that is transformed by the new language of the cityscape, the language of the aesthetic forms around them, and the language they speak and use.

The recent decades have produced much debate about the nature of cosmopolitanism and its roots. In his *Lost History of Cosmopolitanism*, Leigh Penman (2021) takes us back to the long history of cosmopolitan practices without any consideration for its manifestation in the capitals of colonial empires (e.g., Algiers, Cairo, Calcutta, Port Louis). Yet any reader of postcolonial criticism must recall that the enterprise of empire was rooted in a Eurocentric definition of cosmopolitanism. Do postcolonial spaces necessarily follow the same critical history and epistemological order? The twentieth century has theorized the postcolonial. Now it is time to decolonize the discourse, the language, and the tools we use to understand the postcolonial. Of course, in this critical gesture, it is necessary to remember the culturally destructive nature of colonialism. However, to ignore the subtle literary and cultural phenomena informed by this reality is akin to erasing vital parts of the history of formerly colonized regions and preventing the native from writing their own, decolonized history. Addressing the question of "vernacular cosmopolitanism" to the women writers complexifies the reading of colonization.[23]

Self-Subject-Agent

Postcolonial criticism has focused mainly on the reductive and oppositional dimension of colonization without considering the colonial experience as ambiguous and transformative: a "toxic relationship" rooted first in language. As in love, toxicity can be fatal, yet it also has complex ramifications that do not fit a binary reading of the world. French was particularly global and toxic; it killed off aspects of the Indigenous self, but not all of it. Is it the emergence of an agent, a new subjectivity, or a self that is actualized in these writers' books?

There is an important dimension of agency involved in our writers' fictional creations, in the voice of the text, which is why the separation between the narrator and the author is not always pertinent when it comes to postcolonial writings.[24] In any case, it is important to navigate cautiously between the different sources of discourse and knowledge about place shared by our writers, who are fine observers of their changing cityscape and landscape. The expression of the plurality of the self in their writing, its transformation and its self-awareness, the expression of the diversity within the colonial existence trying to control all forms of endogenous manifestation, is the essence of literature as a locus of resilience and resistance. After all, literature is first an act of language, and, as such, its interpretation cannot erase the process of writing in language. Between the text and its interpretation, we need hermeneutical tools that question the nature of this literary language that has forever produced new meanings, new visions. In the case of postcolonial literature, the new meanings are produced in an invisibly multilingual text, which is even more challenging for any act of interpretation. *White Tongue, Brown Skin* thus proposes an aesthetic analysis of the linear relation between the sign and the real, in its vision of the chains of transmission and transformation, occurring in the interconnected life of the self that writes: the poetic relation between the self and its conflicting worlds in words.

1

WHO IS THE SUBJECT IN TRANSLATION?

What Subject?

The Western philosophical tradition on the subject/*sujet* as the origin of being has a genealogy of its own. It begins before Descartes's "Cogito, ergo sum" with Augustine's *Confessions* and is followed by Ibn Rushd (1126–1198) in medieval Islam, and by Michel de Montaigne in his *Essays*. This tradition of the subject continues to be developed today by Alain Badiou, *Théorie du sujet* (1982; *Theory of the Subject*, 2009), Jean-Luc Nancy, *Être singulier pluriel* (1996; *Being Singular Plural*, 2000), and Julia Kristeva, *The Crisis of the European Subject* (2000). Although this genealogy is not exhaustive and is overly simplified, Saint Augustine (354–430) historically establishes the first well-known, detailed reflections on the subject other than as a critical agent of history;[1] among his meditations are ones dedicated to the pleasure of writing in a foreign language (i.e., Latin) instead of his mother-tongue, Tamazight.[2] The Western literary tradition of inwardly expressed subjectivity has historically been automatically gendered male and is distinct from those histories and cultures experienced by the postcolonial women writers studied in this book. However, the underlying Western tradition nevertheless informs postcolonial women writers in many subtle ways.

Past works on "the subject" have been informed by myriad subfields and traditions of thought, and there are as many subjects as there are discourses: ethical (the agent of political thinking or action), ontological (the being), psychological (the psyche), and so on. Of course, there are also different philosophical traditions surrounding the concept of "the subject," and it is vital to avoid the assumptions rooted in Western vs. Eastern claims, as well as the general belief that subjectivity is a Western concept. The genealogy of the subject defined here is different from that of the "being" (*être, dasein*) commonly addressed in philosophy. The subject here is the enunciator of a complex text, self-conscious about being interconnected to multilayered colonial history and the experience of imposed languages as an essential experience of alienation.

Indeed, the main distinction between a postcolonial theory of the subject and any other Western theory of subjectivity is that the former incorporates the modern trauma of a forced historical encounter. This historical trauma is at the origin of the complex use of language that emerges from such contexts. Applying both textual and comparatist poetic approaches, as well as moving between the various discourses of power (patriarchal, colonial, national), makes a more complex understanding of writing in colonial/postindependence situations visible. Abstract theoretical approaches cannot replace the need for a direct textual understanding of multilingual subjects, which can be found in the poetics of the syncretic languages that so often arise in postcolonial spaces.

A multilingual existence is now dominantly associated with the postcolonial condition, but the world of interpretation and reading is still informed by a monolingual approach. The interrogation of this specific construct of the subject as a being of plural, forced cultural (including linguistic) encounters therefore constitutes the core of this project. Although sociology, anthropology, psychology and even postcolonial theory have fruitfully explored the concept of a plural subjectivity, a systematic reflection on the poetics of multilingual colonial and postcolonial subjectivity has been undervalued in postcolonial studies and comparative literature.[3]

The plurality of forced encounters can be elucidated through a study of the aesthetic and cultural experience of a *multilayered colonialism* only visible in the practice of literary language.[4] The differentiated poetics, or the fabric of the subject, is informed by a historical, cultural context which no general discourse about the subject can express. The core component of postcolonial subjectivity is the multilayered dimension of language that arises from colonization, a foundational source of both alienation and liberation from the recent history of colonialism. The subjectivity in question here emerges from the subject's experience of their own alterity, or what is also understood as the "otherness" of the colonized subject. Agent and patient, this unbalanced "Caliban and Prospero" subject dynamic is structured through relationality and interconnectedness,[5] becoming the idealized subject of literary aesthetics in a context where plurality, diversity, and transcultural poetics become the shared expressed reality of our humanity.[6] In modern European thought, the subject, as agent, is someone who possesses *choice* and can be *self-determined*. This active subject is defined mainly through Western canons: the achieved actualization of this ideal subjectivity is the enlightened subject. The postcolonial subject seems to represent the dark side of this subject as defined through Western criteria, wherein the decline of the enlightened subject began with the emergence of the postcolonial subject, whose birth is conditioned by the fabric of plurality of languages.[7]

Postcolonial thought on "the subject" maintains its own genealogy—from Fanon and Albert Memmi (1920-2020) to Edward Said (1935-2003), Gayatri Spivak (1942-), and Homi Bhabha (1949-). Each defined the postcolonial subject using different sources and from different discursive positions: Fanon, mainly through his experience as a psychiatrist engaged in an anticolonial war, first analyzed a contemporaneous Black masculine subjectivity by predominantly using a psychoanalytic and phenomenological grid of interpretation. Memmi developed his definition in his famous psychological and sociological portraits of the colonized and the colonizer, *Portrait du colonisé* (1957; *The Colonizer and the Colonized*, 1965). Said was informed by a more historical and literary tradition, but also by a masculine perspective; Spivak, by ontological and gender perspectives; and, finally, Bhabha, following Fanon, theorized the split or division of the postcolonial subject without considering their gender perspective as determinant. The assumption of the divided nature of postcolonial subjectivity reveals a lack of understanding of the work of multilingual ontologies and a pathological Western vision of its plural nature.

Two dimensions of this postcolonial subjectivity are missing throughout studies of its expression in literature, though: the inherently unbalanced linguistic positionality of its writers and its resulting ambiguous gender dimension. In other words, how will a theory of the postcolonial subject expand if it is reconsidered when taking into account multilingual writings produced by women?[8] The history and positionality of the postcolonial subject have mainly been analyzed from the perspective of a guilty choice or an abnormality.[9]

The first occurrence of a theory of the postcolonial subject after W. E. B. Du Bois's (1868-1963) *The Souls of Black Folk* (1903) was Fanon's *Peau noire, masques blancs* (1952; *Black Skin, White Masks*, 1967).[10] In this seminal work, Fanon describes the pathologies of the Black masculine psyche first and foremost through "language," based on the traumatic experience of colonial domination, which he refers to as "The Black Man and Language." The imposed model of normality, according to psychoanalytic terms, is that of the unified, modern European subject, or the "subject of modernity," as defined by Anthony Cascardi: "Thus while the modern self (more accurately, the 'subject') must be in principle open to those forms of criticism and self-revision that are consistent with the project of an enlightened critique, this same self is likely to be found at sea among its various desires, not knowing how to choose appropriate ends. And while modern society offers the self the potentially liberating experience of choosing from among a variety of different roles, the modern psyche is reflected in the image of a scattered, fragmented, or 'disseminated' whole" (*Subject of Modernity* 39).

Because Fanon holds a white-normative notion of subject, his theoretical background already harbors its own structural crisis. Thus, Fanon's reflections on postcoloniality inevitably carry the burden of history and create a hyperconsciousness of internalized otherness and divide. Indeed, Fanon's notion of experience is based on pathologies of trauma: his postcolonial subject can be described as the fragmented subject of modernity, the result of a failure of the accomplished and powerful enlightened subject of the end of eighteenth-century Europe. Division and opposition seem to be inherent to the psychology of the colonized. The theoretical structure of Fanon's subject is heavily informed by a Freudian framework, cultivating the opposition between unity and plurality (i.e., fragmented-scattered-disseminated), an opposition that can also be read as the normality of unity versus the chaos of plurality. The Freudian framework of Fanon's subject also hints at a hidden coherence with the concept of "the unconscious." Psychoanalytic discourse usually tries to fix the gap of the scattered, subjective structure of the plural being. "Scattered" is taken here to mean an expression of inner conflict. An important discovery of Fanon's has remained unexplored—namely, the relationship between the imposed language and action of the colonizer as a pretext for the continued domination of this "scattered postcolonial subject" in the colonial context. This project therefore goes from the reading of literature through the lens of texts in several languages to the construction of a plastic subjectivity, meeting Fanon in the middle where the subject leaves the speech in order to *act*.

Homi Bhabha is another fundamental critic who conceptualizes a more recent theory of postcolonial subjectivity. This chapter will provide a critical reading of Bhabha's "Third Space," defined as a space of cultural hybridity in colonial contexts, and how this idea announces the conceptual implications of the linguistic turn as a form of resilience. This in-between space is modeled by the plasticity of all languages and is also the medium of their interconnectedness, a notion that needs further excavation. In looking precisely at the nature of symbolization from an informed linguistic perspective, the "Third Space" becomes more than just an abstract concept, taking shape in the nature and poetics of texts. Cultures are not unitary or binary; they are plural and plastic. This plasticity is truly visible in the language of literary expression. This chapter also intends to demonstrate that, because the discourse of colonization rendered subjectivity into a form of oppositionality, models of multiple subjectivity did not emerge as rapidly in people's actions as they showed up in theory and poetry in the late 1960s in the work of two major philosophers, Khatibi and Édouard Glissant (1928–2011).

Well before Fanon, certain models of cultural development privileged a view of subjectivity that aimed, through the appreciation of aesthetic experience, for multiplicity and transculturality, without explicitly ignoring the traumatic experiences of colonialism.[11] Authors such as Dutt and Ziyadah, followed by Djebar and Devi in the twentieth century, were already thinking from their complex linguistic situations as postcolonial women writers and intellectuals, promoting models of cultural development that were transcultural precisely because transculturality was embedded within their specific histories and experiences of their landscape. While these first feminists were not puppets to be manipulated by the West, they each experienced the ambiguous position of a disloyal gratitude vis-à-vis their European education, at the same time as they were unable to betray their countrywomen, countrymen, and their native landscape. The languages in which they express this confusion are mediated through the prism of literature.[12] Because they wrote in the language of the other, they were read as traitors, misread as modern figures of La Malinche.[13] For some of them, their invisibility was the result of the misreading of their work or due to the confusion regarding their political and ethical positions. As translator/traitor, positioned in the margin of the margins, they embraced complexity instead of adhering to the oversimplified rigidity of normative national identity. A gender studies lens that makes use of psychoanalytical discourse is helpful here to think through notions of basic power structures and the complex links between three major components of their subjectivity:[14] first, multilingual subjectivity as plastic;[15] second, the language of aesthetics and literature, in particular as the unique *substance* that provides space for this complexity;[16] and, third, cosmopolitanism as its political manifestation beyond oppositionality.

Fanon's "The North African Syndrome" and *Black Skin, White Masks*

"Le Syndrome nord-africain" ("The North African Syndrome") and *Peau noire, masques blancs* (*Black Skin, White Masks*), two major works by Fanon, do not demand expertise in psychiatry for them to be read and used critically. These two texts offer insights that help narrow down the relationship between language and subjectivity in colonial contexts. The result of this narrowing down can only be described as deviant or expressed as one of the *pathologies of language*.[17] Fanon was the first to direct attention to colonial language as a tool of physical, psychological, and symbolic alienation, which results in, as he put it, the loss of the soul of colonized folks. Fanon's theory offers a comprehensive perspective on two major historical systems of alienation, slavery, and colonialism: colonial language acts as a whitening mask.

"The North African Syndrome," first published in the journal *L'Esprit*, described in broad terms, for the first time in the history of psychiatric scholarship, a clinical portrait of the North African subject exiled in France.[18] Fanon's observations were based on patients who were exiled in Lyon (mainly living in the neighborhood of Rue Moncey) and were generally North African. In this short article, he declares that, per his analysis, exile is a state of morbidity: "Psychoanalytical science considers expatriation to be a morbid phenomenon. In this, it is perfectly right" (*Toward the African Revolution* 15).[19] This was his first confrontation with fresh colonial trauma. Fanon did not know much about Algeria in 1952. He thought of himself as a Frenchman from Martinique and as culturally white, except that his experience in Lyon drastically changed his self-perception. For the first time, he felt his skin as a color and a problem.

"The North African Syndrome" and *Black Skin, White Masks* were the first widely read observations of colonial domination and alienation imposed through language. But the language Fanon considered was not in written form, which is certainly a major distinction from the literary approach to colonial language. Fanon *listened* first and foremost to language as it expressed forms of pathologies in speech and in body, exploring oral colonial language as a medium for the elaboration of a physical alienation. Although I analyze written works in this book, Fanon's observations on speech in colonial language as a tool of domination, deculturation, and alienation laid essential groundwork for thinking about colonial language as a form of forceful translation of the self.

In the first chapter of *Black Skin, White Masks*, "The Black Man and Language," Fanon makes the following lucid statement about the link between colonial languages and the colonized: "We attach a fundamental importance to the phenomenon of language. [. . .] All colonized people—in other words, people in whom an inferiority complex has taken root, whose local cultural originality has been committed to the grave—position themselves in relation to the civilizing language: i.e., the metropolitan culture. The more the colonized has assimilated the cultural values of the metropolis, the more he will have escaped the bush. The more he rejects his blackness and the bush, the whiter he will become" (1–2).[20]

Fanon claims there is an imbalance of power embedded in the act of the colonized using the colonizer's language, which results in the negation and repression of local language and culture. While this is certainly true, the native language does not fully disappear; rather, it finds its way in the symbolic realm of the subject in translation.[21] Postcolonial writers use colonial language as a tool to *disalienate* themselves from the traumatic dimension buried in its very usage.

In his "Journal de bord" ("Practice Log"), Fanon takes a deep dive into the effects of colonial trauma and its expression in language. He also extends artistic expression into a form of mental health therapy. He knew that language is a plastic tool that can undo its own alienation. But, instead of trusting the plastic power of the colonial language, Fanon transfers this same ability to the body as the main locus of resymbolization.

Fanon saw the pathology within the language as a site of experimentation, the *split*, the narcissistic wound that deteriorates the subject's ability to form a direct link with the world. Colonial language becomes a screen imposed on the colonized, preventing them from apprehending the world. The colonized's power of referentiality, embedded in their native tongue, is broken by the interference of French, imposed as a new indexing language—the words used to label the world—coexisting with the native language(s).[22] French language becomes a mental prison for the colonized, intimately haunting the colonized by replacing their modes of symbolization, displacing their reference to the world, and changing their ability to interpret and symbolically react to the world. The colonial language becomes a tool to *translate* the unique, inner self into terms that are familiar to the colonizer. This statement is equivalent to Fanon's notion of the "black man" in *Black Skin, White Masks*: colonial language is the tool at the heart of alienation. Fanon studied in depth how indexing is affected by the traumatic experience of colonization: "By referring to other research and our personal observations, we would like to try to show why the black man posits himself in such a characteristic way with regard to European languages. We recall once again that our findings are valid for the French Antilles; we are well aware, however, that this same behavior can be found in any race subjected to colonization" (9).[23]

Fanon spent a time developing his observations about the language of the Black *man*, yet the women writers examined here explore these pathologies of language, too. Is it an illusion to imagine a different effect on women under colonial scrutiny, particularly when some of them become writers in the dominant languages?

As colonized subjects, their positions regarding the language of the colonizer remain ambivalent. They are, however, sharing the knowledge that the use of this language (French or English) gives them a new, *ambiguous* power, and they cannot completely repress their sympathy for the culture that gave it to them.[24] For women, writing in colonial languages changed their social gendered position and masculinized their voice. For example, Dutt's countrymen assumed she was a man when she published her first volume of poems translated from French into English, A Sheaf Gleaned in French Fields, in March 1876.

Beyond the absence of a much-needed chapter on "The Black Woman and Language," other aspects of Fanon's work have been criticized, although this should not be read as detracting from its importance. Rather, it should be seen as the sign of an incredibly productive line of thought. The following paragraphs summarize some overriding critiques made against Fanon's ideas, mainly those found in Black Skin, White Masks. The first is a perception that Fanon read the colonial situation from an oppositional perspective that left no room to reevaluate the ambiguities of colonialism without moral condemnation.

Colonial Language, Trauma, and Binary Opposition

For decades, perspectives on the postcolonial subject have been structured through the binary oppositions of colonizer and colonized, dominant and dominated, and the like and have thus limited the horizon of new insights in the field.[25] In this way, critics have emphasized a model of oppositionality, particularly in the reading of identities within the formerly colonized world, sometimes missing the subtle adaptations and survival strategies developed by writers, particularly women writers, who were among the first to learn how to subvert colonial languages from within: taking advantage of the freedom it gave them to overthrow its domination and heal the deliberately fragmented psyche. But how exactly did these women accomplish this subversion of colonial language, as well as its symbolic and plastic power of transformation? In other words: How can we understand the language of domination from within?

Black Skin, White Masks ends by proclaiming the complexity of subjectivity and the need to overcome historical determination through the experience of the body that always questions. Fanon's conclusion to the text insists:

> The misfortune and inhumanity of the white man are having killed man somewhere. [. . .] It is through self-consciousness and renunciation, through a permanent tension of his freedom, that man can create the ideal conditions of existence for a human world.
>
> Superiority? Inferiority?
>
> Why not simply try to touch the other, feel the other, discover each other?
>
> [. . .] At the end of this book we would like the reader to feel with us the open dimension of every consciousness.
>
> My final prayer:
>
> O my body, always make me a man who questions! (205–6)[26]

Yet the active legacy that remains is the binary structure of *affect* expressed within social behavior like that found in this excerpt: "The black possesses two dimensions: one with his fellow blacks, the other with the whites. A black man behaves differently with a white man than he does with another black man. [. . .] the more the black Antillean assimilates the French language, the whiter he gets—i.e., the closer he comes to becoming a true human being" (1–2).[27]

Fanon's incipit outlines the schism (*schize*) inherent to the *psyche* of the colonized person surrounded by a dominant white tongue.[28] In the conclusion of *Black Skin, White Masks*, Fanon finds his way out of the alienated, divided self through the claim of subjectivity, of self-determination, in a personal interrogation of History, the empowerment of the self against social and historical determination, and, last but not least, a mindful presence in his own body. Yet the white tongue remained a minefield:

> A normal black child, having grown up with a normal family, will become abnormal at the slightest contact with the white world. [...] What do we see in the case of the black man? Unless we use Jung's postulate of the *collective unconscious,* so vertiginous it unhinges us, we can understand absolutely nothing. [...] Very often the black man who becomes abnormal has never come into contact with Whites. Has some former experience been repressed in his unconscious? Has the young black child seen his father beaten or lynched by the white man? Has there been a real traumatism? To all these questions our answer is no. So where do we go from here. If we want an honest answer, we have to call on the notion of *collective catharsis.* (122–24)[29]

The colonized—here, namely, "un enfant noir normal" ("a normal black child")—is described by a tendency of becoming "abnormal" from only the slightest contact with the white (colonizer). Shall we assume that this slight contact is mainly mediated by language? The operative statement in this passage compares the normality of the white man to the abnormality of the Black man, which issues from traumatic contact mediated by the alienating language.[30]

In a different perspective, Gwen Bergner emphasizes Fanon's de-essentialization of "both race and psychoanalytic models of subject formation," which allows for more critical approaches to the established canons of subject construction:

> Fanon transposes psychoanalysis—a theory of subject formation based on sexual difference—to register where it accounts for race as one of the fundamental differences that constitute subjectivity. He asks how sexuality and language, the primary constituents of the symbolic, are inflected by race, as well as how they construct categories of race [...] By making explicit the cultural construction of racial subjectivity, Fanon de-essentializes both race and psychoanalytic models of subject formation: psychoanalysis becomes a tool with which to evaluate relations of power and cultural hegemony. ("Who Is That Masked Woman?" 76)

This de-essentialization constitutes a vital first step in questioning the role of colonial language as crafting a dominated subjectivity in order to understand the underlying (self-) translation process. Benita Parry writes that Fanon's "colonized as constructed by colonialist ideology is the very figure of the divided subject posited by psychoanalytic theory to refute humanism's myth of the unified self" ("Postcolonial" 29). Fanon was trapped in the alienating power of the white tongue and could not resolve its contradictions (both therapeutic and pathologic), particularly during colonial times.

Another dimension that appears in Fanon's work is a complex homoerotic relationship between the white male (dominant, father-like figure) and the Black male (dominated, childlike figure). Bergner has noted that Fanon, like Freud, "takes the man as a norm" ("Who Is That Masked Woman?" 77). Fanon's work displays an inversion of the common reading of the Oedipus complex, resituating the triad around the figure of the father and not around the mother. The father, who is also constructed as the figure of "white god," becomes the center of the comparison. Such a scheme doubly alienates feminine subjectivity and its desire. Within the postcolonial context, colonized boys are alienated by a destructive white colonial father figure and a silenced *native* mother, who very often does not speak or read the language of colonial power, whose language is limited to the intimate sphere. The native language thus becomes the internalized language translated into the dominant masculine language used at school, in the outside world. The intimate tongue is feminine for any writer under the regime of colonial alienation. As Bergner puts it: "So while it is not surprising that Fanon, writing in the early fifties, takes the masculine as the norm, it is necessary not only to posit alternative representations of femininity but also to consider how his account of normative raced masculinity depends on the production or exclusion of femininity" (77).

Another point of discussion, outlined by both H. L. Gates and Bergner, is the elitism of Fanon's position, which reproduces the same structure of domination it denounces, since, as they argue, Fanon "did not identify with and even found distasteful the common people of the cultures he championed theoretically and politically" ("Who Is That Masked Woman?" 77). In Fanon's thought, alterity is seen, understandably, as a threat synonymous with insanity, or the reason for it, which is overcome only by the strong affirmation of his corporeity at the end of *Black Skin, White Masks*. For Fanon, the colonized must transcend the overdetermination of history as a structural discourse and speech to survive in the present. Seen from the perspective of the texts explored in later chapters of this book, the plurality born from colonial trauma is not only self-destructive or annihilating. The power structures Fanon described accurately justified the anticolonial struggle during colonization and even during the first decades after decolonization, but some questions about the use of colonial language are worth revisiting. In this regard, there is an important distinction to be made between the open-ended direction of Fanon's therapeutic discourse as a psychiatrist and the rigid understanding of his conclusion by his readers. A correct reading needs to balance the two movements of his thought: as psychiatrist and as anticolonial FLN (Front de Libération Nationale [National Liberation Front]) fighter.

Homi Bhabha, the postcolonial critic, tried to go beyond the schizoid construction of postcolonial subjectivity. Bhabha's *The Location of Culture* (1994) perspective simultaneously acknowledges and criticizes the oppositionality with concepts such as "Third Space" and "hybridity." Let us now discuss both concepts as tools to overcome the divided postcolonial subjectivity.

Bhabha's *The Location of Culture* (1994)

Three major terms or concepts from Bhaba's *The Location of Culture* interest us here: the "Third Space," the split of postcolonial subjectivity, and modalities of hybridity. In the chapter "Articulating the Archaic," Bhabha develops his understanding of the other through E. M. Forster's *A Passage to India* (1924) and reinterprets once again the famous scene of the Marabar caves:

> What happened in the Marabar caves? *There*, the loss of the narrative of cultural plurality; *there* the implausibility of conversation and commensurability; *there* the enactment of an undecidable, uncanny colonial present, an Anglo-Indian difficulty, which repeats but is never itself fully represented [. . .] In the epistemological language of cultural description, the object of culture comes to be inscribed in a process that Richard Rorty describes as that confusion between justification and explanation, the priority of knowledge "of" over knowledge "that": the priority of the visual relation between persons and objects above the justification, textual relationship between propositions. It is precisely such a priority of eye over inscription, or Voice over writing, that insists on the "image" of knowledge as confrontation between the self and the object of belief seen through the mirror of Nature. Such an epistemological visibility disavows the metonymy of the colonial moment, because its narrative of ambivalent, hybrid, cultural knowledges—neither "one" nor "other"—is ethnocentrically elided in the search for cultural commensurability. (180–82)

Bhabha envisages the existence of an elision creating the *invisibility* of the narrative of cultural plurality. What is visible from the perspective of *A Passage* to India is the perception of difference from the colonizer's point of view, more a differentiation vis-à-vis colonial norms. The comparison between the colonizer and the colonized in the context of Forster's *A Passage to India* is equivalent to the position of Fanon's "The Black Man and Language." The failure of this reading, the inherent misunderstanding of the other as a comparable part of the self, encourages the transformation of the other into an antagonistic part of the self. Bhabha goes on:

> In these instances of social and discursive alienation there is no recognition of master and slave, there is only the matter of the enslaved master, the unmastered slave. What is articulated in the enunciation of the colonial present—in-between the lines—is a splitting of the discourse of cultural governmentality at the moment of its enunciation of authority. It is, according to Frantz Fanon, a "Manichean" moment that divides the colonial space: a Manichean division, two zones that are opposed but not in service of a "higher unity." [. . .] Splitting constitutes an intricate strategy of defense and differentiation in the colonial discourse. [. . .] Splitting is then a form of enunciatory, intellectual uncertainty and anxiety. (*Location of Culture* 188)

Bhabha, like Fanon, reiterates the essential "'Manichean' moment that divides the colonial space: a Manichean division, two zones that are opposed." For him, the "splitting is then a form of enunciatory, intellectual uncertainty and anxiety." This splitting dominates the essence of the third space and the intellectual forms it generates:

> It is significant that the productive capacities of this Third Space have a colonial or postcolonial provenance. For a willingness to descend into that alien territory—where I have led you—may reveal that the theoretical recognition of the split-space of enunciation may open the way to conceptualizing an international culture, based not on the exoticism of multiculturalism or the *diversity* of cultures, but on the inscription and articulation of culture's *hybridity*. To that end we should remember that it is the "inter"—the cutting edge of translation and negotiation, the *in-between* space—that carries the burden of the meaning of culture. It makes it possible to begin envisaging national, anti-nationalist histories of the "people." And by exploring this Third Space, we may elude the politics of polarity and emerge as the others of our selves. (56)

The third space is "the 'inter' [...] the *in-between space*." Bhabha is programmatic in stating that "by exploring this Third Space, we may elude the politics of polarity," an answer to Fanon's oppositionality. For Bhabha, the Third Space is a space of translation, the dynamic space of negotiation. Bhabha's comment on the term "hybridity" aligns with the present preoccupation of locating the functionality of this Third Space in language and its power of symbolization:

> What is irremediably estranging in the presence of the hybrid—in the revaluation of the symbol of national authority as the sign of colonial difference or evaluated as objects of epistemological or moral contemplation: cultural differences are not simply there to be seen or appropriated.
>
> Hybridity reverses the formal process of disavowal so that the violent dislocation of the act of colonization becomes the conditionality of colonial discourse. [...] It is crucial to remember that the colonial construction of the cultural (the site of the civilizing mission) through the process of disavowal is authoritative to the extent to which it is structured around the ambivalence of splitting, denial, repetition. (*Location of Culture* 163)

In fact, what is described here in terms of "hybridity" is the process that leads to the freedom to choose and desire without being condemned, as claimed by Fanon at the end of *Black Skin, White Masks*. Hybridity as the reversal of "the formal process of disavowal so that the violent dislocation of the act of colonization becomes the conditionality of colonial discourse" means that hybridity is a dialectic moment of opposition, where the present organization of powers are reversed. Both Fanon and Bhabha seem to generalize a theory of the postcolonial subject without concretely acknowledging what accounts for the specific complexity of historical diversity, looking back and forth between two dynamic maps of the self that superpose geographies of language and nation. These were exactly the criticisms addressed to Fanon by Bhabha: "It is one of the original and disturbing qualities of *Black Skin, White Masks* that it rarely historicizes the colonial experience" ("What Does the Black Man Want?" 118). Fanon does not consider the complexity of colonial diversity or a sort of "géocritique"/geocriticism of coloniality.[31] In other words, by prioritizing an ethical reading of colonialism, Fanon did not recognize the poetics of a plastic postcolonial subjectivity expressed within new ways of linguistic symbolization produced at different moments in the long history of colonialism.

This literary production, not filtered by an already canonized discourse of struggle, is probably the best space to explore the various answers to colonial cultural hegemony beyond any kind of binary opposition that is, in a sense, the very structure that reproduces dichotomies and encourages the emergence of power structures still affecting politics in the Global South as the major place of the postcolonial. It is time to reexamine literature per se out of the blind gaze of *ideology*.

The Healing Power of Literary Language

The labeling of cultural phenomena is a way to decipher and control a part of the world not yet objectively defined by uniformity. Literature has always escaped normative models of understanding. Beyond criticism, the fabric of poetry reveals to the "lecteur absolu" / "absolute reader" (Djebar, *Oran* 378) the human essence, which ideologies tend to hide from us.

Fanon's argument about pathologies of colonialism was extensively debated by writers and critics of the first wave of postcolonial studies and the decolonizing power of literature. However, they did not analyze the *ambiguities* surrounding the use of the colonial language. Mayy Ziyadah and Toru Dutt and, later, Assia Djebar and Ananda Devi addressed the violence of colonization by embodying multiplicity and plurality as a historical given, the hybridity described by Bhabha. They perform an enunciation based "not on the exoticism of multiculturalism or the *diversity* of cultures, but on the inscription and articulation of culture's *hybridity*" (Bhabha, *Location of Culture* 88). Dutt's fictional diary, *Le Journal de Mlle d'Arvers* (1879; *The Diary of Mademoiselle D'Arvers*, 2005), and Ziyadah's volume of lyrical poetry, *Fleurs de rêve* (1911; Flowers of dream), as well as Djebar's *L'Amour, la fantasia* (1985; *Fantasia: An Algerian Cavalcade*, 1993) and Devi's *Ève de ses décombres* (2005; *Eve out of Her Ruins*, 2016), likewise approached the conjunction between the use of an "I" and the culture's hybridity located first and foremost in the joyful use of languages. Today, we need to see the deep process at work in the language of hybridity.

Women's writing at the end of nineteenth century already defines another postcolonial subject by acknowledging the plurality, plasticity, and fluidity within a creolized (unified but not uniform) self,[32] as is the main idea in the postcolonial feminist critique developed by Bergner, Flax, Lionnet, and Shih in the late twentieth and early twenty-first century.[33] Dutt, Ziyadah, Djebar, and Devi represent countermodels to the aim of uniformity. This point allows me to comment on the necessity of this model to achieve a *multicultural citizenship*, that is both vertical, in how it considers all social spaces from popular to elite culture, and horizontal, in both a transcultural and transregional perspective (i.e., Algeria is not just Arab and Muslim but African, Amazigh, and Francophone). Through the recognition and confession of their constitutive plastic and fluid plurality, these authors avoid the "split" due to power divisions, which is, consequently, a "masculinized" understanding of history as well as a denial of the power of aesthetics, to translate the inner language into the outer language in a way that is both plastic and dynamic, and consequently *joyful*.

Our writers aim to transcend the splitting. As women, their strategy was and is to preserve that plural unity and show the profusion of possibilities, the enjoyment of difference, within the colonial context and its divide. The melancholia and anxiety of the split is reversed into a Kristevan *jouissance*, or celebration, of the creolized multiple.[34] My critique of the split subject is both an acknowledgement of its existence and its *de*pathologization; that is, this split will be perceived differently if another, female-authored body of texts is taken as a core corpus to rethink postcolonial subjectivity. In fact, recognizing plurality as inherent to a *hybrid* subjectivity is the position of those who have no choice over whether to keep the copresence of their differentiated languages. By choosing not to deny any part of their languages and cultures, the creolized writers accepted their hybrid selves without agreeing to be silenced.

In the process of acknowledging the *plurality of the self*, the subject is in a position to neutralize oppositional powers. For instance, in nineteenth-century Bengal, or during the Nahda, some women writers responded to colonial domination by promoting plurality and a cosmopolitan approach to subjectivity, and by providing a novel understanding of both the Bengali Renaissance and the Nahda not just as an anticolonial epistemology, but as the foundation of a creolized cosmopolitan self.[35] Women can suggest such a position because they were caught for centuries in-between different authorities and their languages. Their only way to survive was to develop subversive strategies of resistance to elude power structures and, very often, other languages specifically shared by their community of women (colloquial Arabic embodies this gender dimension and its equivalent in Indian languages). Therefore, it is time to revaluate a masculine-based elaboration of postcolonial subjectivity and to accept that the counterpoint position in epistemology begins with acknowledging the paradigmatic difference of the production of women postcolonial writers, inclusive of all the languages, both those spoken at home and those used in the wider world. Plurality is not a division of the self, but its multiplication, not the loss of a divided entity, but its growth.[36] Division and loss are the seeds of coloniality.

To summarize, the famous "Manichean" moment reimagined by Bhabha (*Location of Culture* 187) quoting Fanon, a kind of delirium, still informs modes of interpretation of *native cultures* that are now transformed into the myth of rigid *nation-states*. The fixedness of a reaction to the West prevents any kind of dialogue about possible fluidity, possible creolized universality, possible differentiation between cultural identities and fixed national community. Before and after Fanon's seminal idea of the postcolonial subject, some women writers were already thinking from the perspective of a nonoppositional plurality, fluidity, and constitution of a plastic multiple subjectivity that could coordinate histories to address the anxiety of the postcolonial condition. Now that those independence movements are over, maybe it is time to rethink the reified oppositions through the use of models of creolized writers. Within literary texts, the pragmatic model of multiplicity and fluidity occurs through the act of self-translation. Our poetics of a postcolonial subject in translation is based on the contention and critique of any discourse advocating for an internalized antagonistic position. It is a subject that claims plurality without ignoring the trauma of colonialism. Its Third Space is the active locus of *languages* and *literature* as a space of fluid plasticity representing protean worlds. The situations of this subject in translation are the recognition of literature as aesthetics beyond ideology, an answer to the need to think about *multiple* interconnected selves. In the realm of postcoloniality, the dimension of the political and the ethical prevents any claim of an aesthetic dimension of the postcolonial subject, probably because of the common understanding of the aesthetic as an ethics of ambiguity. The attention to beauty is felt as a threat to ideology. There is a hidden link between the denial of a *transcultural* postcolonial subject and the denial of aesthetics. The discourse of aesthetics, because of its nature—grounded in interpretation—is unclear, ethically confusing, and inefficient in the realm of the struggle, where nationalism advocates for a clear idealism. Beyond the violence of a schizophrenic answer to the complexity of history, the subject in translation performs the "higher unity" without indulging uniformity, claims inner plurality as the *only* answer to rigid ideologies of colonial and anticolonial powers. The following section addresses more specifically the "translation" aspect of this subjectivity, inherently linked to the pleasure of the fluid and plastic plural.

Translation as the Pleasure of the Plural

The pleasure of the plural is the joyful consciousness or jouissance that blossoms from the historical split of the postcolonial subject; a resolution to the schizophrenia of the postcolonial situation. Accepting the multiplicity of histories and filiations, different time periods overlapping, but also the multilingual aesthetics that builds postcolonial societies are ways of acknowledging their unique configuration, the first steps toward understanding the place of the subject in the postcolonial dynamic. Less obvious, however, is the need to describe the emergence of the multilingual aesthetic that gives order to that subject under the schizophrenic duress of postcolonialism.

A comparison of the myriad histories of the postcolonial subject will consolidate the aforementioned broader reflections on multilingual subjectivities. An extensive tradition on the subject already exists, yet there remains an urgent need to address the specificity of the complexities of a subject who is surrounded by several languages shaped by colonial power structures. This subject emerges from a poetic and aesthetic experience: the experience of the colonial language encountering native languages as *different soundscapes*. The point of origin is the unpredictable contact between several languages and aesthetic traditions expressed through all media, all visual (e.g., architecture, fashion) and acoustic senses (the languages spoken, the musics played). This first experience of internalized differences seems to take a specific form in writing through the invisible work of translation.

Derived from the Schillerian tradition, this subject could be described as "I feel, therefore I am."[37] The aesthetic subject expresses itself in relation to the sounds and sensations of the new culture, despite the violence of the encounter. This subjectivity (grounded in a plurality of languages and aesthetic forms) expresses resilience through its daily survival. It results from the postcolonial aesthetic experience and exposure to its hierarchy of languages: its acoustics, its graphism, its existence as sensual, sensorial encounter.

In essence, this subject's aesthetic experience is rooted in differentiated signs and the need for translation as a way of being. This state of existence, both in relation and in translation as a form of relationality, has been theorized, respectively, by Glissant in *Poétiques I à V* (Poetics 1 to 5) and by Khatibi, in several works.[38] It is in the last of these that Khatibi develops, precisely, the concept of "bi-language" (*bi-langue*) to explore postcolonial cultural production (textual, visual, acoustic) as informed by both a popular and a native tradition transformed by a European colonial presence.[39] The critical perspective in this chapter is a continuation of works by these Francophone postcolonial theorists on processes of cultural creolization and is highly informed by a Fanonian approach to ontological questions in postcolonial contexts, each of which pursues a cartography of postcolonial difference.

Khatibi and Glissant have established a catalog of concepts with which to examine difference in a variety of postcolonial contexts, from the "double-critique" (a resurgence of Du Bois's "double consciousness") in *The Souls of Black Folk* to the "bi-language," from "poetics of relation" (*poétique de la relation*) to "créolisation." Here, their conceptual framework is applied to female authors whose work exemplifies the concrete realities of their theories. In a few simple words, creolization is the system of the bi-language, and the bi-language is the manifestation or discernible aspects of the process of creolization. The praxis of translation in the *langue littéraire* (literary language), as exemplified in the work of Khatibi, is both systemic and specific to each author vis-à-vis the linguistic configuration of each instance of languages under examination.[40] This phenomenon of the subject in translation needs to be addressed historically and to be related to gender.

Khatibi's complex analysis of the work of the bi-language in his seminal chapter on Meddeb's *Talismano*, "Bilinguisme et littérature" (Bilingualism and literature), in *Maghreb pluriel*, offers a methodology to approach multilingual writers who are exposed to more than two languages. Their positionality is not static but dynamic, and, more importantly, this "being in translation" is an ontological principle that structures their *relation* to the world and to the language that speaks the world. The multilingual positionality is the consequence of a historical trauma that inscribes any postcolonial subjectivity into an essential existence in translation. This being in translation is not merely a theoretical discourse, but a praxis that draws from all sensorial experiences. This existence in translation is perhaps more pronounced in places of the world belonging to the former French Empire, whose language politics were brutal, based on a systemic erasure of native languages and cultures, but the same can be said of the former colonies of the British Empire and other European countries. The being in translation is therefore aligned with Khatibi's theory of a double-critique (*Maghreb pluriel*; Plural Maghreb). The not only double but plural episteme is the result of this exposure to languages with differentiated power dynamics, with one tongue holding the power to destroy and silence the other. This book's textual analysis of how writing in bi-language (or, in more than two languages; for me, in dia-language) transforms the sign is a tribute to Khatibi and a continuation of his thought.[41]

The Dia-language

In colonial contexts, the encounter with the *sounds* of the colonial language is a brutal, transformative aesthetic experience.[42] *Aesthesis* means "sensation," or, in the discipline of psychology, physiological traces of our embodied relation to the world.[43] Our reaction to the world is then recognized and actualized by our speech and allows for individual subjective differentiation, which can be understood as resulting from aesthetic experiences. Contrary to subjectivity in a precolonial condition, the postcolonial subject is crafted by the forced and rejected relation between a colonial language and native languages.

This dynamic is most acute when it comes to women writers. In colonial contexts, colonization and modernization fostered access to education for native women, adding new forms of expressions into their life experience with a new language (mainly French or English). Schools for girls developed in North Africa and Egypt in the 1880s. Meanwhile, in India and Egypt, some aristocratic families hired women preceptors to educate their young ladies.[44] Such a deep transformation of society led to a new intersubjective relation to the colonial world. The subject as theorized by Fanon and Bhabha must be differentiated from the colonized feminine subject (under scrutiny in this book), who was exposed to poetry and literary forms in a colonial language, gaining a bitter freedom while discovering new sounds, new words, new realities. A form of feminine subjectivity was likely already present in some aristocratic milieux in India and Egypt, but traditional structures limiting women's artistic production usually prevented the affirmation of such a subjectivity. One proposed catalyst for the emergence of women writers and a specifically feminine subjectivity at this time consisted of their access to secular education, whether private or public.[45] Whatever insights our critique of colonization morphs into, it remains true that European education gave voices to women who traditionally belonged to marginalized classes: thus, colonization opened spaces for subaltern women within their own cultural milieu.[46] Shall we ignore this transformation because it is an inconvenient truth?

As colonization imposed its norms and language, translation became, both literally and metaphorically, the medium of relation between the two spaces of the native and the colonial. For many writers of the colonial era, the figure of the mother often represents the sounds of their native tongue. In *Love in Two Languages*, Khatibi dramatically describes this complex positionality with respect to both aural traditions, which were generationally transmitted by women, and written traditions, transmitted by the Quranic schools and colonial public schools. In between the two traditions there emerged a permanent movement of translation. Women writers are the heirs to both. Their reception of the colonial language constructs a singular chaotic positionality, which has been thoroughly studied in relation to Assia Djebar vis-à-vis her theory on languages, among them the language of the body.[47]

Translation is correlated to the process of the bi-language as described by Khatibi and Gauvin's notion of the linguistic overconsciousness. The bi-language—or, in my own interpretation, the dia-language, because multilingual writing can involve more than two languages—is the process of this particular language, while the linguistic overconsciousness is the psychic state related to the bi-language: translation is its perpetual movement toward its resolution.[48]

Translation is also the work of moving a text from one language to another in both its visible and invisible dimensions. Additionally, it is meant to embody the experience of plurality. There is, therefore, a linguistic and an ontological dimension necessarily grounded in experienced sensations. Instead of conceiving of the colonial encounter one-dimensionally, as a discourse of loss and trauma (which it is, without reservation), we must recontextualize colonial subjectivity as aesthetic experiences of plurality and acknowledge the resilient and plastic literary responses offered by women writers in such extreme situations of cultural ambiguity. As a response, the language of literature informed their daily life strategy; they decided to make their stand in writing, to preserve their integrity without renouncing one or the other language. Finally, it was through the work of translation that the plurality of the languages of colonization unified.

As Khatibi beautifully describes in *Love in Two Languages*, translation is the active resistance of plurality in language. While there is always the possibility of shutting down this process and submissively remaining in one language, the act of translation is irrepressible, as it is the *process* of recovering emotions and sensations in the repressed hidden language: Bengali, French, Arabic,

Tamazight, and Creole. In each situation, the language of domination needs to be analyzed outside of the overdetermined ideological categories that very often prevent critical thinking about them. In each context, it is important to evaluate the power dynamics where the personal meets the political.

Among the previously mentioned theorists on colonial subjectivity, Gauvin has extensively explored the work of multilingual Francophone writers in a diverse body of literary texts, both linguistically and culturally, and analyzed this subjectivity's semantic and symbolic implications within the corpus.[49] The path opened by Khatibi and Gauvin acknowledges French as specific in Francophone postcolonial writing. But, as it often is with pioneers, while Khatibi, Gauvin, and others have elaborated on a select amount of the potentially fruitful inquiries revealed by their earlier work, what has been left unrealized must now be uncovered by contemporary critics.

In my perspective, writers' nuanced relationship to colonial language provides a space for the continuation of this intellectual lineage. The experience of colonization destroys the cultural foundations of native lands, leaving its victims naked and dispossessed, but not broken. Women writers inverted the dynamic of resistance and resilience—from destruction to reconstruction through the plasticity of poetic experiences, and through the remodeling of their colonial world to welcome the worlds in words. In this inverse dynamic, the translation at the heart of the process contaminates both the colonial language and the native language, charging their interstitial relation. Textual analysis is the praxis to reveal this modus operandi, a tribute to the writers working in the only material given to resist all iterations of oppression.

In the following chapters, each writer is discussed in her specific multilingual context. The being in translation is analyzed through poetics expressed in various literary forms: poetry, novels, essays, and letters.

2

BEING COSMOPOLITAN IN NINETEENTH-CENTURY CALCUTTA

Toru Dutt (1856–1877)

In his essay *Towards Universal Man* (1961), Rabindranath Tagore (1861–1941) expressed the need for a universalist perspective, probably to avoid the dangers of a growing nationalism in a region where a diversity of languages and religions immediately displayed the paradox of the nation. In Bengal, during the same period, Toru Dutt (1856–1877) wrote her first novel in French, probably the first francophone novel by a female writer, *The Diary of Mlle D'Arvers* (published after the author's death, in 1879), with an explicit desire to repress her Indianness. It is considered the first Francophone novel written by an Indian woman. Her other novel, in English, *Bianca, or The Young Spanish Maiden* (1878), also published after her death, explicitly expressed her being plural, just as her languages and cultures were. Her original choices as a translator of poetry, from French into English, in the only volume published during her life, *A Sheaf Gleaned in French Fields* (1876), reveal the resolution of her divided self. Is this to say that the language of poetry contains the space of a plastic reinvention of the multilingual self, per se? Either way, these early modernist texts reveal the inner tensions between Dutt's nationalism and a desired cosmopolitanism as they invite us to analyze contradictions inherent in the circulation of cultural components through languages and political structures, both often moving from the European center to the peripheries in nineteenth-century India.[1]

As in the chapters that follow, I will begin this chapter by trying to capture the nature of coexisting and competing ideological structures of domination and their translation into poetic language. In the nineteenth century, the circulation of aesthetic forms was predetermined by the trajectory between empires and their colonies. In colonized regions of the time, cultures were not limited to the modern structure of the nation, however. Cultures precede the nation-state, a concept that is still an epiphenomenon, with respect to a long history of cultural exchanges. Thus, we must adopt a transcultural perspective regarding cultures and territories that are not nationally defined.[2] While transnationalism (circulation between nations) is an etymologically recent form of "relationality,"[3] the transcultural is foundational (because nations are more recent than cultures), even if its understanding changes throughout the history of human societies, adapting to the way human groups are organized (tribes, empires, cities).[4]

The building of a modern sense of community and displacement of cultural components, including ideological and aesthetic forms, can be reinterpreted according to a poetics of the subject. The expression of subjectivity in creative writing, as in Dutt's production, reveals a plastic cultural imagination beyond predetermined territory, be it linguistic, religious, or national. I argue that approaching the polymorphism of the subject through textual analysis reveals a complex and ambiguous conception of cultural circulation. My reading of the text will also show, through the recorded experience of cultural diversity, how Dutt unconsciously built literary worlds that allowed for hospitality. Being cosmopolitan, a "citizen of the world," during the emergence of Indian nationalism, was understood as a provocation going against the grain of the nation.

Toru Dutt was a poetess and writer, educated in different languages and possessed of knowledge of diverse cultural worlds (French, British, Bengali). Her life during the Bengali Renaissance exposed her to the cosmopolitanism of Calcutta, the Raj's capital during that period.[5] Her experiences as a reader, traveler, translator, and writer allowed her to elaborate on the complexity of being a colonized female subject informed by multiple cultures and languages. Dutt's texts illustrate an ambiguous and misread cosmopolitan ethos close to what Amit Chaudhuri observes about Tagore: "Imperfectly perceived, partially known, unnamed presence—whether it represents the spiritual source of the pre-colonial world now made semi-visible and nameless, or the regeneration of the new one" (*Clearing a Space* 83). Through a close reading of Dutt's language strategies, I will question Dutt's convivial position to otherness as opposed to the exclusive nationalist discourse, represented by Bankim Chandra Chatterjee, the father of Indian nationalism. I will then attempt to deconstruct the misreading of indigenous cosmopolitanism as only an indigenous imperialism. Finally, I will suggest a retrospective reading of cosmopolitanism in nineteenth-century Bengal as a form of cultural inclusiveness, as an essence of the subject in translation emerging within the poetics of the text.

Portrait of a Multilingual Bengali Author

Toru Dutt was born in March 1856 to "a Hindu family in Rambagan (Calcutta). Her father, Govin Chunder Dutt, was a good poet and linguist. Her mother, Kshetramoni, was well-versed in Bengali and English" (Dwivedi, *Toru Dutt: A Literary Profile* 1). She was the niece of Michael Chandra Dutt, a famous historian and the author of several novels in English. As A. N. Dwivedi asserts, "[Her] conversion to Christianity caused a temporary estrangement between Toru's parents, her mother being a devout Hindu lady" (2). The family experienced several tragedies, the first of which occurred in 1865, with the death of Dutt's eldest brother at the age of fourteen. In 1869, the Dutt family left for Europe, where Toru and her older sister Aru learned French while studying in Nice from 1869 to 1873. The world of young Toru Dutt was animated by the poets she read while in Calcutta in the company of her father, the instigator of her insatiable passion for literature.

In what follows, I will provide an intimate map of Dutt as a reader, a projection of a dreamed world putting all of her different personae in relation to each other: first, as a translator of French poetry into English; as a writer of two novels in colonial languages; as a poet (through her posthumous 1883 volume of poetry, *Ancient Ballads and Legends of Hindustan,* a mix of her own creation and an adaptation of ancient legends and ballads); and, finally, as a letter-writer, where she freely exhibits her unpredictable use of different languages (French, English, Sanskrit) as well as her ambiguous political posture toward her native culture. The letters especially are a space where Dutt evoked the contradictions of being cosmopolitan but colonized, her uncomfortable political position, her struggle against her own internalized colonial biases. Taken together, these texts allowed room for complex contradictions, a multi-dimensional construction of the *self.*

The two sisters, Aru and Toru Dutt, worked together to translate more than a hundred French poems into English in *A Sheaf Gleaned in French Fields.* Even though it was a family enterprise, Toru was the main translator. *A Sheaf* was a personal anthology, probably inspired during her stay in France. The volume received critiques praising her genius in the mastery of both French and English poetry rules; indeed, the French poems had been rendered in English verse. *A Sheaf* contained 156 poems, of which 155 were translations and the last her own creation, written for her father. There is no real thematic order or any visible structure to the volume. For example, there are several poems by already-famous French poets of the time, but the work is not ordered by poet or by school (i.e., *parnassien, romantique*). The volume opens with a poem by Leconte de Lisle, "The Sleep of the Condor" / "Le Sommeil du condor," and closes with "To Pépa," by Alfred de Musset. Victor Hugo is the most represented poet (30 poems), followed by de Musset (3 poems), Théophile Gautier (3 poems), Gérard de Nerval (3 poems), Alphonse de Lamartine (3 poems), Alphred de Vigny (2 poems), Charles Baudelaire (2 poems), Sully Prudhomme (2 poems), Du Bartas (1 poem), Chateaubriand (1 poem), Charles Nodier (1 poem), and Joachim du Bellay (1 poem). The work also includes one anonymous poet and several lesser-known poets by today's standards, such as Pierre Dupont (1821–1870, 2 poems) and N. Martin (1814–1877, 2 poems). Among those names, there are also French poetesses of varying notoriety, like Madame Henriette Bourdic-Viot (1744–1802), Madame Desbordes-Valmore (1830–1871), and Louise Victorine Ackermann (1813–1890). The themes evoked are representative of a diversity of genres and tones: the elegiac, epic, and political, in poems by Victor Hugo ("After the Battle," "On the Barricade," "The Political Prisoners"), including the famous satirical poem "Napoléon le petit," whose title Dutt did not translate into English. There are also poems about travel and exile, such as Du Bellay's famous sonnet about Odysseus. Most express romantic feelings and suggest how isolated Dutt was—far from a real intellectual life, translating was a promenade among poets and texts she liked and wanted to share with other readers. The poems follow the flow of her readings, much like a bee flying from flower to flower. It is thrilling to see all these texts in a creative disorder. It could also be the accumulative process of the bucolic reader that would have pleased Montaigne.

By choosing to translate French poetry into English, Dutt aimed to experience literature organically, balancing the rigor of historical studies that had developed in the nineteenth century with her urge to explore new territories as a poet. As a Hindu-raised woman translating from French into English, Dutt became a mediator between the two imperialist languages without ignoring the Sanskrit tradition. For example, in *A Sheaf*, she quotes verses in Sanskrit from the *Ramayana*, which she found relevant for illustrating how Victor Hugo's poem "On the Death of His Daughter" (180) expresses a similar sorrow to a verse in Sanskrit. She adds in her notes on Hugo's poem, "Have we not here the same cry that thrilled the hearts of hearers three thousand years ago!" (232). The quotation is followed by the Sanskrit verses. It is rare to see Bengali or Sanskrit texts quoted as equals in texts by European authors, as if the social and political boundaries imposed by imperialism were transmitted to textual spaces, reproducing a mental divide and preventing any intertextuality from easily occurring. When *A Sheaf* came out, Dutt declared that she would "be able to bring out another 'Sheaf,' not gleaned in French but in Sanskrit Fields" (Dwivedi, *Toru Dutt: A Literary Profile* 3); this would be her *Ancient Ballads*. Dutt accepted that she would need to reconcile her vast European culture with her equally vast Indian culture. Without reference to borders or differentiated spaces, her unique aim was to appreciate texts for their aesthetic values, the pleasure they gave her as a reader. Her movement from one text to the other is an expression of her inclusive perspective, which allows the *Ramayana*, the *Mahabharata*, and the *Vishnu Purana* to be compared to poems by Hugo, Leconte de Lisle, de Musset, and de Lamartine.

Ancient Ballads is a series of texts adapting historically important Indian legends. Some of her essays were published in the *Bengla Magazine* and show her ambition to create connections between the English language and her Bengali roots. Dutt wanted to celebrate all of her languages, poetry, and cultures without exception, guilt, or fear. She "never ceased to be Indian," and her *Ancient Ballads* "seemed to answer to a profound inner need for links with the living past of the country as well as [. . .] serv[ing] her poetic purpose" (Dwivedi, *Toru Dutt: A Literary Profile* 61). Dutt received recognition for her talent as a poet, as shown by the following quotes from literary critics. As Edmund Gosse puts it in the introduction to *Ancient Ballads*, if she were alive,

> she would still be younger than any recognized European writer, and yet her fame [. . .] is already considerable. [. . .]. Within the brief space of four years which now divides us from the date of her decease, her genius has been revealed to the world under many phases, and has been recognized throughout France and England. (7)

> She brought with her from Europe a store of knowledge that would have sufficed to make an English or French girl seem learned, but which in her case was simply miraculous. Immediately on her return she began to study Sanskrit with the same intense application which she gave all her work, and mastering the language with extraordinary swiftness, she plunged into its mysterious literature. But she was born to write, and

despairing of an audience in her own language, she began to adopt ours as a medium for her thoughts. (13)

Ancient Ballads follows the structure of the *Ramayana*. At the end, the volume contains the *Miscellaneous Poems*. The first section, *Ancient Ballads*, is divided into nine parts, each part dedicated to a specific character, some from the *Mahabharata* and others from Indian legends: Savitri, Lakshman, Jogadhy Uma, the Royal Ascetic and the Hind, Dhruva, Buttoo, Sindhu, Prehad, and Sita. As an example of her *Ancient Ballads,* let me quote a few verses:

> Savritri was the only child
> Of Madra's wise and mighty king;
> Stern warriors, when they saw her smiled,
> As mountains smile to see the spring.
> Fair as a lotus when the moon
> Kisses its opening petals red,
> After sweet showers in sultry June! (1)

The verses introduce Savitri, a major character of Hindu mythology. Here the form and versification is in the pure English romantic tradition, while the character and landscape are Indian. Words like "Savitri, Madra, Lotus, Moon" belong to the Indian poetical tradition. Themes and metaphors like "Fair as a lotus when the moon / Kisses its opening petals" draw on an established Oriental tradition that we also find in Arabic and Persian poetry, particularly around the symbolism of the moon. The reader sees here another sort of translation, a creolization and transfer of figures, symbols, and metaphors from Sanskrit to English in European versified form. Dutt accomplished the transformation of Indian literature—she did indeed glean sheafs in "Sanskrit Fields."

At the end of the literary history *Essais de littérature anglaise*, written by James Darmesteter, the young Indian lady appears after Lord Byron, described in these terms: "This child of Bengal so admirably and so strangely gifted, Hindu by race and tradition, British by education, and French in her heart: poet in English, prose writer in French."[6]

In her two novels, *The Diary* and *Bianca, or The Young Spanish Maiden,* Dutt explores characters totally immersed in French and British contexts, respectively. It is as if she translated her inner being from her Indian location to other cultures and languages. Dutt's decision to write her first novel in French was not an easy one. I hypothesize, perhaps too much in the vein of a postcolonial perspective, that French represented neutral territory for her. In a sense, French was a space safe from the historical conflicts that plagued her country, colonized by the English, and from all the local tensions she experienced as a Christian in a Hindu milieu.[7] Another anecdote sheds light on Dutt's relation to poetry and fiction. In the introduction to *The Diary*, Clarisse Bader, a French critic of the period, recounts a story told by a family friend:

> Toru Dutt did not direct her studies towards history. One day, lord L . . . visited the Babu and his family in Calcutta, and having surprised Aru with a novel in her hand, he told the two girls, "Ah! You should not read too many novels, you should read histories."
> Toru replied, "We like to read novels, lord L . . ."
> "Why?"
> The bright young girl replied smilingly, "Because novels are true, and histories are false." (De Souza and Pereira, *Women's Voices* 17)

The truth of the novels is what fiction teaches us about the complexity of our emotions, those hidden by historical accounts.

Her letters are treasure troves of reflections and interesting comments that allow us to see the making of a subject in a multilingual context. Through her different readings, we can see how she also identified with some women writers. In a mix of French and English, she comments to her friend Miss Martin about her passion for the Brontë family. She implicitly compares herself to Charlotte Brontë as she shares her love for *Jane Eyre*:

> **MARCH 24, 1876**
> I wonder what the papers will say of my book. Of course there will be *for* and *against*, and I have already armed myself with stoicism.
>
> When *Jane Eyre* was first brought out, of course there were some papers which cut up the book. Thackeray, who was a friend of Miss Brontë, went to see her the day after, to observe how she read and took an attack on her book which had appeared in one of the leading daily papers.
>
> **MAY 13, 1876**
> The *Life of Charlotte Bronte*, by Mrs Gaskell, induced me to read some more of Miss Brontë's works; *Shirley* is well-written and interesting; *Villette* is a failure; there is one character which [*sic*] is interesting, M. Paul Emmanuel. (*Letters* 156)

Dutt jumps from one space to another one, putting them in touch in her own creative writing and creating bridges that will link different shores, recreating the bridges any colonial culture destroys. Dutt's aim was to refuse to acknowledge the existence of the divide, even if it would have been more comfortable from a bourgeois Bengali position to feel prepared to embrace the world.

As a female writer in a highly patriarchal society, she was sensitive to gendered assumptions as another form of discrimination. For example, in her letter dated May 13, 1876, we read: "There was a very good and favorable criticism of my book in the *Madras Standard* a few days ago, only the critic had taken me for a gentleman, and used 'he' and 'his' every time! I was rather amused and (shall I confess it?) perhaps a little flattered at this mistake" (*Letters* 157).

Amazingly, because she was well ahead of her time, she insisted on using feminine forms of the word "author," typically gendered masculine, to describe herself. In her translations, she added women poets to reach a balance not even found in recent anthologies of Romantic French poetry. Dutt also tried to avoid the same divide in her native Hindu culture and cites, in her writing in English, names of ancient Hindu female figures such as Sita and Sakuntala. Though repairing and healing colonial divides was central to her poetics, the next section addresses ideological contradictions and colonial fractures that induced interpretations of Toru Dutt as an imperialist.

The Politics of Languages during the Bengali Renaissance

In 1864, Bankim Chandra Chatterjee published his first book, *Rajmohan's Wife*, considered to be the first Indian novel written in English. After this experience, he suddenly decided not to write in English anymore, but in Bengali. In fact, after *Rajmohan's Wife*, he was harshly criticized for his use of the colonial language. "'To be original in an acquired language is hardly feasible,' according to [Aurobindo] Ghose (who himself, incidentally, only wrote in English); for an Indian, the enterprise of writing in English has 'something unnatural and spurious about it—like speaking with a stone in the mouth'" (*Rajmohan's Wife* 137). Comparing *Rajmohan's Wife* with other of Chatterjee's novels, Meenakshi Mukherjee comments: "*Rajmohan's Wife* never had that kind of visibility, partly because the book was not easily accessible, but also because most commentators and critics of Bankim Chandra have regarded his foray into English as 'a false start' after which he is supposed to have found his true métier in Bangla" (*Rajmohan's Wife* 5). Bankim Chandra Chatterjee is still today identified as the father of Bengali nationalism, which fast became Indian nationalism, mainly in recognition of his famous novel in Bengali, *Anandamath* (*The Abbey of Bliss* 1882). Chatterjee chose not to write in a "foreign language"—even though he was educated in English, he defended the use of a regional language (one of the numerous Indian languages). In his writings, he built a model of nationhood based on the praise of historical Hindu mythology, Hinduism, and the use of Bengali to assert a modern sense of community.[8]

Years after Chatterjee's decision to stop writing in English, Dutt published her *Sheaf*. The criticism she received from her countrymen sheds light on the way she was read by the Bengali society of her time: "Sri Aurobindo [. . .] regretted, 'That unhappy and immature genius, who unfortunately wasted herself on a foreign language and perished while yet little more than a girl'" (*Toru Dutt: Collected Prose and Poetry* 353). Even though most critics admired the genius of her writing in English and her perfect knowledge of French, some, like Aurobindo, deplored the fact that she squandered her time writing in a "foreign language." Aurobindo affirmed the first condition of the emergence of a modern nation: the constructed superposition between language identity and national identity, implying that English could not be an Indian language. From a European perspective, too, Dutt's Indianness was minimized: in 1881, Edmund Gosse and James Darmesteter stated that "nothing in the book [*The Diary*] betrays the fact that the writer is a foreigner."[9] Bader wrote, "Toru showed me the native qualities of a Hindu woman developed and transformed by the Christian civilization of Europe" (*Collected Prose* xxi). In each case, Dutt is represented as an imperialist brilliantly using European languages. Indians saw her as a corrupted product, and Europeans as a perfectly adapted product. The choice of which language to write in was corrupted by political interpretation and partisanship, particularly in the colonial period.

Of course, it is easy to understand why, at the time of the rise of Indian nationalism, some Indian intellectuals would associate cosmopolitanism with the elite position offered to upper-class Indians suspected to be British sympathizers because they were so Europeanized. Just like Dutt, women intellectuals were often misread as imperialists if they chose to write in the language of the colonizer, reaffirming that "the word 'education' had come to be synonymous with English education" (*Rajmohan's Wife* 148). Yet, in fact, it was easier for these women to use English (as it was for Algerian and Egyptian women writers to use French) to avoid the gendered segregation and subjugation of male-dominated Indian society. Many women gained the right to express themselves specifically through their education in English. For these reasons, Dutt was seen as an imperialist.

The ambiguity of her position—Dutt often felt guilty about her imperialist self—can only be resolved by examining her writing; the complex unfolding of her voice as a *double-nature* subject finds room in the text.[10] In her letters to Miss Martin, we find examples of her ambiguous but sincere position toward the colonial culture. Some could be understood as racist comments, but let us keep in mind that she was not even in her twenties when writing these letters:

[BAUGMAREE GARDEN HOUSE, MAY 12, 1974]
[...] Our grandfather and grandmother never can hear of our return to Europe; the latter weeps at even the mention of it. I wish you knew her: she is, I am sad to say, still a Hindu, but she is so gentle and loves us so much. (*Collected Prose* 228)

[CALCUTTA, OCTOBER 12, 1875]
The *Doorga-Poojah* holidays have come, and all business men [sic] have left town for a change. Last Sunday was the day that the Hindus threw the goddess Doorga into the river, after three days' worship! The streets were crowded to excess, processions, with the goddess, I mean with her image, borne in a triumphal throne and with music, marched towards the river. We thought we should be able to escape all the noise and crowd by going to Baugmaree for a day or two, but somehow we were prevented. (*Collected Prose* 247)

[CALCUTTA, JANUARY 13, 1876]
[...] There is a good deal of talk at present about a Bengali gentleman and a pleader, Babu Juggodanundo Mukherjee, because he permitted the Prince to see his zenana. All the papers conducted by natives are loudly crying out against this "Outrage on Hindu Society." (*Collected Prose* 259)

[CALCUTTA, MARCH 13, 1876]
Thank you very much for what you say about calling my countrymen "natives"; the reproof is just, and I stand corrected. I shall take care and not call them natives again. It is indeed a term only used by prejudiced Anglo-Indians, and I am really ashamed to have used it. (*Collected Prose* 263)

Dutt carries with her the superiority complex of educated Indians who were Westernized and, in her case, Christianized. As we can read in her letters, she was probably ashamed in her youth to be Hindu, although she eventually reverted to more constructive and productive feelings toward her Bengali Hindu background. Reading the letters, we can see how conflicted and "really ashamed" she was to have called her countrymen "natives." As we will find below, her trajectory as a writer and thinker exposes different strategies of harmonization between her conflicting cultural systems.

In a comparative reflection about languages and political systems, Tagore offered another understanding of the "split" nature of the colonized subject. For example, as far back as 1892, he argued about the dissociation between the English culture and language and the structures of meaning in Bengali: "From whatever angle we consider the matter, we find that our life, our thought, and our language are not harmonized. Because of this fundamental disunity, we cannot stand on our two feet, cannot get what we want. [. . .] Let us pray that He would unite our language with our thought and our education with our life" (*Towards Universal Man* 48). Through this politics of languages, the plea to "unite our language with our thought and our education with our life," Tagore outlines the inadequacy between forms that are mainly discourses, or structures of meaning that are imported, and the local structures that are not adapted to receive these forms. In another famous article, "Society and State," he argued:

> The inmost creed of India is to find the one in the many, unity in diversity. India does not admit difference to be conflict. [. . .] Since India has this genius for unification, we do not have to fear imaginary enemies. [. . .] Hindu and Buddhist, Muslim and Christian shall not die fighting on Indian soil; here they will find harmony. That harmony will not be non-Hindu; on the contrary, it will be peculiarly Hinduistic. And however cosmopolitan the several limbs may be, the heart will still be the heart of India. (50)

> We must remember that we shall not always have to receive the learning of Europe as mere students. (65–66)

Tagore's discourse represents the other as internalized in the form of a "cosmopolitan[ism]" equated with a localized and historicized praxis of universalism.[11] The other becomes the world, cosmos, or universe, sliding slightly toward Europe, toward England.[12] On the opposite shore is the representation of India as the womb that will feed the community.

In a sense, Tagore implies that if we take the nation-state as a model for the building of a people, the Indian community should address differences between the structures of meaning that were imported and the social reality specific to India, its territories, its inner diversity of languages and religious groups.[13] Tagore pointed out the inadequacy between the two layers or structures of discourses that do not fit with each other. Like two conflicting maps, the national model does not correspond to the Indian cultural reality. He was predicting the partition, showing through structures of discourses the split meaning from which social crisis would result. Tagore was looking for harmony between cosmopolitanism as a form of universal thinking and India, offering to his readers a revised definition of "universal" that would no longer be European, but "truly" global. Arjun Appadurai has described the circulation of political forms as being composed of "ideoscapes," or "images which are associated with state or counter-state movement ideologies which are comprised of elements of freedom, welfare, rights, etc." ("Disjuncture and Difference" 10–11). The cultural components circulating in the nineteenth century came from literary and historical texts, representations, but were also grounded in the experiences of the colonized.

Dutt's works function as an example of the encounter between contradictory structures as she looked for a solution to handle her internal "hybridity." Her representation of literature is built using analogy, bringing together writers from France, England, and India. Consequently, her desired assimilation—which is an ideological position—is defeated by her praxis of cultural and aesthetic discourses. There is a contradiction between her claimed position as a fervent supporter of "France," and her literary praxis that in fact transforms what is first perceived as differences into a fluid circulation between objects of desire. The result of the encounter is a reflection upon her inner creolized self, or a subjectivity in translation.

Being in Translation

In his introduction to Dutt's *Ancient Ballads*, Gosse comments on *A Sheaf* as follows:[14]

At that moment the postman brought in a thin and sallow packet with a wonderful Indian postmark on it, and containing a most unattractive orange pamphlet of verse, printed at Bhowanipore, and entitled "A Sheaf gleaned in French Fields, by Toru Dutt." This shabby little book of some two hundred pages, without preface or introduction, seemed specially destined by its particular providence to find its way hastily into the waste-paper basket [. . .] A hopeless volume it seemed, with its queer type, published at Bhowanipore, printed at the Saptahiksambad Press! But when at last I took it out of my pocket, what was my surprise and almost rapture to open at such verse as this:—Still barred thy doors! The far east glows, / The morning wind blows fresh and free. (viii–ix)[15]

Gosse's comments perfectly illustrate the aesthetic and political effects of reading and translating from a minor, transnational position in the world. The configuration of French literature, as seen from a little town in India that is not even a former French colony like Pondichéry, demonstrates how the circulation of texts is not just the displacement of texts, discourses, forms, and languages from the center to the peripheries: it exemplifies the transformative function of the acts of reading and translating in unexpected comparative and transnational perspectives.[16] The two acts also partly deconstruct certain structures of power through their intimacy, which allows for reconfiguration at different levels of meaning (e.g., poetic, discursive, symbolic).

The encounter between the reader and a text is always a very special, transformative moment. During her stay in France, Dutt cultivated a particular feeling and sensibility for French literature and poetry.[17] Yet it is still important to determine how she came to read certain texts.[18] Indeed, although she was probably not reflexive about the process—at least not openly—the result of her choices is interesting and strikingly diverse. Dutt's collection of poems implies a certain history of French poetry that is uncommon: one made from the peripheries. As mentioned previously, the anthology illustrates a most comprehensive perception of French poetry, mixing minor poets with major ones, the political and the intimate, the grand and the minor genres, women and men and allowing for a critical comparative perspective on reading. Emotionally and cognitively speaking, Dutt experienced reading as a fundamental act of comparison and analogy. This is not to say that we need to limit our understanding of the phenomenon to the lens of analogy, but that, by comparing (therefore connecting) similar cultural phenomena, we can identify patterns that guide the circulation of knowledge in specific directions on a larger scale.

The act of reading that led to this anthology resulted from analogies established between texts from a constellation of French authors and texts grouped by their proximity to and difference from other European texts and authors. As Lootens explains, "Dutt's critical scholarship speaks from Calcutta: it seeks to interpellate, by assuming, an audience whose conversance with Indian writing is as much a matter of course as is its familiarity with British, American, and French poetry and poetic criticism" ("Bengal, Britain, France" 583).

In *A Sheaf*'s notes section, Dutt draws certain analogies and described her readings of the French poets she translates in a very consistent paratext. When mentioning the song "My Vocation," by French poet and songwriter Pierre-Jean de Béranger, she notes: "This song was a great favorite of Thackeray. The reader may perhaps remember his reference to it in his lecture on Goldsmith" (192). In another note, on Charles Nodier, she writes: "His stories are charming, and remind one very much of Washington Irving. His 'Souvenirs' also are very interesting. A very graphic account of his life and works has been given by Alexandre Dumas who was a personal friend of his. Nodier travelled in England and Scotland, and some verses addressed by him to Sir Walter Scott after a visit will be found in one of the earlier numbers of *Blackwood's Magazine*" (193). Her practice of reading and translation makes visible an implied history of connections and relationships. She formulates the act of reading as a comparative process, where translation plays a major role in connecting and building intimate cartographies of knowledge whose circulation is determined by larger power structures and by intimate pathways. For instance, about Nicolas Martin, a poet who remains unfamiliar to most scholars, she writes: "[. . .] Nicolas Martin is deeply imbued with the grand poetry of Germany. He was born at Bonn, and his mother was a German lady,—a sister to the poet Karl Simrock, the learned translator into modern language of the old and magnificent *Nibelungen*, which Victor Hugo considers to be one of the three great epics of the world,—the other two being the *Mahabharata* and the *Ramayana*. M. Martin's landscapes are very beautiful, and his German leanings have not spoiled his French at all. It is very clear and idiomatic" (194). We see in her remarks on Martin an explanation tying the citation to the claim preceding it.

In another note, she comments on the translation from Goëthe and Schiller by Emile Deschamps: "[. . .] Emile Deschamps like his brother Antoni Deschamps has paid much attention to foreign literature. His translations from Goëthe and Schiller,—*La Cloche, La Fiancée de Corinthe, Le Roi de Thule*, may stand side by side with the admirable originals, and his imitations of the Spanish Ballads are as good as those of Mr Lockhart. As an original writer he belongs to the Romantic school founded by Lamartine and Hugo" (*Sheaf* 195). Obviously, her notes bind texts together in an infinite possible network. She does much the same regarding Gérard de Nerval, reminding us of certain elements of his work and trajectory as a writer and a translator: "[. . .] His tastes led him towards the legendary, the mysterious, and the supernatural, and German literature, had, as a consequence, a fascination for him. He translated the Faust of Goëthe and the ballads of Bürger and of Koerner. He knew Hebrew and Sanscrit well, and has left us some translations from Calidasa and Solomon" (196).

Moreover, Dutt explains the connections between the authors in her anthology as if building bridges between them is necessary to understand their poetry. Indeed, different scales of networking are implied by the figure of the reader she explicitly represents. The network is thus established not only between texts but also between places and temporalities. Her notes shape an intimate cartography where Bonn, Paris, Calcutta, and London are closer than in real life; places and texts are therefore seen as mapping a circulation of meaning and its transformative function. The same is the case with temporalities. While the relations between writers defeat periodization, Dutt engages in a diachronical understanding of literature: in her notes the *Nibelungen* (twelfth century AD) meets the *Mahabharata* (fourth century BC); the poet Kalidasa (fifth century AD), Du Bellay (1522–1560), Pierre Corneille (1606–1984), Jean de La Fontaine (1621–1695), Molière (1622–1673), Racine (1639–1699), Hugo (1802–1885), and Goëthe (1749–1832) share the same space of meaning. The literary bridges also connect languages such as Sanskrit, Hebrew, French, and German. This intimate literary map implies encounters between ancient Indian literature and classic European literature. Nevertheless, it has some blind spots, such as African literature and the Mediterranean tradition. Indeed, the Islamic tradition is not represented at all, although it impacted Hindi and Urdu poetry through the experience of the Mongol Empire (1526–1857). Was this a conscious choice for such a widely read writer?

Dutt's literary formation shapes her translation, which I argue represents the ultimate act of reading: beyond rendering the literal meaning of the original text, the possibility of seeing an invisible text—the reader's understanding of the text emerging from the translation—opens new spaces of symbolization and reveals processes that produce dynamic and interconnected meanings. When Sartre writes that "la lecture est une création dirigée" (*Le Lecteur* 51; reading is a creative act), he points toward this unfolding of meaning through a productive interpretation of the text. Gaps of meaning constitute the text; they are a space for the reader to inhabit. Translating takes a new turn as an ultimate act of reading-comparing and is no longer ancillary. Translation as transfer, as a dynamic networking between languages, meanings, and other texts in other languages, can produce slight displacements that show the construction of knowledge as a "What if?" Translation becomes not just the limitation and loss of the original meaning, but a space of creation and exploration of other ways of reading the original text. Dutt's translation of "Le nid solitaire" by Marceline Desbordes-Valmore is a good example of how her work stands as an act of comparison and resymbolization:[19]

> "THE SOLITARY NEST"
> Go my soul, soar above the dark passing crowd,
> Bathe in blue ether like a bird free and proud,
> Go, nor return, till face to face thou hast known
> The dream,—my bright dream,—unto me sent alone.
>
> I long but for silence,—on that hangs my life,
> Isolation and rest—a rest from all strife,
> And oh! from the wild pulse my nest unvexed by a sob
> To hear the wild pulse of the age round me throb.
>
> The age flows like a river,—on, on, and alas!
> It bears on its course like dead sea-weeds,—a mass
> Of names soiled with blood, broken vows, wishes vain,
> And garlands all torn that shall bloom not again.
>
> Go my soul, soar above the world and the crowd,
> Bathe in blue ether like a bird free and proud,
> Go, nor return, till face to face thou hast known
> The dream,—my bright dream,—unto me sent alone. (*Sheaf* 67)[20]

This poem is a perfect illustration of Darmesteter's description of *A Sheaf* as "translating recent French poetry not merely into English, but into an English nurtured with Indian literary undertones" (278-79). In fact, Dutt's translation not only rerenders the original but offers a new symbolization because of very specific word choices.

While in French we are invited to think about water through the present participles "grondant" and "entraînant," which connote flowing and water without explicitly mentioning any body of water, in English the use of "river" manifests the distance and appropriation of the text by Dutt, transferring the meaning into another sphere of values and symbols. Namely, in ancient Indian mythology, the river—mainly Ganga, deification of the Ganges—represents time, life, and death. It is the place where the body is consumed by fire to be transformed into new life.

A similar transformation is at stake in the choice of "garlands" to translate "bouquets purs." The original indicates flowers brought together into the shape of a bouquet; the equivalent in the Indian imaginary is the garlands that are often offered to gods and goddesses as a tribute in recognition of their power. The garlands are "all torn" and "shall bloom not again," rendering the expression of loss and melancholia present in the original with the terms "ensanglantés" and "vains serments"; their destruction accentuates the loss and identification of the garlands as a spoiled present to Ganga. The "bouquets purs, noués de nom doux et charmants" evidently refers to former loves that are softly forgotten; they belong to human time and are detached from the sacred time of gods. In the translation, by contrast, the garlands are part of the sacred realm and time of gods and as such are destroyed, "torn," and "shall bloom not again."

Dutt's translations establish new textual and symbolic networks. Through the diffusion of images, themes, and word choice transferred from Indian poetics into European imagery, Dutt's translations construct a dynamic space of interpretation. This act of translating hybridizes representations at the level of the symbol. It creates an association between the bouquet, with its specific meaning, and the garlands, generally present in Indian celebrations. Mediated by the *effet texte*, the poet openly imports—at a deep level of meaning and exegesis—modes of feelings and structures of affective knowledge into the host language.[21] It is the result of a transpoeticity at work.[22] The English version of the French poem becomes a hybrid form whose poetic and symbolic hybridization is explicit.[23]

At another level, an important dimension emerges within the notes providing a biography of each poet and describing the network they belonged to while extending the connectivity to other poets, thus reaffirming the historical connections between authors and forming a constellation of writers around each text and each poet. Dutt's critical discourse in her notes is perceived as "concerned with questions of cultural circulation" (Lootens, "Bengal, Britain, France" 579); "with *Sheaf,* Dutt may in fact have inaugurated the publication of serious comparative poetry criticism" (582).

Dutt not only makes visible poets' connectedness through explicit intertextuality; she also perceives the relations between writers diachronically, thus tracing the unexpected map that resulted from her analogies and comparisons. She connects writers like Du Bellay, Corneille, Molière, La Fontaine, and Racine with Goëthe, Gottfried August Bürger (1747–1794), and Carl Theodor Körner (1791–1813), while establishing connections between languages, as previously developed. About Hugo, whom she contrasts with Marceline Desbordes-Valmore, she writes: "It would be absurd to make any comment on Victor Hugo in a short note at the end of a book. His name is among the great ones of the earth, with Shakespeare, Milton, Byron, Goëthe, Schiller, and the rest" (*Sheaf* 197). She compares Musset to Byron in her note on the poem "Chanson de Fortunio": "[. . .] He is one of the most popular poets of France, and his countrymen regard him as their Byron. In truth he possesses the spirit, the power, the wit, the brilliance, and the love of nature sometimes real and sometimes affected, which mark the writings of the English poet. Like Byron, he has no great depth of thought. Like Byron, he is sometimes eccentric and wild" (207). It is not just an analogy, because she enumerates the many points of convergence between their works. Her intimate literary map and historiography establish a relationship between ancient Indian literature and ancient European literature, as well.

Reading obviously implies building connections and networks, an act based on analogies and poetics of genre, which become channeled by common emotions. The figure of the reader, in Dutt's words, is accumulative and systematic. This figure transcends moment and place and aims for a universalist position found in the language of poetry as a form of music. The act of translation is a claim for the idea of a universal transmission and communication of meaning through poetry, without the imperialist prejudice of a hierarchical order from the peripheries to the center. Behind each translation, there is the assumption that the text and the life of the poet are intertwined. The act of reading for Dutt was an act of imagining worlds, lives, and patterns of behavior. Reading appears to have fostered an immersion in another dimension of life, beyond the physicality of time and space; reading became an act of travel and construction of meaningful encounters. Rethinking "translation" as "exegesis" is not new but can be productive when imagining the process of reading in a multicultural and multilingual context.[24] Does a multilingual reader process reading the way a monolingual reader does? The multicultural/multilingual reader develops a sense of connectivity that allows for a circulation between different words and different worlds—at least, this is the strategy of reading promoted in A *Sheaf* and Dutt's subsequent works, where she explicitly exhibits connectivity and compares different linguistic universes and symbolic construction of knowledge. Translation as exegesis illustrates the process of reading as not only understanding but also as interpreting and transferring meaning from one space to another.

Writing in Dia-Language: From the Postcolonial Split to a Poetics of the Creolized Self

Dutt's initial attitude toward her European host cultures is explicit in *The Diary*, where she tries to represent the "perfect life" of a bourgeois French girl, Marguerite, a young demoiselle growing up in Brittany. It is written in standard French, without showing any hybridization of language. The world represented is culturally and linguistically monolithic; the unique detail connected to the author's Indianness is her protagonist's dark skin. Nonetheless, Brittany represents Bengal (B/B) through their many similarities: their proximity to the sea, their marginalized position relative to the larger nation state, and their important religious and nationalist commitment, expressing a strong sense of regionalism. An aesthetic of "cleanness" dominates the text, written as a daily diary in prose. Despite the lack of hybridization of language, *The Diary* has different levels of potential structural hybridity, particularly in Dutt's experiments with genre and narrator.

Dutt's chosen format is not a fairy tale but a diary, which implies a high degree of realism. In French, the style itself is close to the anachronic expression *écriture blanche*, which is the search for simplicity without ornamentation. This choice implies a departure from the traditional flourished style present in Bengali literature during the same period; in novels by Chatterjee, for instance, the systematic use of metaphors evokes the ornamented style of traditional Indian poetry (Boutaghou, *Occidentalismes* 102). It is important to remember that, in the context of emerging literary forms, the genre of the novel and romance are not universal forms across all languages. The hybridization of *The Diary* resides in the use of French to narrate an English genre—Dutt has interpolated a gothic narrative into the diary. Additionally, Dutt's use of different points of view participates in the implicit hybridization: at the end of the text, it changes from Marguerite's first-person perspective to third person as an unknown voice narrates Marguerite's agony.

At the same time, the choice of the journal format offers an important flexibility. At the core of the diary, the reader finds quotations of poetry, songs, and legends, counterbalanced by the homogeneity of the dominant French linguistic and cultural representations. The journal also allows Dutt the opportunity to portray different social classes, such as the poor, peasants, bourgeois, and aristocrats: "I visited mother Grestine today. She is the oldest woman in the village, and then I went to the Corraine's place. I found Jeannette boiling some meager soup; I threw in a piece of bacon and cauliflower which I had in my box. I cooked a dozen potatoes under the ashes." (*Diary* 26).[25] The clichéd representation creates an effect of déjà vu, at the same time an "effect of the real," as if the use of the cliché were a way to neutralize Dutt's ethnic difference from her protagonist. The cliché becomes the expression of a desired neutrality or a way to repress her inner colonized self, as in the following example: "This morning, Papa and I went to the woods; we met the count and his brother there. I was eating blackberries and wild berries whose juice had coloured my lips" (24–25).[26] For an Indian reader, in terms of cultural behavior, the erotized suggestion "le jus avait coloré mes lèvres" ("whose juice had coloured my lips") creates both a transgression of Indian cultural codes, where women do not explicitly evoke their pleasure in a prosaic manner, and where betel leaves are used to naturally color the lips. Although an important Indian tradition of highly erotic poetry written by women exists, here the transgression consists of representing an erotic detail in a novel rather than in poetry.

In *Bianca, or The Young Spanish Maiden*, Dutt's second experiment with fiction led her to a different strategy. Here she scrupulously follows the conventions of the romance genre; the hybridization appears within the language, projecting a simultaneous sense of unity and disparity.[27] The novel is written in English and set in England, with numerous passages in French, mainly in the dialogue, though Bianca and her father are Spanish immigrants. This plurality of European languages can be understood as an attempt to give a cosmopolitan touch to a bourgeois milieu, but this is probably an overly simplistic answer; rather, I think it is tied to the author's attempts to erase her Indianness: "'Tu l'aimes bien, dis.' 'Plus que ma vie.' 'Tu la rendras heureuse?' 'Oui, Dieu en soit témoin.' And a flush came over his pale face. 'Alors, je te la donne mon fils.' Garcia's eyes were misty, and he turned aside to conceal his emotion. 'Merci!' said Lord Moore" (*Collected Prose* 111).[28] Even if the critics considered *The Diary* a more accomplished text, probably for the very bad reason of its visible coherence, *Bianca*, her incomplete text, is much more interesting. The unfinished narrative reveals the inner contradictions defining a new poetics of the subject rising beyond the conflict of a cultural split. In *Bianca*, the ambiguous ethical position of the character's voice is repaired in the linguistic conviviality and inclusiveness, not as a way of blending differences but as a fluid circulation between fragments of beings, morphing into a magnified plastic self. The unapologetic multilingual dimension in *Bianca* is not just the sign of a rough draft but of Dutt's willingness to expose her reader to the inherent plurality of languages by not conceiving of the text as a monolingual space. Her literature "tells us that Toru had begun to be aware that she did not quite belong with the Imperial Centre" (Lokugé, *Toru Dutt: Collected Prose* xx), although neither was she exclusively Indian. Even if she was in the position of being a stranger to her own culture, Dutt tended to avoid exclusion of what she also was, a *plural native*. By this process, she aimed to include multilingual modalities of reading.

Dutt also translated this inclusiveness with tropes in her poetry, the only flexible language allowing for the invention of complex selves without guilt. Her experience of being multiple others is configured in metaphor. Her volume of original poetry, *Ancient Ballads*, is an in-between creation and transcription of Sanskrit legends transmitted to Dutt by her mother. The volume is described as having "complex moments when the boundaries between European and Indian literatures dissolve to offer a rich symbolic hybridity,"[29] but a part of it, "Miscellaneous Poems," including "Near Hasting," and the two sonnets, "Baugmaree," and "The Lotus," represents her most original production.[30] In "Near Hasting," written while Dutt was in England, we read: "Strangers,—we were alone / [. . .] Sweet were the roses,—sweet and full, And large as lotus flowers." The apparition of "lotus," the Indian flower par excellence, as the second term of comparison reminds the reader of the passion for roses shared by both Bengali and English gardening traditions. In the sonnet "The Lotus," we see that the flower can be interpreted as the representation of Dutt's inner, constructed self, which is equal parts Indian and European. She could express this mosaic through elements of nature, rooting her sensibilities in her Bengali landscape and affirming them in English.

"The Lotus" contains a dialogue between two voices, Love and Flora: as allegories, Love asks Flora: "What 'flower that would of flowers be undisputed queen'" (*Collected Prose* 210)? The poem provides us with the answer:

> "[...] Give me a flower delicious as the rose
> And stately as the lily in her pride"—
> "But of what colour?"—"Rose-red," Love first chose,
> Then prayed,—"No, lily-white,—or, both provide";
> And Flora gave the lotus, "rose-red" dyed,
> And "lily-white,"—the queenliest flower that blows.

Through her choice of the rose, the lily, and the lotus, one can see the connections with Dutt's creolized self (English, French, Bengali). The red-dyed lotus is the symbol of India, the one that brings together all of her selves, the one that welcomes her otherness. We find again the drive to creolization: the lily, the rose, and the lotus are all parts of the same poem, the illustration of the formula by Jean-Luc Nancy, the *being plural-singular.*

"Baugmaree" was the name of the Dutt's house in Calcutta. Some critics claim that, in this poem, Dutt shows a "native genius" (Agrawal, *Toru Dutt: The Pioneer Spirit* 90):

> A sea of foliage girds our garden round,
> But not a sea of dull unvaried green,
> Sharp contrast of all colours here are seen:
> The light-green graceful tamarinds abound
> Amid the mangoe clumps of green profound,
> And palms arise, like pillars gray, between:
> And o'er the quiet pools the seemuls lean,
> Red,—red, and startling like the trumpet's sound.
> But nothing can be lovelier than the ranges
> Of bamboos to the eastward, when the moon
> Looks through their gaps, and the white lotus changes
> Into a cup of silver. One might swoon
> Drunken with beauty then, or gaze and gaze
> On a primeval Eden, in amaze. (*Collected Prose* 210)

The poem shows a balance between the regularity of prosody (repetition and internal rhyme: "a sea of" repeated in lines 1 and 2, "red-red" in line 8, and "gaze-gaze" in line 13) and the expression of the uniqueness of the location and the scene. The sonnet is mainly a description of the garden, although a narrative arrives at the end of the poem with the apparition of the moon ("when the moon looks through"). There is also one major metaphor at the end, in the heart of the scene—"The white lotus changes / Into a cup of silver"—evoking a metamorphosis. The sea of the poem's beginning is contained in the cup of silver that one is going to drink. A reader familiar with the raga aesthetic might think about a Monsoon raga because of the power of evocation and the radiance of nature in the acoustic image evoked by repetition of sounds and words, as in "red,—red, and startling like the trumpet's sound." The European reader will think about Rimbaud's famous poem "Voyelles" (1871), where sounds are colors. The poem goes back to the essential link between poetry and music (signifier as both a visual and an acoustic image), highly represented in traditional Indian poetry, like in the lyrical tradition of Orpheus. Only a few verbs are present in the whole poem, which is composed mainly of nouns and adjectives that outline the referential power of language. The lotus is the symbol of India, and Eden the symbol of Dutt's Christian faith. Both of her cultures are assembled in the text; she realizes the perfect harmony, in a sense the one evoked by Tagore. Her Eden becomes a Bengali Eden. This poem resolves the dichotomy between her "creolized self" and her native Indian inner landscape.

Dutt's poetry certainly does not illustrate simplistic ideas about Indian-English poetry where the "thematic is Indian," and "the form is foreign."[31] The poem reveals a new form, which would be confirmed with Tagore's *Gitanjali*, and that is even visible in his English translation. In "Baugmaree," the sobriety of ornaments, the simplicity of the vocabulary, expresses the purity of the language. The apt term to describe this universe is "sensuality," all produced by the encounter between the sonority and the evocative power of the poem's words. With this text, Dutt reached a level of artistic production that was universal, not only as a reproduction of what was perceived as European but also as the creolized historical moment she belonged to. It is the pioneering work described here that allows us to begin thinking about modernism as a first attempt at a cultural universalism. Through this text, Dutt creates her own creolized universal location of culture. It is not a mere opposition between abstract European form and content, or the outside versus the inside, being instead the production of a new poetic language without any visible split but, rather, the more subtle sensation of the *pli* (fold) à la Deleuze (1988).

In the following section, I will question the oversimplified and rigid view of identity constructed during the rise of Indian nationalism that voluntarily ignores the complex desire for a *creolized self*. Indeed, Dutt's preference for complexity is rooted in the Bengali landscape, but not expressed in Bangla.[32] Toru Dutt's conscious choice was to be *grounded in a cosmopolitan ethos* to allow for enough plasticity to manage all her filiations: French, English, and Indian. Her cosmopolitanism was not just the default choice of evasive subjects escaping a rigid and narrow construction of cultural identity homogenizing everyone; it also announced the notion of fluid identities. Most likely, Dutt was caught between the complex structures of ideological meaning and conflicting emotions. Through her characters and narration, she explores the distortion of her own inner self to express the internalized "other" without irony. The community around her in Calcutta perceived the difference between European culture and Indian culture as a potential cause of division, but Dutt's work was all about showing her creolized yet fluid self.

Through her writing, shaped by her travel and her cosmopolitan education, Dutt gave voice to the intimate creolization of her subjectivity. She translated this experience through her use of multiple languages. In this case, the poetics of the subject is the personal economy of languages as manifested in the literature Dutt produced. As in the language of dreams, when material is transferred from one place to another, its trajectory is interpreted as much as the material itself, representations originating in different locations are revealed through Dutt's use of mixed poetic structures that display the plasticity of the brain exposed to plurality. This mixture is comprised of poetic structures in several languages that circulate and give the text the complexity of a dream. Because the metaphoric ground of a colonized culture is unstable, the effect of cultural flows is notably visible in colonial cultural production. As seen in "The Lotus," Dutt is an exemplary split subject trying to balance her several inner selves.

Through the specific example of Toru Dutt, one can see how a multicultural/multilingual reader develops a sense of connectivity that allows for a circulation between different worlds. Reading in a multilingual context is not just an intertextual actualization; it is a guided critical reading to the multiple possibilities of interpretation or exegesis codified by the signifier, extending the text to a broader symbolic network. In other words, the multicultural and multilingual reader is always comparing languages because of the importance of the signifier as a dissonant emotional trace of a particular cultural experience.

The act of reading is essentially constituted by this fundamental relation to the materiality of language (sounds and/or graphemes). Dutt fosters the circulation of emotions, knowledge, and ideologies in a colonial context and creates new, intimate, unexpected connections leading to new ways of saying, new ways of describing the world around her, beyond the monolingual colonial vision. She creolizes the reader, centering them in her landscape. The poem "Baugmaree," as a creolized form, illustrates a model of harmony. The language is imported into a new land and submitted to new forms of imagination, which are linked to the landscape, containing both the lotus and the rose, reaffirming cultural production as essentially organic and local while acknowledging the European transformation of the landscape and the language to describe it.

The connections between texts are transcultural; a relation where atavistic representations of precolonial and prenational time, of other cultural moments and other languages, are interconnected in the web formed by the text. The poetics of relation actualizes the nature of poetic encounters beyond all kinds of institutionalized mediations, colonialism being one form of institutionalized relation. The poetics of the subject realizes another meaning in the colonial relation; it transforms colonialism's toxicity into art. Colonialism is an imposed toxic "relationship." It is the reason why the poetics of the subject as the expression of a poetics of relation represents a cultural turn: the inner transformation of the subject from victim of a language to its creative agent. In terms of location, the subject is formed by both fixed structures and structures of meaning informed by migratory flows. For example, the inner process of the poetics of the multilingual subject can be compared to the process of dreaming, a process of translation: outlining the organic nature of cultural flows and their effects. A poetics of the subject, in multilingual contexts, creates its own transcultural constellations of texts, meanings, and forms transmitted with and by the languages the subject has read, heard, and spoken. There are plenty of Baugmaree-esque poems that fail to be noticed because readers ignore the borderless mapping of cultures, which reside in the shadows of nationalist powers of homogenization to which we have become accustomed through our understanding of nations *as* cultures and vice versa. It seems appropriate to evoke Lionnet's now well-known argument: "Transcultural exchange has always been 'an absolute fact' of life everywhere" ("Logiques métisses" 104). To push it a step further, shall we say then that universalism could only be a creolized absolute?[33]

In the following section, I will develop an analogy between cosmopolitanism as a subjective position and Calcutta, the visibly cosmopolitan city, which Dutt saw as a creolized city.

Being Cosmopolitan

Dutt's understanding of diversity was grounded in the experiences that shaped her creolized constructions of meaning through languages. Dutt's cosmos was built through her experience as a reader and traveler, composed of select visions of worlds informed by her experience as a colonized person, a mosaic without a fixed center, an accumulation of foundational sceneries, sounds, and smells. She did not claim any particular ideology and avoided political discussions of her time in India. In fact, Dutt did not define herself as cosmopolitan, but her discourse indicates that her preferred intellectual and political position stood against any kind of exclusion. For Dutt, being cosmopolitan meant being both European and Indian, without any split. Her cosmopolitanism was the acceptance of and the free circulation between her multiple filiations and the result of her experience as a complex self that looked like a community of texts and spaces despites walls erected around her, be they in her use of languages or in space occupied by the modern narrative of the nation. Of course, this counterposition to nationalism à la Bankim was mainly available to highly educated Indians. In the nineteenth century, a part of the discourse around cosmopolitanism implied that cosmopolitan Indians were thought of as Westernized.[34] Though cosmopolitanism was "discursively constituted" (Chaudhuri, *Clearing a Space* 66) in colonial India, it was also a position resulting from the praise of diversity and resistance to monolithic identities that contradict the reality of the colonial trauma: the abusive imposition of a new language on a landscape and its people. Cosmopolitanism could be understood as the necessary, empirical answer to nationalism, an inclusive model matching subjective rootedness in a complex space. This cosmopolitanism à la Dutt allowed for permissive and fluid representations creating a harmonious construction of the self and the world, here the city of Calcutta. In a letter to Miss Martin dated February 28, 1876, Dutt wrote, "A new Zoological Garden has just been started in Calcutta; it is far from being complete yet, but specimens are pouring in of all kinds of animals; the tigers, elephants, Cashmere goats. [. . .] The zoological grounds are also to contain an aquarium. Calcutta will soon be quite a European city!" (*Collected Prose* 263). In her statement about Calcutta, the explicit comparison with a European city shows a hierarchy of values: Dutt admires the fact that Calcutta "will soon be *quite* a European city." Dutt's cosmopolitanism was partly Eurocentric and reflects the same mimicry she, as a writer, was able to transcend.

The relationship between a *cosmopolitan space* and a *cosmopolitan discourse* can first start with the obvious analogy between the city and the text. Like a text, a city is a network. The urban space is a space of relationality and commonalities, of circulation of representations. Space and discourse echo one another. (The terms "cosmopolitanism" and "politics" share also the same root, *polis*.) Calcutta in this letter and elsewhere mirrored and informed Dutt's imaginary. Her cosmopolitanism can be understood as an empirical response to transcultural situations, one that lessened the gap between a cultural imaginary and political models of cultural construction. Beyond colonial imperialism vis-à-vis nationalism, as competing ideologies, cosmopolitanism was the only secure and flexible mental position that could accommodate the plurality of her languages and aesthetics. Dutt, like any colonized writer, was condemned to being cosmopolitan.[35]

In pictures of late nineteenth-century Calcutta and its diverse neighborhoods, one can still see a transcultural space resembling the imaginary map of a colonized subject. Like its diverse selves, Calcutta was characterized by European and Indian influences, especially regarding its architecture. This multicultural and multilingual urban space in a sense matched the internal creolized self of the colonized.[36] Evidently, the colonial city was also the space of social disruption, separations and boundaries between classes, religions, and ethnicities. Colonized urban spaces contain the exclusiveness of both imperialism and nationalism.[37] In fact, for an important part of the Bengali population, the urban space was mainly a space of social order, hierarchies, and a disruptive model of cultural identity, a space with more boundaries than room to move (Mignolo, "Many Faces of Cosmo-polis" 740). To be cosmopolitan, one needs to be intellectually authorized to see the creolized space and to feel like one is a part of it. This is probably why only upper-class Bengalis were able to identify with the discourse of cosmopolitanism and see its conviviality. The materialistic cosmopolitanism of the urban space matched the transcultural subject as an urban subject, and therein lay its modernity. Cosmopolitanism, both the "world in the city" and the "citizen of the world," in this context, is the privileged position offered to subjects able to handle multiplicity because of an elite position, where multilingualism was already acknowledged as valuable. But cosmopolitanism is not simply elitism. It helps us understand the circulation between the imaginary of a transcultural colonized subjectivity and the transculturality of the city—in this case, Calcutta. Cosmopolitanism becomes the only possible answer to an experience of difference rather than an abstract elitist construction informed by the domination of imperialism. Dutt as an intellectual did not represent a social movement but offered an example of hospitality through her textual negotiation of difference, poetically translating her experiences of diversity. Even if cosmopolitanism was simultaneously the most relevant model to embrace and the least popular, Dutt chose it to avoid the internalized split imposed by a nationalist understanding of cultural identity.[38] In Bengal, cosmopolitanism was the materialized vision of mixed cultures and could be seen as the intimate experience of difference. In the nineteenth century, cosmopolitan cities such as Calcutta were the location of visible but shameful creolization; Dutt's gaze helps us understand the need for a transcendent, inclusive political model for postcolonial nations and how to actualize it in discourse.

This cosmopolitanism à la Dutt is an attempt to find a way toward a better praxis of difference, for a recognition of difference, avoiding its repetitive violence. The metaphor of the lotus is the trope representing the space of encounter between differences—or, as Seyla Benhabib puts it, an attempt to poetically "imagine forms of political agency and subjectivity that anticipate new modalities of political citizenship" (*Another Cosmopolitanism* 47) The materiality of Dutt's cosmopolitan subject could be the plasticity that allows circulation between the self and the world, by which I do not mean a political dismissal but, rather, acceptance of a complex and ambiguous relationship to one's colonial past—accepting the fascination and the fear as a part of the relation without denying either.

The creolized subject of postcolonial descent is diverse and multilingual because their cosmopolitanism is not only a textual construction but also the experience of a cosmopolitan landscape. From there, one can get a better sense of cosmopolitanism as the political result of an urban and pragmatic experience of both cultural hospitality and inhospitality. Prospective political discourses have a duty to design a cosmos that is not exclusionary, either culturally or socially. The negotiation of a better praxis of multiplicity in Dutt's writings was already the subjective manifestation of an internalized multiculturalism that we want to call a "creolized self," a self that mimics creole languages, the way they absorbed linguistic structures from all around and morphed into living languages in several former plantation colonies. I view writing from within colonialism as a pragmatic experience of multiculturalism, as a manifesto for cosmopolitanism opposed to an *idealist nationalism*. Dutt's writing in particular laid a claim for the positive recognition of a Bengali cosmopolitanism exemplifying other cosmopolitanisms in colonized contexts, what Paul Gilroy names "cosmopolitanism from below" and Sneja Gunew calls "vernacular cosmopolitanism" (*After Cosmopolitanism* 2). We have yet to find a response to the issue regarding the relationship between the need for a community to find a convivial definition and the need for a subject to avoid oppression and to become harmonious citizens of the world. One way out of this conflicted position is to acknowledge (without forgiving) and transcend the ambiguous reality of any colonial experience as a multicultural, transformative reality originated by a traumatic encounter.

3

BEING COSMOPOLITAN IN NINETEENTH-CENTURY CAIRO

Mayy Ziyadah (1886–1941)

Mayy Ziyadah, a famous intellectual, writer, and translator from late nineteenth- and early twentieth-century Egypt, and one of the main voices of her time, was deeply involved in the modern Nahda movement, or the Arab Awakening. During the Nahda, issues of languages were more important than one might imagine. There were two common hegemonic elements discussed as ways of supporting nationalist cohesion within the collapsing Ottoman Empire: language (Arabic as opposed to regional languages such as Turkish, Tamazight in North Africa, and distinct Semitic languages; e.g., Aramean, spoken by the Syrian Maronite community) and religion (Islam, in its normative version). These two elements shaped communitarian discourses held by intellectuals, mainly journalists, among them Ziyadah. This chapter explores her paradigmatic works as an original reader and a translator bridging European literature with the old concept of *adab* (producing a modern Arab version of both *urbanitas* and *humanitas*), creating a new shift toward a more distinctive understanding of what became, in her writing, an *inclusive* practice of world literature acting as a path to a "vernacular cosmopolitan" ethos.[1] Ziyadah's voice, not yet present enough in discussions about world literature in academia, is surprisingly complex, providing insight into the lively discussions about multiculturalism and multilingualism occurring in Cairo's influential intellectual milieux in the 1920s. This conversation about cosmopolitan culture in Arabic should become a part of our understanding of modern Arab culture.

An Intellectual Portrait of a Multilingual Arab Author

Two major biographies give us access to Ziyadah's turbulent life: one by Raif Georges Khoury (2003), and the other by Boutheina Khaldi (2012).[2] Both describe Ziyadah's exceptional gifts as an intellectual of her time, a lady of the Nahda. Ziyadah's famous platonic relationship with Gibran Khalil Gibran, author of the best-selling book *The Prophet* and pillar of the Mahjar's movement in the United States, transformed her life. Khoury and Khaldi also suggest that she was gay—unfortunately, the most likely cause for her forced hospitalization by her family. This chapter aims to capture her contribution to the field of literary studies and cosmopolitanism through her writing, which has not yet received world-wide recognition and visibility. In it, I will analyze certain aspects of her critical writing in Arabic as well as her unique volume of French poetry; some examples of her work will lead to a discussion of multilingualism, comparatism, and cosmopolitanism vis-à-vis the traditional *adab* on which she based her conceptualization of a modern Arab citizen. The complex relationship between language and identity will be examined in a selection of Ziyadah's articles that give expression to what Deborah Starr terms the relationship between cosmopolitanism and empire.[3] I hope to do Ziyadah justice and break the silence around her legacy as an exceptional thinker who, like Toru Dutt, deserves room in the literary arena of so-called world literature.

A paradoxical comparison can be made between the following quotation taken from Ziyadah's 1924 article "Speak Your Language," and a citation from Jacques Derrida's *Monolingualism of the Other*.[4] Both imply a contrastive conceptualization of the link between language and identity:

> Yes, I only have one language, yet it is not mine. . . . When I said that the only language I speak is *not mine*, I did not say it was foreign to me. There is a difference. It is not entirely the same thing. (Derrida, *Monolingualism of the Other* 2)

> Speak whatever languages you want, people of mine, but don't forget your language.[5]

While Ziyadah claimed language as a belonging and possession of the subject ("your language"), Derrida aimed for detachment incarnated in its practice ("one language, yet it is not mine"). For Ziyadah, identity was sustained by the use of a "communitarian" language and tended to be mirrored in one's mother tongue; for Derrida, conversely, language and identity were distinct, it was both *his* and *not* his language. In the same work, he discussed the rigid location of cultural identity and subjectivity as well. For Derrida, there existed a pure form of French, identified as the unique location of Frenchness: "An accent—any French accent, but above all a strong southern accent—seems incompatible to me with the intellectual dignity of public speech. [. . .] I have contracted a shameful but intractable intolerance: at least in French, insofar as the language is concerned" (*Monolingualism of the Other* 46).

In contrast, Ziyadah—a writer and thinker who expressed her ideas in Arabic while also having an advanced knowledge of several European languages (French, English, German, and Italian)—constructed a discursive space that bridged European and Arabic languages in a cosmopolitan cultural locus. Such an approach might have facilitated the construction of what was then an emergent Arab-Egyptian nation, establishing a critical space that would, perhaps, have allowed for the existence of located identities within the linguistic diversity of Cairo at the end of the Ottoman Empire. By analyzing how Ziyadah's thoughts and cultural reflections proffer a prototype for cultural interaction, this chapter questions the complexity of this emerging discourse. I therefore propose to approach Ziyadah holistically, as a prolific intellectual figure: a critic, poet, and translator who opposed the hegemonic ideological powers at stake in 1920s Cairo (i.e., pan-Islamism, pan-Arabism, and the consequences of the Young Turk Revolution, whose regional effects have been ignored in the scholarship about the Nahda).

Intellectuals who formed part of the Nahda, beginning with the first generation's eminent figures such as Rifa'a Rafi' al-Tahtawi (1801–1873) and al-Mu'allim Butrus al-Bustani (1819–1883), followed by Mohamed 'Abduh (1849–1905) and Jurji Zaydan (1861–1914), among others, held very elaborate views on language politics and produced well-defined discourse on cultural theory, with the aim of achieving modernity via different strategies, such as modernizing *fusha* (classical Arabic). Ziyadah's discourse on the philosophy of languages also circulated among intellectuals in Syria and Egypt in the early 1900s. An overview of the contemporaneous debate surrounding Arabic, *al-àmmiyya* (i.e., *darija,* name given to colloquial Arabic in Maghreb), and *fusha* will help us understand how Ziyadah's work dialogued with that of several leading figures from the Nahda, like Haykal.[6] As an intellectual in a milieu where language politics held a central position, Ziyadah's voice was unique in that it bridged the gap between languages and cultures, placing Arabic in conversation with European languages.[7] In doing so, she adopted a comparative perspective, inserting Arabic literatures and cultures into a world-language framework that differed, of course, from Orientalist ones. She opened new dimensions of comparison and inclusion of Arabic as a part of world literature that harmonized with the ethics of *adab,* putting them into practice each week in her literary salon.[8]

Ziyadah was also deeply involved in the women's awakening at this time, known as *al-nahdha al-nisa'iyyat.* Indeed, her writings presented a very interesting mix of Arabness, women's awakening, and cosmopolitanism; this latter was not only an intellectual position; it also derived from the fact that she read, wrote in, and translated from European languages. During the 1920s, her main intellectual network was located across three major cities: Damascus, Beirut, and Cairo, all of which were cosmopolises and leaders in the production of knowledge in Arabic. At the same time, while hosting her weekly salon between 1913 and 1936, she advocated for a more cosmopolitan culture in Cairo. "takalamu lughatakum" (Speak your language) was written in 1924, a few years after the official collapse of the Ottoman Empire, which is usually associated with the end of World War I.[9] It is in this context that one should read her prose, which is not just about Arabic, but about the competing languages in the region within intellectual milieux informed by both European imperialism and 1920s cosmopolitanism. In the field of comparative literature, cosmopolitanism is traditionally understood as having its roots in the European Enlightenment.[10] Recent scholarship, however, has outlined a nostalgic strand of cosmopolitanism in certain Islamic contexts, one that can also be traced in urban studies concerning the Arab world.[11] Ziyadah's critical theory and literary production suggest a pluralized approach to cosmopolitanism, one that attends to its diverse historical and cultural manifestations within Muslim and Arab contexts.[12]

Ziyadah's production furthers current debate on differing varieties of cosmopolitanism.[13] Following critical voices such as Stephen Sheehi, my reading aims both to explore the complexity of being a cosmopolitan Arab and to "unpack the native subject" (*Foundations* 15). By linking transformative historical processes to cosmopolitanism within a tradition that emerges via the culture of *adab* and not merely through mimicry of the West—as suggested by Amit Chaudhuri in his discussion of the Bengali Renaissance and class privilege in

Clearing a Space[14]—and by positioning her own writing within a *geopoetics* of powers that counterbalanced a *geopolitics* of powers, Ziyadah opened a space for debate in both French and Arabic.[15]

Ziyadah's volume of French poetry, *Fleurs de rêve*, can be read as a manifestation of her inner multiculturalism. It reveals many of her internal conflicts, confronting the difficulty of being a gay Christian woman writing in French at a time where the uprising of a strong Arab national identity was considered the only way to resist Western colonization. The collection provides insight into the power structures underlying her internal linguistic and cultural conflicts, and the ways in which she traversed such an unstable plurality as a unique reader-translator. Becoming a cosmopolitan reader brings with it the demands of constructing a complex identity as well as the need for specific individuation—at once rooted in pan-Arabism but open to the world—to create a sense of self that is simultaneously political and cultural. In other words, Ziyadah's cosmopolitanism must be analyzed through the lens of a poetics of relation, both of which exist in *adab*. In this historical context of the emergence of national identities, translation functioned as a key juncture in the complex path toward a transcultural and cosmopolitan consciousness, one that offered an antidote to religious and cultural homogenization.

Functioning as the Arab equivalent to *weltliteratur*, Ziyadah invested *adab* with new meaning. The concept of *adab* is close to that of belles lettres and implies a multicultural approach to literature.[16] Indeed, it constituted the main tenet of Arabic culture during the Abbasid era. During this period, texts (mostly poetry) written in several Oriental languages circulated among a large community of educated readers. The term *adab* was first associated with education in the sense of a habit, a practical form of conduct, and was extended at the beginning of the 'Abasid epoch. This meaning is equivalent to the Latin *urbanitas*, "the civility, courtesy, refinement of the cities in contrast to Bedouin uncouthness." The humanistic concept of *adab* was initially an imperial one, referencing the knowledge transmitted from *ayyam al 'arab*, but, with the extension of the Arab conquest and owing to contact with other cultures, it changed from *Arab humanitas* to *humanitas* in general, including Indian, Persian, and Hellenistic literatures. During the modern Renaissance, Gabrieli asserts, the meaning of *adab* was associated with "literature in the most specific sense of the world. [. . .] But beyond the limits of technical nomenclature, the conscious usage of certain writers (e.g. Taha Husayn) tends to give back to the word something of its former elasticity and amplitude."[17] Ziyadah, in turn, added something new to this definition, going beyond Husayn's conceptualization to suggest that *adab* extended to European literature as well. This was a rather unusual approach, given that it placed emphasis on the language in which the literature was produced rather than on the nation-state to which it was putatively attached. Ziyadah's transnational experience of literature in early twentieth-century Cairo encouraged her to question the relationship between speaking a language and the citizenship to which that language was attached. Out of her conception of the relationship between language and literature emerged, therefore, her inner political identity, which was caught between the different antagonist forces and conflicting knowledge during the Nahda: pan-Arabism, the cultural Turkish revolution, cosmopolitanism, and pan-Islamism, which was seen as a threat to pluralism. Here, it serves as a framework for analyzing the complex interactions between her longing for, on the one hand, cosmopolitanism, and, on the other hand, a durable, enlightened Arab cultural identity grounded in a rich Arabic literary heritage.

Like Dutt, Ziyadah offers us a renewed way to think of world literatures and cultures as rooted in the practice and recognition of modern Arabic literatures *in relation to* European literatures. Ziyadah's development of *adab*, although close in many ways to the notion of weltliteratur, is indicative of her own individualization and signals the development of her consciousness as a multilingual reader. For Ziyadah, *adab* enabled a movement from the particular—the subject as a specific reader mirroring their own choices—to the projected vision of a complex Arab community based on three compatible elements, rootedness, hospitality, and diversity, in the face of the growing power of hegemonic movements in the region.

The World within Her Languages in *Fleurs de rêve* (1911)

This collection, published in Cairo in 1911, constituted the first volume of poetry published in French by a Lebanese women writer and Ziyadah's first foray into literature under the pseudonym of Isis Copia.[18] It is interesting to note how this rather disorganized text illustrates and modernizes the idea of *adab*. The literary world at stake is largely European and only came into contact with Ziyadah's Arab imaginary when she touched upon Lebanese and Egyptian landscapes and place names. Moreover, it is notable that Ziyadah made no mention of Arabic writers within her text, despite the fact that, as the daughter of Ilyas Ziyadah, the editor of the newspaper *al-Mahrusa*, she was surrounded by writers from the *Nahda*. The fact that Ziyadah wrote in French, the language of colonial domination, distanced her somewhat from the judgments of her paternalistic Arab society, affording her more autonomy to hone her own subjectivity and aesthetical convictions.[19] The volume is dedicated to Alphonse de Lamartine, the French Romantic poet, and is composed of two parts: the first part is a series of poems written in French, some of which have English-language titles, such as "Remember Me!," "Good-Bye!," and "Nothing More!" In the last chapter of the book, written as a diary (with sections in both English and French), Ziyadah exuberantly—and in no apparent order—expresses her admiration for several authors, including Lamartine, La Rochefoucauld, Voltaire, Shelley, Byron, Shakespeare, Aristotle, and Edgar Allan Poe.

For example, "Good-Bye" opens with the epigraph "Cairo farewell! / I love thee well!" (Ziyadah, *Fleurs de rêve* 72). The use of the archaic form "thee" is certainly not inadvertent, accentuating as it does the linguistic disjuncture at stake in a French-language poem that bears an English title. In this poem, Ziyadah expressed (in French) her "dislocated" position as a subject moving between Syria and Egypt who also sought to find a balance between her various adopted cultures. Her poetry evokes multiple locations, including Egypt, Syria, Lebanon, and the Mediterranean Sea, and cities such as Cairo, Alexandria (71, 73), Nazareth (113), Tibériade (102), Bet-Saïda (106), Galilé (108), and Antoura (48).[20] This intimate cartography gives expression to rather personal, obsessive metaphors that locate sentiments and experiences within specific geographies.[21] In discussing figures such as Byron, Lamartine, Rousseau, and La Rochefoucauld in both English and French, Ziyadah places cultures in conversation with each other, all the while nostalgically embracing the Romantic position that complements her ethos. The text functions as a safe haven, allowing for the encounter between languages, their literatures, and her landscapes.

Ziyadah commented humorously on writers as friends who can be boring; her lightness and free spirit are signs of how she integrated literature as a part of her life. The following citation shows her being playful with Pascal, a major pillar of French philosophy: "Pascal bores me, he was neurasthenic, his only glory is his discourse on the passions of love."[22] In another passage, she dialogues with Byron's *Childe Harold*:

> It is half past ten in the morning, and I have been alone in the forest for more than two hours now. Alone with Byron, the sweet, savage poet that the English ranked in fourth place, perhaps because he was such a

good rhymer, and who, after Shakespeare, deserved to be in first place. [...] Did he know, poor Byron, could he have known when he was writing this sad and charming poem, that a young Syrian girl would spend with him, with what remained of him, long solitary hours in the sweet Lebanese forest?[23]

In this passage, Ziyadah's intimacy with the poet enables her to explicitly represent her sense of uniqueness as well as conveying the Romantic experience of solitude and self-consciousness. Indeed, to read *Childe Harold's Pilgrimage* alone in a forest figured as an ideal Romantic experience in a time that could no longer be deemed Romantic. That such a Romantic image could be translated by a Syrian woman into an Oriental context (namely, the Cairo of 1911) can be read as an example of aesthetical *dischronia*.[24] Not only did *Childe Harold* give Ziyadah the opportunity to proclaim *I*—that is, to be in the position of the lyrical narrator, and experience the possibility of her own existence as a poet—but it also allowed her to establish an explicit *intertextuality*. In other words, this "diary" entry offered an image of a joyful circulation of texts freed from their ideological burdens. Indeed, what we see here is not mimicry or servile imitation, but, rather, a conscious strategy utilized by a creolized subject resisting, repairing, and emerging within the domination of imperial cultures. Ziyadah gave expression to the ambivalent subject of the Nahda, the originality of which lay in her inscription of a personal cartography of reading within an *unfamiliar* landscape. This creative encounter is underscored by various literary strategies—for instance, highlighting the stark contrast between the landscape of *Childe Harold* and that of the pyramids and employing analogies such as those set up between Lamartine's poetic landscapes and Lebanese topographies. By introducing such original textual encounters between Oriental landscapes and European literature, Ziyadah constructed a new "geopoetics," leveling the differences between colonizer and colonized.

Notably, this is far removed from the position of Orientalist writers and painters such as Eugène Fromentin, who visited Algerian territories on three occasions between 1846 and 1853, and Lamartine, who traveled to Lebanon during 1832–33. Fromentin, for example, described seeing something new and tried to give shape to this novel vision; his eyes were not used to the intense light of the North African landscape. Ziyadah instead responded to the violent acculturation that was forcible linguistic and cultural imitation by incorporating images of her Syrian, Egyptian, and Lebanese landscapes into the language of Byron and Lamartine, making a "home" of their imposed languages. In this sense, she proposed a new cultural order beyond the schizophrenia of colonialism that perceived cultural pluralism as abnormal. Her strategies were far removed from those of the Orientalists: if, for Lamartine, the Orient was the land of his imaginary, for Ziyadah there existed an inherent split between the imposed, new languages and the known landscape of her first language, Arabic (*al-ámmiyya* and *fusha*).

"Un matin" (One morning) focuses on a minaret, a symbol of Islam described in Orientalist writing as an eternal and rather astonishing architectural object in the eyes of Westerners, who focused on its "newness." "Oh que le ciel est doux dans son azur qui brille! / Au loin le minaret dresse son bout pointu" (*Fleurs de rêve* 42; Oh! How the sky is sweet in its shining azure / Afar the minaret erects its sharp end). The minaret is incorporated into French in a natural way, becoming a new cultural object that belongs to, or is assimilated by, the language. The *unheimlich* (uncanny) and exotic effect of the minaret as described by Orientalists is, in this context, transferred from the object to the language used to define the object; the unheimlich effect thus relates to the French-language labeling of the minaret, which loses the exotic charge that would figure it as belonging to a different cultural and linguistic universe. The subtle differences between a formidable Arabism and a longing for cosmopolitanism do not figure as contradictions but instead offer new insights into early twentieth-century Egyptian practices of cosmopolitanism, which were too often associated with imperialism and Westernization, and were therefore caught in a bind between *muslihin* (modernist) and Islamist conservatism.[25]

Ziyadah was very much a product of her time. Indeed, questions concerning the construction of an Arab identity were crucial to the writers who came before her. Jurji Zaydan (1861–1914), the editor of the journal *al-hilal* and author of *riwayat tarikh al islam* (novels from the history of Islam), was one of these (Boutaghou, *Occidentalismes* 59), but his strategy was the revival of Islamic history, whereas she promoted a *poetics of relation* between languages in literature.

Being in Relation: Ziyadah's Critical Discourse on Languages

Although Ziyadah was educated in French and taught the language in Cairo for several years, she focused on improving her Arabic. She had a sound grasp of several European languages—among them English, Italian, and German—and, as a journalist and literary critic, was an active member of the local intelligentsia.²⁶ Ahmad Lutfi al-Sayyid (1872–1963), "ustadh al-djil" (the master of the generation), an intellectual from Cairo, counseled her on what to read. Because she was a Christian, he suggested she read the Quran to better her Arabic. Khoury described her in the following terms: "Mayy is so imbued with Arabic and European culture that she is able to draw what she needs from her experience of reading an impressive number of sources in order to bestow upon the theme under study, or the idea in question, the contours of world citizenship. Didn't she dedicate her *Fleurs de rêve* to Lamartine, whom she was fascinated with, and who had said, among a vast cortege of European writers, German, French, and others: 'I am the fellow citizen of each man who passes by.'"²⁷

Khoury also affirms the influence of Ibrahim al-Yazidji on Ziyadah's thought. Al-Yazidji left Lebanon to establish himself in Cairo, where he founded several journals, such as *al-nadjah* (1872), *al-tabib* (1884), *al-bayan* (1897), and *al-diya'* (1898). His translation of the Bible into Arabic is still the most celebrated version, and he remains known for his thoughts on the usage of Arabic in the cultural environment of his time. For instance, he authored a treaty, published in 1897, on *al-lugha wa-l-ásr*, in which he tried "to modernize the reflection on Arabic and to show how language is the mirror of society" (*Mayy Ziyadah* 227). He was a very important figure among thinkers of the Nahda, particularly regarding the morphology and semantics of Arabic.²⁸ Cairene intellectuals knew all too well that to change society, they first needed to modernize the main tool of communication—that is, language. Ziyadah positioned herself at the crossroads of this dialogue on Arabic. She was also influenced by Djubran's thought on creativity as a tool that could revive the poetical power of language, which he developed in his *mustakbal al-lugha l-árabiyya* (the future of Arabic) (228).

Most importantly, as demonstrated by Khaldi, Ziyadah led significant intellectual discussions at her parents' home in Cairo, where she hosted her literary salon for some twenty-three years, between 1913 and 1936 (Khaldi, *Egypt Awakening*, 54). Inspired by French *salonnières* and not dissimilar to Mallarmé's Tuesdays (les Mardis de la Rue de Rome), her salon was very well attended every Tuesday. Eminent writers of the Nahda met there to discuss important issues regarding the country.²⁹ Discussions concerning language occupied a central position, and Ziyadah's standpoint arose out of an ongoing quarrel with other intellectuals, itself the result of Egypt's inherited multilingualism, particularly in cities such as Cairo.³⁰ Debate surrounding the use of colloquial Arabic, the simplification of classical Arabic, and the eventual status allocated to English and French dominated this intellectual space. This dialogue confirmed the dangers of a cosmopolitanism that would mirror the very Eurocentrism that Ziyadah opposed. Taha Husayn, among others, had a very interesting idea about "bringing classical Arabic (*fusha*) into conversation with Egyptian society and its standard language, the language of the press" (Khaldi, *Egypt Awakening* 125). Ziyadah herself was concerned that the "emphasis on classical Arabic is no ordinary feat when understood and seen against a background of heated discussions about possible reconciliation between scientific knowledge, its appropriation into usable Arabic, and the so called complexity of classical Arabic" (126). Indeed, literary Arabic was the language of choice in Ziyadah's salon, rather than *al-ámmiyya* (colloquial Arabic) or European languages: "In other words, Ziyadah's enforcement of this practice served Arab nationalism as well. It combatted the counter-revitalist movement that called for *al-ámmiyya* and the conservative revivalists whose preservation of *fusha* and imitation of the ancients deprived the language of its adaptability to modernity" (127).

In this regard, Ziyadah did not follow Muhammed Husayn Haykal's initiative to impose the use of *al-ámmiyya*. In fact, her stance against the use of colloquial Arabic, as well as her focus on cosmopolitan literary culture, were expressions of a coherent mode of cultural thought. While her salon and the publications discussed during these sessions were informed by her imitation of European salonnières and the Enlightenment, she was also convinced that the use of *fusha* alone could implement the changes needed to modernize society. She thus enacted a kind of *cultural imitation* inherited from her familiarity with ancient Arabic literature; indeed, her mention of Sukayna bint al-Husayn (669–736) suggests that her vast literary knowledge figured as the actualization of the spirit of *adab*, itself informed by an anticolonial stance (128). In other words, we can detect what Starr describes as the "relationship between cosmopolitan and empire"; it is the specificity of this relationship that renders each claim or position as historically cosmopolitan but locally defined, one "that resists clear identification with either side of the colonial or postcolonial binary" (*Remembering Cosmopolitan Egypt* 153).[31] Ziyadah, like some of her contemporaries, including Haykal and Zaydan, developed a distinct sense of *tamaddun* (urbanization) through the importation of "Western" knowledge, all the while attending to the strong specificity of Arab culture via her desire to use *fusha*.

Her constant use of comparison as a means of understanding cultural phenomena opened a space of dialogue between Arab and European cultures. In "Speak Your Language," Ziyadah relates how, while in Italy, she addressed an Italian bookseller in French, asking for the works of Gabriele D'Annunzio (Mayy Ziyadah, *bayna al-jazr wa al-madd* 463). He asked whether it was intended for her or for someone else, to which she replied that it was for her. The bookseller then proceeded to criticize her for speaking to him in French rather than Italian, arguing that Italian was the more beautiful language. Back in her hotel after this encounter, Ziyadah had a conversation with her Egyptian friends about Arab people's lack of interest in their own language, realizing that many of those around her did not value Arabic. Some considered it to be a harsh language lacking in melodic harmony. Her article suggests that, before speaking or revering other languages, Arabs should value and love their own language in much the same way foreigners did theirs. She disapproved of any hierarchical linguistic order that would discriminate between center and peripheries.[32]

In a famous article entitled "fadlu al adab" (Apology of literature), published in April 1918, Ziyadah explains how societies have been mixed since the beginning of trade ventures, and that such miscegenation is also the origin of civilization: "The consequences of production and trade informed social relations long before the arrival of the Phoenicians on the shore of the Greeks for the first time, and this reality will follow us until the end of our civilization. Without these relations, the societies would not have been mixed, mixed ethnicities would not have been possible, and the establishment of cities would not have been envisioned, if the different populations had stayed far removed from one another."[33] Literature, according to her definition, unites people and functions as the sustenance of its people and, more broadly, of humanity:

> The different nations are like individuals that can understand each other only through intellectual dialogue and they don't isolate themselves from the dialogue of minds. Any production or results from a work will keep the signature of the people who were behind its creation. But intellectuals and scholars don't have any stamp and address for the whole of humanity, without exclusion. They speak, work, write, explain themselves about their theories, and their feelings in Greek, Latin, Arabic, Hindu, they just translate human issues and their desire for a humanism issued from their great, sensitive minds.[34]

Ziyadah suggests that people can use literature to express their sense of belonging to the vast soul that is humanity. She thinks of literature and culture as the consequence of relation or *alálaka*, reminding us of the link between culture and urbanity and the importance of *tamaddun* in Arabic.[35] In fact, she considers movement and hybridization as the main processes driving civilization. Moreover, in the second part of the quotation, she addresses the issue of the circulation of knowledge as free and open but nonetheless marked by the language in which it was produced. For Ziyadah, the practice of borrowing constitutes part of the intellectual and humanist traditions of all civilizations throughout all periods; the inner process of cultural production relies on circulation, imitation, and reappropriation, which should arise without shame or guilt. According to Ziyadah, humanity is a fluid entity, and literature operated as the main locus of human singularity. At the same time, literature localized differences between communities; it figured the very essence of identity as a site of resistance and inclusion:

> And what is the purpose of literature and rhetoric but the expression of a thought, feelings with words and writing, and the translation of hidden mental images into the realm of analysis and representation. Each nation (people) will stay singular in its style, and each will create poetry and prose full of sadness and softness. [. . .] And with the use of *kalam* [speech, utterance] as the tool of rhetoric, and with *kalam* only, each nation will show its own literature, in other words the "juice of its soul" and it will be a part of the juice (or essence) of the soul of humanity.[36]

In her critical discourse, Ziyadah not only links literature to a particular "nation" but also to a specific language since, as she would later put it, "each language has a literature." It is particularly noteworthy to see this differentiation occurring in the Arab context. In fact, it is possible to think of the relationship between literature and language in the Arab world as being stronger than the one between literature and nation, because Arabic was shared by many different ethnicities, peoples, and nations that formed part of the larger Arab world even under Ottoman rule. In her critiques of literature and language, Ziyadah put forth a "transcendental" view of literature that can be read, in a sense, as a nascent conception of world literature. It is important to reiterate that it was not a question of mimicking the West. Her approach to world literature counterbalanced her desire for an enduring Arabic literature. Her attempt to build a transcendent, universal space was shared by the people of the Mahjar, the Arab diaspora of New York, in particular its famous leader Gibran, with whom Ziyadah shared a deep, platonic relationship.

In the same article, Ziyadah quotes the following sentence, attributed to an anonymous ancient poet: "ina kula lisanun bil haqiqati insanun" ("fadlu al adab" 79; indeed, each language is a human being). Literature and language were represented as organic and alive. Her cosmopolitan reflections on "world literature" parallel her thoughts on the usage, reinforcement, and modernization of Arabic. In her article "tatawur al-lughat al 'arabiya" (Evolution of Arabic), she rightfully claims Arabic as a shared regional language across religions.[37]

Ziyadah thus figured Arabic as the cement that bound all emergent Arab nations, allowing for the creation of national communities regardless of tensions between religious factions (in this case, mainly Jews, Christians, Copts, and Muslims in Egypt). This period also marked the birth of the Muslim Brotherhood movement (1928) and the resurgences of modern Turkish culture. Ziyadah's comparative cultural thinking, generated by and related to the practice of translation, can be read as "performing" the cosmopolitan space. Her attitude clearly exemplified a shift from the old tradition of *adab* (relating to both literature and education) to the attractive concept of "world literature," which was based on her readings of Goethe and open to European texts. Notably, these European works did not function as mere models to imitate, but instead were to be reappropriated by Arab intellectuals via a "culture of translation" (Zubaida, "Cosmopolitanism and the Middle East" 33).[38]

Being in Translation, or Translation as a Dialogic Discursive Space

Ziyadah translated works from European languages into Arabic—for example, Sir Arthur Conan Doyle's 1917 novel *The Refugees* (*al hubb fi al 'adhab*), a love story set during the time of Louis XIV, and *Deutsche Liebe* (1882), an autobiographical narrative by Max Müller (1823–1900). In the preface to the second edition of her translation of Müller's text, its literary genre is not even mentioned. When Khoury compared Ziyadah's translation to the original, he found it to be too far removed from the meaning of the original and frequently incorrect. Indeed, she deliberately translated *Deutsche Liebe* as *ibtissamat wa dumu*,' which means "smiles and tears" and is an inversion of Gibran's title *dam'a wa ibtissamat*, an intertextual tribute to their platonic love. Her title is more an interpretation than a translation, and her inversion of Gibran's title explicitly reveals how she viewed translation as a medium through which to speak of herself and her own place in the world.[39] In fact, the politics of translation into Arabic at that time, as established by scholars like Rifa'a Rafi' al-Tahtawi (1801–1873) and later Mustafa Lutfi al-Manfaluti (1879–1924), encouraged a process of revision that targeted the demands of a Muslim audience.[40] Moreover, although Müller was a well-known Orientalist in the Indian intellectual landscape, if Ziyadah paid attention to him, it was not only because of their shared interest in Romanticism; it also enabled her to express her desire for an exchange, an interconnectedness, that would allow for the return of Orientalist discourse to the East, thus reversing the Orientalist movement of translation and promoting and confirming a new perspective on translation that could be labeled "Occidentalist" (Boutaghou, *Occidentalismes*). For the same ambiguous reasons, she highly admired Pierre Loti, but decided against translating his novels, because they would give young Egyptian readers a conservative view of their own culture.[41]

In her preface to *ibtissamat wa dumu'*, Ziyadah explains her relationship to Müller's text, commenting upon her own interpretation of it and relating it to her personal library (13). The work of translation created a domesticated space of mediation through which she could fearlessly challenge the uniformity of the dominant culture and defend the singularity of her Lebanese Maronite culture. Through her choice of texts, she was able to make visible a personal and ideological trajectory that reflected a new Arab configuration beyond dichotomies and symbolic violence. Of course, Ziyadah herself was caught in a double movement—horizontal and vertical—at once asserting the need for a located community that supposedly shared the same language while avowing the importance of a transcendental, cosmopolitan culture made visible through translation and literary comparison. In early twentieth-century Cairo, Ziyadah's sense of belonging hinged upon the discourse of world interconnectedness, while her sense of an elusive place found expression in the building of a more convivial, solid, and self-confident Arab identity. This double philosophical goal protected her, in Cairo, from the growing risks of radical ideologies (pan-Arabism and pan-Islamism). During virtually the same period, in 1921, Walter Benjamin developed the idea that "languages are not strangers to one another but are [...] interrelated in what they want to express," which is strikingly reminiscent of Ziyadah's own account of literature as the expression of our shared humanity.[42] Benjamin also went on to explain that "all translation is only a somewhat provisional way of coming to terms with the foreignness of languages" ("Task of the Translator" 75). This assertion of similarity ran counter to that of the Babelic "otherness" of so many theories of translation, including those of the *belles infidèles* (beautiful infidels). The same polarities were evident in cultural theory and thought at the turn of the twentieth century, when all languages came under the radar of the phenomena of translation and cosmopolitanism beloved by the elites and artists of capitals such as Barcelona, Paris, Brussels, Vienna. Needless to say, such reflections on translation were relevant to Ziyadah's interrogation of the status of her culture and language within the collapsing Ottoman Empire. In Cairo, Ziyadah was also the product of an era that might be labeled "the century of translation" (Gaha, *al-tarjama* 240). The task of the translator was to be understood as linking cultures from the periphery to the center without, as yet, the establishment of any boomerang effect that could lead to the real building of a "world literature" or *littérature monde* or literatures of the world.[43] This last coup would be today's reading of her work. As Itamar Even-Zohar puts it: "It is clear the very principles of selecting the works to be translated are determined by the situation governing the (home) polysystem: the texts are chosen according to their compatibility with the new approaches and the supposedly innovatory role they may assume within the target literature."[44] Antoine Berman deems this kind of translation "ethnocentric," which "means here: that which draws everything to one's own culture, to its norms and values, and considers all which is situated beyond it—the foreigner—as negative or just good enough to be annexed or adapted in order to increase the wealth of one's own culture."[45] For Ziyadah, translation becomes a dynamic relation, a bridge from the others to the plurality of the same—that is, from European languages to Arabic, the language used by diverse groups (yet to be nations), which was at once the center of her world and a new inclusive space, for a renewed *adab*.

As stated previously, this period was marked by conflicts between different reforming trends (*al-muslihun*) and more conservative movements. This battle of ideologies evidences the antagonism of philosophical orientation and political decision-making concerning the evolution of Muslim/Arab culture. The Arab intellectuals who made decisions regarding the future viewed it as a conflict with the West; linguistic and cultural issues were at the core of *al-muslihun* and were very much caught within an East/West dichotomy. Khoury discusses how Ziyadah's transcendent conception of a cosmopolitan literary community can be gleaned in the European authors she referenced as paradigms: for instance, Frédéric Mistral (1830–1914), the Nobel Prize–winning (1904) Occitan writer rarely mentioned in histories of French literature, and Sir Walter Scott (1771–1832), whose work focused on the reemergence of

Scottish popular culture and language (Khoury, *Mayy Ziyada* 230–40). For Ziyadah, each literature had its own located identity and origin. Oddly, perhaps, she also—against a predominant use of classical Arabic as a unifying language—defended the plurality of the colloquial as the manifestation of the plurality of the Arab world. She even compared the Occitan, Scottish, and Irish languages to the multiple varieties of colloquial Arabic that prevailed, ultimately defending the existence of such forms of Arabic (240). As mentioned earlier, Ziyadah, like the more famous Gibran, stressed the need to modernize Arabic in opposition to all kinds of conservatism. She hailed France and Great Britain as nations composed of a multiplicity of minor cultures, but nonetheless failed to address the imperialism of French culture vis-à-vis minor languages and cultures within the French territory, similarly overlooking the prohibition of what was ironically called "patois." She might not have discussed the hegemony of French culture in her article to avoid being accused of implying an analogy with Arab culture as hegemonic. Indeed, both Arabic (as *fusha*) and French were and are still languages of Empires. Are these ambiguities of her being in translation?

By way of conclusion, it is helpful to turn again to Even-Zohar's theory of literary polysystems to understand the various locations and hierarchies that relate translated literatures to their target languages and attendant literary systems. Ziyadah's achievement as an intellectual was not the proposition of a naive, positivist, or transcendental humanism, but a transcultural model of communication between cultures that would foreclose any threat of totalitarianism. For Ziyadah, all cultures and languages were welcome in a system of world literature insofar as each literature in its language represented a territory—that is, a defined place such as a region or a geographically located nation. The idea of "world literature" was somewhat removed from the humanist cultures that developed around the classical concept of *adab*, probably owing to the fact that the former can be linked to the emergence of the nation-state in eighteenth-century Europe, while the idea of *adab* relates to a family of languages and texts as the expression of an imperial culture. Such was the case in the old humanist cultures in which Greek and Latin literature made up the knowledge of the educated elite, configuring the culture of empires as "a cosmopolitan society *par excellence*" (Yerasimos, "Cosmopolitanism" 36). *Weltliteratur* emerged with the birth of modern nations, giving rise to a certain tension between the longing for a modern universal literature and the emergence of cultural territories that were defined by a shared religion and language.⁴⁶ The concept of cultural universality was an exciting but remote ideal, without any visible impact on the development of nationhood and its resilient borders. Of course, several transcendent historical moments and their attendant concepts overlap—humanism, universalism, cosmopolitanism—and exist alongside their literary counterparts: *belles-lettres, humanitas, adab,* and *weltliteratur*. In the case just discussed, the configuration is slightly different, since Arabic emerged as the dominant language, of a religious empire, in several future nations that were in the process of defining their new national identities against a colonial presence. By shifting the hegemonic definition of Arabic and returning to translation and comparison, Ziyadah revived the organic link between literatures in Arabic and the emerging idea of world literature. In "fadlu al adab," in which the values of *adab* and *weltliteratur* coexist, translation and comparison simultaneously provided a means of stressing the difference between cultures, of asserting the existence of modern Arabic cultures and literatures, and of promoting solidarity between Arabic speakers with respect to the rest of their minor worlds (e.g., Tamazight, Turkish, Aramean, Hebrew). Her cosmopolitanism resided in this tension. Ziyadah's thoughts on culture resulted from the concomitance of a communitarian discourse and a projected cosmopolitan space in which translation acted as a conduit between a plurality of geopolitical systems.

Ziyadah's cosmopolitanism must be understood as an idealistic system in which minor literatures form part of a larger territory. Minor literatures, in the Arab context, are those produced within the same literary system by minority groups; there is only a subtle linguistic difference between what was produced by Muhammed Husayn Haykal (1888–1956), Taha Husayn (1889–1973), Zaydan, or Ziyadah herself, or later on by Maghrebi writers like Mohammed Choukri (1935–2003) or Tahar Outtar (1935–2010).⁴⁷ By encouraging sectarianism, the pan-Islamist movement created differences between religious groups and imposed an illusory Arabo-islamic identity that opposed any attempt at accepting plurality. In fact, Ziyadah called for the acknowledgment of minor literatures within the regional ensemble formed by the rising pan-Arabism. She evoked regional cultures through the concept of a spectrum of identities, which, in her writing, was figured according to a particular hierarchy: regional, national, and imperial. Her cosmopolitanism was first and foremost a kind of transregionalism that operated as a compromise, deflecting the terrible couple formed by pan-Islamism and pan-Arabism that would eradicate all difference, since it emerged under the threat of colonialism. Ziyadah preferred, therefore, to propagate the idea of a plurality of identities mirroring different, interlocked national-regional-cosmopolitan spaces.[48] In fact, it is only possible to destabilize hegemonic powers through the reaffirmation of the intrinsically plural structure of identities; such identities, devoid of any fixed territory, continuously overlap, and it is this fluid plurality (or polysystemic aspect) within each culture that provides an antidote to fundamentalism and totalitarianism.[49] This is primarily why transnationalism remains the cornerstone of hegemonic territorial projects, while a transcultural perspective that moves beyond national boundaries reveals the lived experience of the creolization, hybridization, miscegenation, and so-called chutnification that make up all human language and literature; through an invisible "archaeology of knowledge" and the displacement of texts, it recovers the cultural configuration of older ensembles. In this sense, prospective reflections should rely on the unit or scale of cultural systems as opposed to hegemonic nations that offset and silence minorities living on *unmapped* territories. Literatures as cultures are essentially hybrid and must tackle the supposed purity of an imagined origin within the space of the nation-state.

Ziyadah's work as a critic, translator, and theorist of modernity allows us to visualize how she constructed an upside-down world in which Cairo was the center and Europe's literary production the satellite. Being a satellite does not, of course, equate to distance or rejection; it simply means being part of a system in which the center is Cairo or Beirut rather than Paris, London, New York, Vienna, Barcelona, or Brussels, as was common at the time. Through textuality, Ziyadah crafted a transregional, transcultural network that reconfigured the world according to the tenets of *adab* and *'alaka* (relation). This complex, subjective consciousness, which existed at the junction between several languages, was not clear cut but rather full of ambiguity and ambivalence, destabilizing the stereotype of a precise and observable definition of identity. It is important to evoke Ziyadah's existence as an active model, in order to refer to a time when diversity and difference were part of the understanding of Islam and Arabness. Moreover, in using the oft-criticized term "cosmopolitanism," I have consciously distanced it from the easy opposition between attached/detached subjectivity (Cheah and Robbins, *Cosmopolitics* 1998) and elitism, to suggest that cosmopolitanism can be localized and offer a complex vision of the world from within.[50] Indeed, cosmopolitanism can be linked to an awareness of the relations between the local and the global that is, perhaps, best grasped by the postcolonial multilingual reader-translator.

4

THE MAGHREBI BARD

Assia Djebar (1935–2015)

The situation of Fatima Zohra Imalhayène—a.k.a Assia Djebar—vis-à-vis languages was the genesis of her subjectivity and foundational to perceiving her in translation. Djebar was born under colonial power in Algeria in 1935.[1] In her masterpiece, *L'Amour, la fantasia* (1985; *Fantasia: An Algerian Cavalcade*, 1993), the narrator, a figure close to the voice of the writer, explained how her *ontological* birth dated back to June 1830, when France invaded Algeria, a century before her actual birth. In her essay *Ces voix qui m'assiègent: en marge de ma francophonie* (1999; The voices that besiege me: from the margins of my francophonie), Djebar traced her intellectual autobiography and candidly informed her readers of the core emotional ties she had formed toward her languages and how they became entangled in her writing and filmmaking. It is thus difficult to approach this essential aspect of her work and life without falling into the pitfalls of repetition unless the critic dives into the poetics of this "tangage" (*Ces voix* 51), or the state of being in between languages, whose dynamics were openly displayed in Djebar's film *La Zerda et les chants de l'oubli* (1982; *The Zerda and the Songs of Forgetting*), during the second part of her life as both a writer and film director.[2] Without oversimplifying Djebar's complex poetical expression across various media, it is still important to disentangle the different dimensions that composed her life in languages and see how each language was positioned with respect to her other languages, or how each language is situated. I will not examine any one isolated language but its emotional dynamic *in relation to* the rest of her poetical landscape. It is worth recalling that *langue* in French has many implications, not just linguistics as "language" but as part of the body; "langue" is also "tongue." Djebar's multilingualism was associated with a primitive relation to the experience of the signifier (*le signifiant*) in linguistics as simultaneously an acoustic image and a visual image. This foundational embodied experience of languages as sounds and images informed her "art poétique."³

Being in Translation: Assia Djebar's Languages

This question developed in many ways throughout her novels and essays—particularly in *Ces voix*.⁴ As an Algerian, Djebar grew up in a multilingual culture with competing languages (the Tamazight language from the Chenoua region or Chenoui or Tachenwit, dialectal and classical Arabic, and French). In her volume of short stories, *Femmes d'Alger dans leur appartement* (1980; *Women of Algiers in Their Apartment*, 1992), she reflected upon the plurality of voices in her writings; this aspect was developed later in her fifth novel and the first volume of the quartet, *Fantasia*. In *Women of Algiers*, she italicized some terms to highlight the polyphony taking place in the body of the text (Donadey, "Multilingual Strategies" 30) that revealed the gendered nature of her languages.⁵ Later, in *Fantasia*, Djebar gave a thoughtful, precise description of the use of her four languages (including the language of the body) and their cultural coexistence (*Amour* 254; *Fantasia* 180). Mireille Calle-Gruber summarizes what inevitably became a leitmotif in Djebar's work as she attempted to make her languages visible even in translation: "A woman, a Berber speaker on her grandparents' side, an Arabic speaker on her parents' side, she writes in French, the language of colonization in the Maghreb, the language of her father, a primary school teacher for France in a village in the Algerian Sahel" (*Assia Djebar* 17).⁶

French was, paradoxically, Djebar's unifying language, as she beautifully explains in *Fantasia*: "Ever since I was a child the foreign language was a casement opening on the spectacle of the world and all its riches. In certain circumstances it became a dagger threatening me" (126).⁷ It assembled all of her heterogeneous moving parts. It was the language that readers used to enter her intimate space. As a thread, it was also going to unveil all the other languages and histories embedded in her multivocal writing.⁸ With this movement—and not just this moment—of unveiling came individual narratives and collective memory. For Djebar, French was an analytical tool that dug into the memory of her flesh, one whose traces were those first *sounds* murmured by women in a mixture of Tamazight and colloquial Arabic.[9] But French was not the only written language she learned.

Djebar attended Quranic school during her childhood, so she started learning Arabic script at the same time as she learned to read and write in French.[10] She would also, later in life, learn Greek, Latin, and English, when she went to middle school in Blida. Her extended knowledge of Greek and Latin is perceptible in her literary references. Djebar pictured herself as a daughter of Césarée, the name of Cherchell in Latin, a port city in the west of Algiers, where the family house, on her mother's side, is still located. Her works reflect the classical education she received in preeminent French institutions. Among Algerian writers of her generation, she was unique, being the only one with such an elite background. With her admission to the École Normale Supérieure de jeunes filles (ENS-Sèvre), Djebar became a visible part of the French intelligentsia.

Her other languages belonged to her intimate memory of sounds from songs mainly in Tamazight and colloquial Arabic from the Chenoua region. She liked to refer to her mother's Andalusian songs in Arabic, bearing the weight of her true intimate, emotional self as a woman from Chenoua. Therefore, it is very limiting to read her work but ignore the emotional charge exclusively perceptible to the ear of a North African reader. Djebar used French to poetically translate the affective dimensions associated with each of her languages.[11]

Her experience of languages translated a specific colonial situation and a division of public and domestic spaces. Inside and outside were shifting categories in the North African postcolonial context. Djebar was at the forefront of this shift, as has been described by many critics assessing her language and gender simultaneously.[12] It is high time to analyze the emotional dimensions inherent in these changing categories. As a woman who belonged to a segregated and gendered culture, how were her languages affected by this paradigmatic shift between domestic and public spaces? The outside was carried by sounds and words experienced in the French schools and in the Quranic schools populated by boys. School was her first reason for being outside and learning written languages. There was, therefore, a foundational divide between that outside self and her private self, crafted by women's voices in colloquial Arabic and Tachenwit. When a woman belonged to the upper class, there was no space outside for her. She always moved between different insides. Within that intimate space, there was also an emotional inside: a perfumed skin-to-skin between women. Outside was cold and distant, populated by masculine bodies and strong smells of dirt. The French language as a site of poetical reparation became the vehicle of this complex sensorial and emotional experience.

Yet Djebar received an education in French in large part because her father was a teacher in that colonial context. She had, therefore, a deep emotional bond to the French language, with all its political ambivalence. Despite what certain critiques have claimed, her use of French was not her accepting colonial power. She exemplified what Valerie Orlando describes: "Algerian authors sought to define their roles and places as writers of French expression first in a revolutionary context as contributors to *la littérature heurtée* (jagged style)," and, like many more belonging to the generation of the Algerian New Novel, she "would forever be on the outside, circulating on the periphery of the very nation they wanted to articulate" (*Algerian New Novel* 2). Djebar's *adoption* of French was a transformative mediation deeply rooted in the experience of her love for her father and all the ambivalence implied by her colonial linguistic context.[13]

Her inner multilingualism prepared her to transform this toxic relation to language into a constructive literary exercise of writing in dia-language. Djebar epitomized the colonized writer caught in the ambiguities of a French education, as she was extensively involved in anticolonial work. An active member of the FLN, she and many others who formed the new Algerian elite spent months at the Tunisian border investigating the situation of female fighters, or *moudjahidate*, between June 1958 and August 1959.[14] In 1957, a year before her exile in Tunis, she published her first novel, *La Soif* (1957; *The Mischief*, 1958), which presented the tribulations of a young Algerian woman during summertime in the beachy suburbs of Algiers, and was surprisingly inspired by *Bonjour Tristesse* (1954; 1955).[15] This nonpolitical first novel was highly criticized by the Algerian anticolonial intelligentsia. For Djebar, writing was a distraction, a "what if" that led to her most fictional works. Writing was a space of creation that helped her weather the emotional difficulties of exile and the anticolonial war in which she was actively involved as a student on strike.[16] During the transformative experience of the war, her destiny became even more a part of the Algerian national epics.[17]

It was not until 1982's *The Zerda and the Songs of Forgetting* that she started creating poetical forms to interrogate her various languages.[18] It led her to excavate deep emotions and their transmission through sounds. In *The Zerda*, she reproduced this sensorial experience in the soundtrack: voices in Arabic, murmurs in Tachenwit, songs from tribes in rural Algeria.[19] The oral tradition, transmitted by women in Arabic and translated into French, the language of domination and colonization, became the source of written poetic forms that use translation to transfer sensations from one sphere of experience into another. The language that translates is also the language that destroys native Maghrebi culture. This foundational paradox nurtured and drove most Maghrebi writers of Djebar's generation. Maybe she, more than anyone, experienced this *being in translation* as a necessity to archive the emotions transmitted by her feminine, aural environment, especially because of the *loss* of Tamazight. Sounds as part of Djebar's emotional memory are key to understanding the inner working of her writing. How does the signifier, as an acoustic image, guide the creation and translation of literary languages and new poetical forms that preserve the transmission of aural memory?

The Sounds of the Dia-Language

In the chapter "L'Enjeu de mon silence" (The stakes of my silence), in *Ces voix*, Djebar explains how her time in (literary) silence was a time of deep listening:

> Though this silence was not made of writing, but of attempts at diverse writings, of a different nature, of multiple disciplines—theater, sociological inquiry in rural Algeria, filmmaking . . .
> Ten years without literary publication served this purpose: to search, if not for a way out of my French, the language of my writing, at least to broaden it, and finally to come back to it freely, with the consciousness of a need to inscribe—within the mix of my French tongue, even in the structure of my novels—, all the parts of my personal identity. [. . .]
> Back and forth movements between literature and cinematographic work have influenced me. Cinema brought me to confront the body of my mother tongue, in use, until then, inside me, almost exclusively with family: the maternal dialect allowed me, it's true, particularly the joy of its music (an ancient poetry sung with traditional erudite music, called *Andalus*, but also the Bedouin song from the South and from other Maghrebi regions).[20]

Her experience with cinema guided her discovery of "un arabe des femmes" (a women's Arabic):

In 1975 and 1976, while scouting for in my mother's tribe, I was particularly receptive to a "women's Arabic," to the point that the initial diglossia (dialects used in family settings on one hand, literary Arabic on the other hand, which I wanted to bring closer), this diglossia that I qualify as "vertical," was suddenly doubled by another divide that seemed "horizontal" to me, a real, secret split that reflected the everyday gendered segregation.

It corresponds to a "women's tongue" used in parallel, most often clandestinely and secretly, compared to ordinary Arabic, the one from the community (not to call it a "men's tongue").[21]

This "women's language" is first experienced as a *mother tongue,* through sounds that contrasted markedly to the sounds of the French language Djebar experienced at school. In *Nulle part dans la maison de mon père* (2007; Nowhere in my father's house), she described the experience of hearing the name Baudelaire, for the first time, as "BEAU DE L'AIR" (Beauty of the air):

> Saying now, after so many decades, these three words: BEAU DE L'AIR.
> Slowly, after the first syllable, the image rises: long fingers with long nails, bright red, two female hands united in one gesture . . . of prayer? Of offering? I look, never having seen red nails, long, so long at the end of such slim fingers, and it is a voice that comes back, crossing through decades, cautious and deep, with an accent that I didn't know then, let us say a Provençal accent, belonging to this tall, thin woman [. . .] it is the voice that fixes inside me forever, like the first time her image, she who gave me, yes, the first who gave me the very first French verse to drink, pronounced the way I was used to hearing only verses from the Quran: with a majestic slowness, a gravity, slightly marked, a quiet fluidity, almost fervent in its ending.[22]

Djebar's first experience of French consisted of "signifiers" without "reference" to the world, as Mohammed Dib's narrator describes in the famous passage from *La Grande maison* (1952; The big house) in which the pupil, Omar, questions the term "mère patrie" (motherland).[23] In *Fantasia,* Djebar develops a very similar argument about the referentiality of the French language in a colonial situation:

> I write and speak French outside: the words I use convey no flesh-and-blood reality. I learn the names of birds I've never seen, trees I shall

take ten years or more to identify, lists of flowers and plants that I shall never smell until I travel north of the Mediterranean. In this respect, all vocabulary expresses what is missing in my life, exoticism without mystery, causing a kind of visual humiliation that it is not seemly to admit to . . . Settings and episodes in children's books are nothing but theoretical concepts; in the French family, the mother comes to fetch her daughter or son from school; in the French street, the parents walk quite naturally side by side. . . . So, the world of the school is expunged from the daily life of my native city, as it is from the life of my family. The latter is refused any referential role. (185; ellipses in original)[24]

The intimate world was excluded from the French language. Her writing in French aimed to restore its denied existence.

In the most intimate moments of *The Nouba* and *The Zerda*, the female narrators shift into Tamazight, or into an Arabic colored by Tamazight sounds, that even a native speaker has a hard time deciphering. This intimate language arose spontaneously within the depths of her ambiguous emotions as a child. As St. Augustine experienced before Djebar, between Tamazight and Latin, this transmission of aural memory from one language to another is a recurring experience in the Maghreb, healing the multiple ruptures between the permanent landscape and the sounds of Tamazight:

> Then in my listening, I began noticing some of these reluctances, of these restraints, and some of these understatements from the women's talk—including sometimes, the resurgence of Berber language that reappeared spontaneously in the strong emotional moments, as if it were the language of the repressed (sometimes in the soundtrack of my movie: *The Nouba of the Women from Mount Chenoua*). [. . .]
>
> With all this sound material, apparently never used, I nurtured myself during the years that followed: as much to elaborate the end of my novel, *Fantasia*, as to finally be vivaciously conscious of my horizon as a writer! [. . .]
>
> This female particularism of my native tongues (the one I speak fluently: dialectal Arabic from my region and Berber, lost but not yet erased) became like an ancient sound memory that reappeared inside me, around me, that gave me back my strength—harsh voices, so often dispensing pain, sorrow, loss, but yet making present, to my ear, such a

maternal tenderness, such a deep solidarity, that they still keep me from faltering now.[25]

The Maghrebi *paysage sonore* / soundscape nurtured Djebar's writing. Her poetics derived first from the acoustic image that leads the emotion, which is another way of entering her oeuvre: not only from the visual side, which we are so accustomed to in literature, but alternating between the visual representation, graphic, and its sounds in the mother tongues, and, finally, the possibility of visualization again. The *native* soundscape reinforms the world from which it was expelled by the colonial presence; "mortification de l'oeil" / "the death of the gaze" (*Amour* 261; *Fantasia* 185) is repaired by the emotional charge of internalized sounds carried by mother tongues, as if those sounds inherently held the power to heal the subject and reach the inner self, stuck in a state of terror. The language of writing is the dry tongue, the one inspired and nurtured by the sounds of other languages: Tamazight (also called "libyco-berbère" by Djebar) and dialectal and classical Arabic. One striking example of dia-language is Djebar's discussion of the use of the term حنوني (*hannouni*), whose pronunciation is informed by her dialectal Arabic: "How can you translate this *hannouni*, by a word like 'tender-hearted,' or '*tendrelou*?' Or by 'my darling' or 'my precious heart.' Instead of saying 'precious heart,' we women prefer the expression 'my little liver,' or 'the apple of my eye.' . . . This word '*tendrelou*' seems like the hidden heart of a fresh lettuce" (*Amour* 117; *Fantasia* 80–81).[26] حنوني (*hannouni*) encompassed in its pronunciation the landscape and the stories of Djebar's childhood in Cherchell. Her attempt to translate *hannouni* by using the circumlocution "un coeur de laitue caché et frais" conveys a sense of the untranslatable, of the distance between the word *hannouni* and whatever equivalent is proposed; the musicality is lost even if the French text tries to get closer to the meaning and the affect of the word (Donadey, "Multilingual Strategies" 32). Djebar chose expressions in order to render the effects of dialectal Arabic in French, emphasizing the connotative more than the denotative elements of the words: the signifier as the experience of the acoustic image that conveys the meaning. Because of the absence of possible referentiality in French, the signifier alone is in charge of conveying the experience of initially indexing the world in *darija*. That element of her poetics is central in understanding its *formalism*, grounded in a singular experience of languages.

Another aspect of Djebar's discussion of Arabic is its gendered dimension. In *So Vast the Prison*, the reader can detect this reference to *darija* and the way it was specifically used by women. Djebar has written about how her mother kept notes of traditional Andalusian songs written in dialectal Arabic: "My mother [held dearest her manuscripts] of music. Though she could not write French [. . .] she would open these notebooks where, as an adolescent, she had written down the poetry of the *noubas* of Andalusia. She knew the couplets by heart, and could read and write them in Arabic, so she could not be classified as illiterate, though otherwise she might have been so in our circle" (175).[27] The organic language of Djebar's mother's musical manuscripts are written in *darija*, although it is often forgotten that *darija* has a written tradition. In contrast, a "dialect" is defined as follows: "A language or manner of speaking peculiar to an individual or class or region. Usually it belongs to a region, like the West Riding or East Anglia. A dialect differs from the standard language of a country, in some cases very considerably. Greek, German and Sicilian dialects, for instance, show great variations from the standard. A good deal of literature is in dialect, especially that created in the earlier stages of a country's civilization" (*Penguin Dictionary* 217). This means that what is known as "dialectal Arabic" has its own literature, songs, and recipes, but that it was relegated to popular culture and subsequently lost its cultural value. The other dimension quite specific to Algeria is the process of Arabization. In order to give credence to the standardized version of Arabic, فصحى (*fusha*) or classical, dialectal Arabic was considered to be impure.[28] When one thinks about the dynamic status of Algerian Arabic (*darija*), it is important to remember that the most prestigious institution for Oriental languages in France, the Institut National des Langues et Civilisations Orientales (INALCO), offers a degree in each regionalized form of Arabic. Notably, the divisions are not national but truly regional, which means that someone from an Arabic-speaking region will have no problem understanding that the dialectal Arabic of Oran is not the dialectal Arabic of Algiers or of the M'zab. For instance, Djebar used the expression "les Algéries" (Calle-Gruber, *Assia Djebar* 19) to translate the linguistic situation of different dialects across Algeria, that are subtle variations of the same root language.

The Amazigh tradition was translated first into Latin, and then, after Islamization in the eighth century, the pidgin of Latin, Tamazight, and Arabic became known as colloquial Arabic specific to Algeria and to North Africa more generally. Like a Creole, it is the product of the encounter, and sedimentation, between languages from different groups. Djebar was heir to this tradition of translation as a strategy for cultural and linguistic resilience. She was familiar with the Tamazight language spoken in the Chenoua Mountains (Tachenwit), though she did not speak it fluently herself. For her, the signifier was the acoustic image of her mother tongue with the Cherchell accent.

In an aural culture, sounds are the fluid materiality of languages, the link between the world and the emotions. Sounds can be transformed into meaning, which can disappear *again* into sounds, as the singer, or *meddah*, practices when reading the Quran; sounds recover their pure materiality far from language.[29] This phenomenon is beautifully rendered in *The Zerda*. The sounds of Arabic or Tamazight were first and foremost carried by the voices of women, singing in the house, in the fields, in colloquial Arabic mixed with Tamazight. The signifier was an acoustic image first, with its visual component symbolically related to the signs drawn in any Amazigh jewelry and ornament. This Amazigh ornament and Quranic representation of the sign were both intermingled, entangled, embedded in Djebar's emotional memory.

Being in translation was being in relation among all the different voices that populate Djebar's writings. Sounds travel from one form to another, as Djebar demonstrated in her films (especially in *The Zerda*). The superposition of sounds from different languages in a space can only be rendered as an acoustic reality, not just metaphorically but by the complex work of a subterranean translation. As Djebar understood, cinema as a plastic form allows for a translation of both image and sound; it becomes an intermedial form par excellence. Later, the same poetical phenomenon happened within her novels, where she worked to render the aural narrative tradition in written form. Djebar's creative research was driven by the necessity to preserve the voices of the women around her, and she returned to writing after several experiments with cinema, opera, and even theater.

As a writer, her *art poétique* can be understood as a *mise en écriture* of emotional experiences both written and aural, both feminine and masculine, in Arabic, in French, in Tamazight, and in the experience of her body, whose language also changed in this journey from the space of her sensual, feminine, vocal culture to a space of silence, of men, where her body was seen and represented as something whose understanding she needed to change.

Writing in dia-language becomes, in cinema and in literature, a space of formal invention based on experienced sounds. The main question Djebar wanted to answer is: How can one render the experience of aural transmission in a fixed, written aesthetic form? Aural transmission is digressive, not organized, for a reader, but for a listener. This phenomenon occurs at different levels of the novel *Fantasia:* the narrator changes without notice, from "I" to "she," to "we," and so on; the rhythm of Arabic, its accentuations, interruptions, and repetitions, its lexicon, syntax, and its tropes. At the narrative level, the interviews of the *moudjahidate* become embedded short stories with a complex process of retelling.[30] Although one might think that Djebar was, in a way, producing a colonial historiography about the Maghreb, this biased hypothesis ignores the reality of the Maghrebi landscape and its linguistic complexity, where, indeed, all the Mediterranean heritages mixed: Amazigh, Roman, Muslim, Ottoman, French. In Jean Déjeux and Albert Memmi's 1963 edited volume on poetry in Algeria, *La Poésie algérienne: de 1830 à nos jours (approches socio-historiques)* (Algerian poetry from 1830 until today [socio-historical approaches]), it is obvious that translation was a mode of knowledge transfer from a native space to a dominant, colonial space. Tamazight and colloquial Arabic poetry are archived in translation in French. Though Djebar in this sense reproduced an old colonial habit, she took this *colonial praxis of translation* to a new level of abstraction with strategies to subvert and decolonize French, as if, while archiving, she tried to perpetuate the plastic, unfixed dimension of the aural tradition. Writing in dia-language was a way for her to capture the essence of her aural tradition in tentatively decolonized narrative forms. The following section closely explores several aspects of her translated Arabic syntax and the specific dia-language at work in her texts.

Writing in Dia-language

Much has been written about Djebar's familiarity with French and her complex ties to this intimate enemy.[31] Her relationship to Arabness, which was no less complex, has also been partially analyzed, but rarely do we find remarks on her Amazigh heritage. Here, I explore how dialectal Arabic and classical Arabic informed Djebar's French, and how they are visible to the bilingual reader, allowing for a double mode of interpretation. This field has already been explored on a lexical and narratological level; I extend these studies to show how Arabic is concealed by a specific, distorted form of French syntax.[32] The Francophone reader can interpret this particular way of modifying the syntax as either an effect of style, as the singularity of Djebar's writings, or as a kind of bilingual poetics at work. Excerpts from different texts cited below show how Arabic is not only explicitly present through the use of transliterated terms such as حنوني (*hannouni*), عمتي (*ámti*), حمام (*hammam*), إمام (*imam*), and so on, but also as a form of hidden translation, particularly in dialogic narrative sections.

There is a metaphorical relation between language and the female subject, who must be partly silenced in order to be present in the Algerian context. The hidden presence of Arabic can be seen to mirror the condition of Algerian women, whose Arabness had to be concealed in order for them to explore the streets of the city without their veils. While a large number of studies and books have analyzed womanhood in colonial and postcolonial situations, my objective is to explore more deeply how the structures of groups of languages coexist in the same textual space. Djebar consciously used French in translation, as expressed in parts of her corpus (*Ces voix* 29).

I endeavor to show how the French syntax of her works mirrors her multilingualism. A translinguistic approach—one that alternates between the written text in French and the imagined subtext in (mainly Algerian) Arabic to illustrate the movement between languages in the same textual space, as signaled by the prefix *trans-* (e.g., present in translation, transportation)—shows how Arabic syntax transformed Djebar's French syntax and gave her style its uniqueness.

As I attempt to elucidate this conversation *en abyme*, my argument is rooted in the belief that the reader cannot sufficiently explore Djebar's poetics (in the etymological sense of "making") without taking into account the multiplicity of languages at work within her texts, or without focusing on her internalized struggle between Tamazight, Arabic—itself double, as فصحى (*fusha*) and دارجة (*darija*)—and French. In fact, her poetics were determined by the metaphorical "life" and "death" of languages—that is, their visibility and invisibility, and the interactions between them in relation to the complex political power structures of Algeria.[33] Djebar explained in detail how the concept of dia-language functioned in her own writing: "Multiple voices besiege me—those of my characters in my fictional texts—, I hear them, most of them, in Arabic, in dialectal Arabic, or even in Berber, which I do not understand very well, but whose hoarse respiration and breath dwell within me in an age-old way."[34] At the time her first novel, *La Soif*, was published, French was taught in Algerian schools, but Tamazight and Arabic were not.[35] Indeed, Djebar's relationship to Arabic and French has its origin in her experience of the French educational system during colonial times, as the following excerpt from her inaugural speech to the French Academy demonstrates: "As a twenty-year-old, I was passionate about the mighty Averroes [...] but while I learned English, Latin, and Greek at school, I would ask in vain to improve my classical Arabic, and had to temper my ambition and resign myself to becoming a historian."[36]

When political nationalist movements started to emerge during the 1930s, they often chose to use classical Arabic,[37] such as in the political party of Ibn Badis, leader of the Ulama, whose slogan was "Islam is our religion, Algeria our country, Arabic our language" ("The Swinging Pendulum" 267).[38] Arabic was considered symbolically to be the language of the future nation, a weapon to be used against the French, and a response to the silencing of Algerian culture. There is an easy and understandable slippage between French language and French colonization, but before making any judgments regarding linguistic choice, it is important to bear in mind that, during the rise of Algerian nationalism, most intellectuals used French to build a critical discourse against France, with the best examples being the independence proponents Messali Hadj and Ferhat Abbas. In this section, I do not focus on the political situation of languages in Algeria, but I show how, even when an Algerian writer used French, their language was informed internally by a silenced Arabic, much as it was during the French colonial period in Algeria. Djebar, like many writers, was yet one more victim of a linguistic genocide encouraged by a blind system of oppression. We will see, in Djebar's work, how the "langue 'maternelle' est à l'oeuvre dans la langue étrangère" (*Maghreb* 179; mother tongue is at work in the foreign language).

Mimetic Arabic Syntax and Tropes

Djebar's style presents some syntactic constructions informed by dialectal and classical Arabic. As a reminder, dialectal Arabic largely follows classical Arabic syntax. The difference between the two languages is mainly visible in the lexicon. Some aspects of Arabic syntax should be outlined before going any further. Arabic syntactic structures can be split into two groups depending on the first element of the sentence: the "verbal construction" (or "verbal sentence") starts with a verb and the structure is verb/subject/object; the "nominal construction" (or "nominal sentence") starts with a noun, and the structure is noun/syntagm (that could be nominal or verbal). Djebar's style can be interpreted as a transposition more than a translation of Arabic vis-à-vis a normalized perception of French syntax, which illustrates the idea of style as *un écart* (distance).[39] This distance can be read both as an effect of her style and as the result of a mimetic process of transposing Arabic into French. These two perspectives are interdependent. Elements of Djebar's style are undoubtedly informed by Arabic syntax, though the following list is indicative rather than exhaustive: the repetitive use of short "nominal sentences" (which, in fact, is the construction equating sentences with *être* (to be) due to the absence of an auxiliary *être* in Arabic); the use of anaphora and cataphora to supplement the pronoun in Arabic syntactic structures;[40] and, finally, the use of metaphors and circumlocutions to render specific meanings, with attempts to integrate paronyms in order to mimic the music of the native language.[41]

In Djebar's works, the use of Arabic syntactic structures is common in passages that involve dialogue or first-person narratives. The dialogic parts are signaled by typographical signs such as italics or punctuation—what Veronika Thiel calls "linguistic didascalies" (*Assia Djebar* 54), which are expressions found in the Djebarian narrative that introduce the context of enunciation and language. The presence of a nominal sentence transgresses the basic French grammatical construction, summarized as subject/verb/object, thus sounding strange in this language. It gives an original twist to the Djebarian text, a sort of syntactic smoothness that can be read as mimicking French orality. In fact, it serves to mask Arabic orality.

In the first short story from the eponymous volume *Oran, langue morte* (1997; *The Tongue's Blood Does Not Run Dry: Algerian Stories*, 2006), the reader experiences the translinguistic aspects of Djebar's writings. The female protagonist writes to her French friend and colleague Olivia and recounts the death of her parents, Habiba and Abbas, who were involved as unionists in the anticolonial struggle. I have used italics to highlight three nominal sentences in the passage below:

> J'ai embarqué enfin, et pour la France. *À dix-huit ans, après mon baccalauréat.* Pour mes études, a cru ma mère, enfin ma tante maternelle. Pour toujours, ai-je décidé. *Contre le reniement des gens, des lieux, des choses elles-mêmes. Ma mère et mon père, enterrés là-bas, derrière une colline.* (16, my emphasis)

> I finally embarked for France at eighteen, after getting my *baccalauréat*. My mother—well, my maternal aunt—believed that it was for my studies. I'm going away forever, I had decided. As a negation of people, of places, of things. My mother and my father, buried down below, behind a hill. (14)

In French, the three sentences in italics lack an active verb. The nominal sentence "À dix-huit ans, après mon baccalauréat" (At eighteen, after my baccalaureate) juxtaposes two prepositional segments with an implicit elision of a verbal form, "après *avoir passé* mon baccalauréat" (after *getting* my baccalaureate).⁴² In the last sentence of the passage, the implicit verbal construction in French is "Ma mère et mon père *sont* enterrés là-bas" (My mother and my father *are* buried there). Regarding these grammatical structures in French, the reader recognizes a transgression of fundamental norms, but, in this case, such a transgression is considered to be a creative syntactic shift that is particular to the author's style. Of course, this informal syntax can be understood as a form of poetic license in French, but for the Algerian reader the whole passage can be perceived as a form of dialectal Algerian Arabic that just happens to be in French.

In a nominal sentence with the verb in second position, the verb is constructed using an affix (a prefix or a suffix), thus giving us three indications about the subject: whether they are in the first, second, or third person; singular, dual, or plural; and female or male. In Arabic, if the verb contains information about the subject, then the subject does not need to be explicit. Moreover, there is no infinitive form in Arabic; a verb always indicates a subject. Indeed, in a verbal sentence, if the subject is explicitly mentioned, it is anaphoric, at least semantically, since it repeats the information given by the verbal affix. This is the case in the following example, where the reader can see in French the insistent, repetitive use of personal pronouns: "Ma tante," "elle-même," "elle qui": "*Ma tante elle-même—elle qui* m'a élevée après que 'ce' soit arrivé— s'est remise [...] à fredonner" (15, my emphasis) / "Even my aunt, who brought me up after 'it' happened, started to hum" (13).

The following example illustrates the cataphoric use of personal pronouns, transposing an Arabic structure that could be verb/suffix without explicit reference to the subject: "J'avais dix ans, en 1962. *Ils* vous ont inhumés, un 5 février, à trois heures du matin. *Ils* n'avaient pas voulu nous rendre les deux corps" (16, my emphasis) / "In 1962, I was ten years old. You were both interred on February 5 at three o'clock in the morning. They hadn't wanted to send us your bodies" (14). The passage begins like a witness statement or journal entry: "J'avais dix ans, en 1962" / "In 1962, I was ten years old." The narrator addresses her parents "Ils *vous* ont inhumés" / "You were both interred," and the cataphoric use of the third-person plural "ils"/"they" leaves the door open for interpretation. In French, it could be viewed as a form of oral discourse, where the referent is unclear, yet this structure is quite common in Arabic (classical or dialectal). If a sentence starts with a verb, the meaning is built cataphorically, with the referent often defined later. The reader or the listener must ask the question: "Who are 'they'?" This can be interpreted as a way of maintaining the audience's attention, as is the case with oral narratives.

The following sentences in italics transpose the Arabic verbal/subject structure often built as prefix/verb/suffix into French: "Ma tante, de retour, m'a porté dans ses bras. *M'a déshabillée. M'a mis une chemise.* [...] *Elle* gémissait, *elle*, croyant que je ne l'entendais pas: 'Au nom de Dieu! ... Au nom de Dieu!'" (17, my emphasis; ellipsis in original) / "When she returned, my aunt took me up in her arms. Undressed me. Put me in my nightshirt [...] Thinking that I couldn't hear her, she sighed, 'In the name of God! ... In the name of God!'" (14; ellipsis in original). If I were to translate the italicized parts into dialectal Arabic, the result might be close to "خالتي, كي رجعت, رفدتني, بدلتلي, لبستلي" (*khalti, ki rej'at, refdetni. bedletli. lebsetli*). The two sentences with the elided subject, "m'a déshabillée" and "m'a mis une chemise," are asyntactic in French. They feature the transposition of a "verbal sentence" starting with a verb, its suffix indicating both the subject and the object: "ت" (*t*) indicates that the subject is third person, singular, and female, while "ي/ين" (*ni/i*) indicates that the object is the first-person singular "me." This structure is obviously an Arabic structure transposed into French, as suggested by the absence of any detached subject pronoun.

Since the subject of the verb is denoted by the affix, any mention of the detached form of the pronoun constitutes an insistence in Arabic; this insistence is easily transposed into French by the anaphoric use of the pronoun "elle"/"she," as the reader can see in the following example:

> *Elle! Elle,* son visage de lune, dans sa grâce intacte et son charme. *Elle,* l'orpheline dès l'enfance, la fille de ma mère chérie: Habiba! Yeux fermés, n'importe, elle me regarde; oh oui, je le sais.

> It was she! My sister, her moon face, in its grace and its charm. Orphaned as a child, the daughter of my dear mother. Habiba! Her eyes are closed, but I know—oh yes!—that she's looking at me. (*Oran* 22; *Tongue's Blood* 17)

In this excerpt, dialectal Arabic is again visible in the anaphoric repetition of the pronoun (not always rendered in the published English translation) and in the nominal structure of the sentence: there is only one verb, "regarde." The other aspects that hint at dialectal Arabic are the use of metaphors such as "son visage de lune" / "وجهها كي لقمر" (*wejeha ki leqmer*) and circumlocutions to designate Habiba, "la fille de ma mère chérie." These structures create a feeling of the unheimlich (uncanny) in French, but, in fact, translating a particular word play with circumlocution is, in this case, a way of expressing the multiple existences of the beloved being and the immensity of the pain experienced: Habiba was not only Habiba but also all of the realities that her being expressed. The repetition of the pronoun "elle" is juxtaposed with other expressions that signify the individual: "l'orpheline dès l'enfance" and "la fille de ma mère chérie." It is as if the repetitive invocation of her first name, "Habiba," will make her come back to life, as is the case in Arabic. Indeed, the vocative case is still frequently present in Arabic and is a strong indication of oral culture.

Another aspect of Djebar's style that informs the concept of dia-language is the distinction between the transcription of oral stories and the transmission of written narratives, such as the military archives of the Conquest of Algiers. The short story "Oran, langue morte" involves the transcription of an oral narrative, and this form is employed in several texts, including *Femmes d'Alger*. An example of this oral, often lyrical, narrative can be found in the section "Pour un divan de la porteuse d'eau" (For a diwan of the water carrier), in the titular short story, with repetition producing alliteration. It also forms part of the elegiac tradition performed by women in North African culture, relating to their prayers to the saints of the region. These are common among certain working-class women such as the كياسة (*kiyassa*), the women who perform massages and scrubbing in the حمام (*hammam*). In the passage quoted below, the vocative case is used, along with anaphors: "Endormie, je suis l'endormie," "on m'emporte, qui m'emporte." The first sentence forms part of the narration, followed by a lyrical section. Here the anaphors, repetitions, and expressions do not sound idiomatic in French, indicating that dia-language is at work:

> "Endormie, je suis l'endormie et l'on m'emporte, qui m'emporte . . ." [. . .]
> "C'est moi—moi?-moi qu'ils ont humiliée
> Moi qu'ils ont encagée
> Moi qu'ils ont cherché à ployer; leurs poings sur ma tête, pour me faire couler droit [. . .] moi dans les rocs du silence de voile blanc . . ."

> *"Asleep, I am the one asleep and they are carrying me off, who is carrying me off . . ."* [. . .]

> "It is me—me?—It is me they have excluded, me whom they have barred
> It is me—me?—me they have humiliated
> Me whom they have caged in
> Me whom they've sought to subdue, their fists on my head, to make me drown while standing straight [. . .] me inside the rocks of silence of the white veil." (*Femmes d'Alger* 108–11; *Women of Algiers* 37–39; emphasis in original)

The anaphoric use of the first person accentuates the lyrical form, and the absence of punctuation, presence of anaphors, and repetition of the first-person pronoun "moi" and phrase "moi qui" all confer an elegiac note on the passage. The elegiac tone visible here through alliteration (sounds such as [m], [wa], [ã]) and anaphors (moi / moi qui / moi dans / voile blanc), remind us clearly of سجع (*saj'*), the equivalent of the "rhymed prose" that was frequently used in Arabic.

Similarly, in the first pages of *Ombre sultane* (1987; *A Sister to Scheherazade*, 1993) the connotations surrounding the term "l'Homme" (the Man) (9; 7) on the first page refer to Arabic phrasing. The presence of "il" and "l'homme" refers to "الراجل" (*el rajel*) in Arabic, which means "the husband." The article "ال" (*el*), which is translated by "le" in French, shows specificity and at the same time generalization. Of course, in French "l'homme" refers to *anthropos* and not obviously to "husband." With "el rajel," the narrator indicates a whole gendered culture: "'He' has gone. You hear the regular squeak of his shoes on the tiled floor. 'He' coughs; 'he' opens doors; 'he' has gone'" (*Ombre* 17; *Sister* 8).[43] This sentence exemplifies how the narrative represents him externally, as a stranger and an enemy. The juxtaposition of short segments separated by commas could well be an indicator of Arabic orality as well. Historically speaking, punctuation appeared very late in written texts, having been introduced as part of the نهضة (Nahda) reforms; commas and periods then became the most common form of punctuation.

Djebar also used metaphors to produce semantic equivalents for Arabic expressions, as in the following example: "One who is [. . .] exposed henceforth to the sunlight, while I am tempted to plunge back into the night. [. . .] Your hopeless laughter at dawn, Hajila, after my daughter had called your name over the balustrade. On the blurred horizon, dawn darts its threatening eye at us" (*Ombre* 11; *Sister* 3).[44] The vocative case, "ô Hajila," is used to translate a common form in dialectal Arabic, "يا هجيلة" (*ya Hajila*), which occurs frequently in oral narratives, once again showing dialectal Arabic at work. The first pages of *A Sister* offer the reader a style replete with metaphors that mimic the elaborate Arabic style in which all that is said about intimacy, marriage, love, and sexuality is couched in metaphor. "Toi au soleil désormais exposée"; "Moi tentée de m'enfoncer dans la nuit resurgie"; "Sur la ligne d'horizon noyée, l'œil de l'aurore darde sur nous sa menace"—these metaphors are an implicit allusion to Scheherazade and her sister, and the tension between day and night. Indeed, Scheherazade was condemned to live by night in order to perpetuate her days. The metaphors refer semantically to the same theme, demonstrating a creativity and a newness that results from the need to transpose the Arabic poetic imaginary into French.

The distance inherent in Djebar's style, *l'écart*, reflects the distance internalized by the subject in translation. Word play and sound play even appear within critical scholarship on Djebar, because critics themselves occupy the position of subject in translation, looking for closer interpretations and translations of our emotions.[45] I would venture that Djebar was imitating several voices (Donadey, "Multilingual Strategies"; Thiel, *Assia Djebar*), and that this resulted in different narrative forms with different values. Through her complex use of syntax in which oral and written cultures intermingle, she represented both قلم (*qalam*, pen) and كلام (*kelem*, speech). French, transformed as it is by Arabic, encompasses the variations and plurality of Algeria's voices, "les Algéries" (Calle-Gruber, *Assia Djebar* 19). It signals a multitude of discourses without hierarchies that operate at the same level, on the same page, all the while affirming the singularity of each language.

The following section explores how the palimpsestic reality of languages finds its echoes in the reality of each city represented in Djebar's fictions, where traces of the past are inscribed in different languages of the spaces comprising the cityscape. It is not only a superposition of time as signs of different cultural moments; it is also the literal experience of buildings crafted in another language, transferred and translated in the colonies.

Being in Relation: From Urbanitas to Cosmopolitanism

Djebar wrote several novels and short stories named after cities: *Femmes d'Alger dans leur appartement*, *Loin de Médine* (1991; *Far from Madina: Daughters of Ishmael*, 1994), *The Tongue's Blood Does Not Run Dry*, and *Les Nuits de Strasbourg* (Strasbourg nights, 1997). Yet, even in her other novels, the city is always present. Cities are spaces of projection and experience of the world at large, or cosmopolitanism, the source of its transformation into fiction, urban spaces of aesthetic reinvention of the self. Djebar's characters travel the city perceived as an archive, with a transhistorical map of the Maghreb in mind, its precolonial traces seen and read as a part of everyday life. The narrative of a multicultural Maghreb is not the phantasm of colonialism. It is the reality of the Maghrebi landscape and its lived languages. It is the Maghreb of cities as ancient, distinctive urban centers, like nations, revived through the walking gaze: Césarée, Algiers, Tunis, Oran, Madina, the luminous city. The imaginaries of the cities are ancient, medieval, precolonial, colonial, and postcolonial. They follow major periods of urbanization of the Maghreb as a fluid entity that started to disappear with the growth of nationalism in the region.

Interestingly, cities like Cesaree or Cherchell, Algiers, Oran, Tunis, Paris, and Strasbourg are always related to a long palimpsestic history reflecting the imaginary of superimposed stories and languages in Djebar's work. Already in *The Mischief, Les Impatients* (1958; The impatient ones), *Les Enfants du nouveau monde* (1962; *Children of the New World: A Novel of the Algerian War*, 2005), and in *Les Alouettes naïves* (1967; The naive larks), the reader can follow the character walking in Algiers, Paris, and Tunis. This is striking in her film *La Nouba*, where Leïla is on the road, traveling the Chenoua region to visit her mother's side of the family (Sharpe 2013). The reader encounters this topos again in *Women of Algiers, Fantasia, A Sister to Scheherazade* (1987), and *Vaste est la prison* (1995; *So Vast the Prison*, 1999). In *The Zerda* (1982), the viewer sees archival filmic and photographic representations of Maghrebi cities.[46] Cities are not a colonial invention but a Mediterranean reality in North Africa, and Djebar frequently brought her audience back to this historical fact, often forgotten in contemporary postcolonial discussions about Maghrebi identity. Indeed, the Maghrebi Roman past is not just the product of a colonial historiography; it is an urban reality with ancient ruins in the middle of everyday life for any child growing in Tipaza, Cherchell, Timgad—a past left without narrative in our postcolonial national era.

The City She Walks the City She Feels the City She Writes

The characters traversing these North African cities are emanations of Djebar's intimate relation to the urban space that she conquered as a liberated woman in the postindependence era. She absorbed its sensorial reality, listened to its presence and sounds, its colors and forms. Nomadic, Djebar's narrators always visited or moved from one space to another, in relation between many different spaces, to disappear in the silence and the unknown of a place where her body could go unnoticed. The real sensorial experience of place is impossible to disentangle from its representation in fiction, which makes the distinction between the author's and the narrator's voices ambiguous. Authors who write on Paris have their readers follow their paths and walk the cities represented in the novels; who can work properly on Balzac without visiting Paris? Yet how many literary critics have never stepped foot in the Maghrebi cities about which Djebar writes?

Examples from Djebar's novels capture the sensorial experience within the urban network, life as the source of the text,[47] as a relation to classical Arabic: "This language which I learn demands the correct posture for the body, on which the memory rests for its support. [. . .] And when I sit curled up like this to study my native language it is as though my body reproduces the architecture of my native city" (*Fantasia* 184).[48]

Characters from Djebar's novels walk through cities, feel their bodies through the urban space, their bodies "reproduc[e] the architecture of [their] native city." In *Les Impatients*, Dalila, the main character, discovers the streets of Algiers. She gets lost as she explores the outside, a forbidden space. Dalila lives in the outskirts of the city, Algiers, "la ville." She takes advantage of a wedding to escape the surveillance of her family and wander. She observes Algiers from afar and enjoys the sun on her shoulders and her body moving outside the walls of the house. Dalila is immersed in the transgression of spatial boundaries—the liberation of the gaze and the body. The feminine act of listening to sounds in the house is transformed into gazing outside. For Dalila, seeing and being seen is a learning process.

Coastal cities like Algiers and Cherchell have a particular topography, where the shores are mountains facing the sea. This configuration opens the gaze up to the horizon as a possible escape while characters walk and hide within the meandering medieval walls in Algiers and Tunis. In the case of Algiers, it is almost like a *cité interdite* (forbidden city), only accessible through visual and literary representations, unless one was born there and had already been introduced to the complex cultural layers visible in the landscape.

Djebar portrays the city as a series of connections with a masculine universe in which female characters are immersed without preparation. It reminds us of the beautiful picture of Fatima-Zohra among the boys in her father's classroom

(Calle-Gruber, *Assia Djebar: le manuscrit inachevé*). Her sensorial life, like so many experiences, was thus translated into her characters' lives, shared through their emotions. The visualization of the city happens first through the gaze of Djebar's female characters, modern *promeneuses* claiming the freedom to circulate and belong to the urban landscape:

> I started to walk again. I was hot, so I followed a trail under the trees. The city was not far. Along a curve, Algiers became visible, lain down, lazy; I contemplated *it* at length. The sun itself tried to protect *it*: he shined over it. Stopped at the edge of the show, I fell back onto the grass. After a look around, I turned on my back. I sighed. Penetrated by the cold of the ground, I let myself go to sleep, my half-closed eyes full of the large blue sky like a beast's belly.[49]

Each character inverts her gaze and assumes a new persona, as the reader discovers following Nadia, the main character of *La Soif*:

> That Summer I returned indifferently to the dazzling sunshine of M— and its usual summer visitors, huddled together in small groups and large families for the purpose of parading, half naked, in the noise and heat. [...]
>
> Not that I cared for melancholy or for vague states of mind. I was just twenty years old. The year just passed had slipped by like the rest, to the light rhythm of group excursions to the casino and moving-picture theaters of Algiers, of rainy Sundays whiled away at surprise parties, of mad drives in sports cars as skittish as thoroughbred horses. (1–2)[50]

In *Les Enfants du nouveau monde,* the city is introduced before the main character. The topography of the city, its description as a part of the contextualization of the novel, can also be read as the impact of European realism on Djebar's writing. One can think of the opening of *Le Rouge et le noir* by Stendhal and the description of Verrière, the imagined city:

> In the old Arab quarter at the foot of the mountain, the whitewashed houses all look alike. Before the city grew larger, this was the only place where affluent families would come to find a bit of cool air, near the brooks and orchards at the end of the spring. Each home is at the end of a *cul-de-sac,* where, after wandering through a maze of silent little

alleyways, one must stop. All that can be heard is some vague whispering suddenly interrupted by the shrill cries of children, whom the mothers are trying to keep at home, but to no avail. (1)[51]

Below is another example of a female character wandering and freely feeling her body in the open. In the first pages of *Les Impatients,* Dalila describes a sort of profound joy and excitement after feeling the wind and the sun on her skin as she faces the sea:

> I ran away. [. . .] Tears streamed down my face. The wind, whipping my cheeks, dried them quickly. I walked with a feeling of liberation. Happy to feel my hair on my neck, on my back, happy to be outside in the open air, I ran straight ahead. . . . Now, the city at my feet, I sleep tight, like a queen.
>
> Soon enough the sun beat down on my head. My eyes closed, dazzled, I took off my dress's bolero, which veiled my shoulders. The sun hit my skin; with delectation, I accepted its bites. For the first time in my life, I was sleeping on my own, in the middle of nature. I would decide it was imprudent. But what could have existed besides me and the sky at this hour of the day? For eighteen years, they had prevented me from loving the red sun, the sky full and round like a fresh coupe. I was finally in the light. I fell asleep.
>
> I opened my eyes on a face. A man's face, in which I noticed narrow, laughing eyes. [. . .]
>
> During my trip back on the bus, I wasn't thinking about anything. The night was extending over the city; it got slowly closer to the horizon, to enclose that abundance of light that didn't know where to disappear to. Lonely, surrounded by townsmen who carried their Sunday back in the dust, I felt a sharp, nervous happiness. In the peaceful summer evening, I listened to the world's heart beating slowly in an infinite clarity.[52]

In the fifties, Algiers was not the megalopolis it is today. It was smaller and occupied by the French. Muslims did not have access to all parts of the city, which was epitomized in *The Battle of Algiers* (1966). The sensations Dalila describes are related to her being outside, in nature, which is hard to imagine in today's Algiers cityscape. The city is far away, and Dalila will not reach it until later in the novel. Her inner monologue centers on freeing herself from the burden of traditions, of seclusion. At the time, certain Muslim women were not allowed to go outside, particularly in urban centers. Dalila narrates a story about an old uncle who uses the expression "trek (open the road)" (*Les Impatients* 36), used to alert women when a man is crossing their space. As Dalila walks in Algiers, the reader, as a *promeneur*, follows her gaze, discovering the port, the "studio Aletti," the streets facing the sea. All of it will be part of her forbidden romance with Salim, a young "Arab" like her. The city provides a space of freedom for Dalila, of imagining a new gaze, of consciously educating her body to be in the open, to remember an experience of the city before its independence. In Djebar's first novels, this is a space of transgression and hidden encounters; streets and staircases are everywhere in the hilly city. In Algiers, there is always the sea everywhere you look.

In *Les Alouettes naïves* (1967), the main character, Rachid, discovers the countryside of Tunisia and wanders through the capital, Tunis, starting with this memorable sentence about the smell of the lake, which is still famous today:

> From Tunis, I will always recall the rotting smell of the lake. Each year, we hear about plans to drain it. But the lake is always here. When I need to leave town and I take the *little train*—the treno, as the locals call it, mimicking the Italian minority—I do not regret its presence: its salt shimmers in the sun, oxpeckers fly atop its silver surface, or some elegant aquatic birds. The lagoon is separated from the sea by a slim tongue of land occupied by the railway for several kilometers: therefore, whether we are leaving or getting closer to the capital, for more than half an hour (the train moves sluggishly), we are caught by the sensation of navigating like the old ocean liners that enter the port each day. I like this waving whiteness of the lake, contrasting with the murky layer and the infinitely sad green of the Mediterranean.[53]

The wanderer is always interpreting the city as a space with traces of history. It is an archaeological reading, very much inspired by the omnipresence of ruins in the Maghrebi landscape and cityscape. Traces of other times are superimposed on the present.

The palimpsestic reading of space confirms the experience of the languages, and vice versa, as the wanderer reflects on modernity.[54] The dominant idea here is the consumption of the urban space as a performance, where smell, sound, touch, and gaze are intermingled and produce an amplification of all perceptions. In a way, it is a reappropriation of the colonized space. Djebar's characters are inscribed in this performance, consuming urban space as a reflection of their own palimpsestic subjectivity. Rachid, a member of the FLN in exile, *experiences* Tunis, "[fait] l'expérience de Tunis," the ambivalent city between the Medina and European space. This ambivalence comprises the divide of any colonial space: the past and the present, the order and so-called disorder of the Medina:

> In town, no trace of water: the port was built far from the city, since its birth, it has squatted resolutely on the ground of the interior hills. Its ancient heart smells of shadow, musk, and amber: I often go there looking for a dream of silence. Since the beginning of the century, new neighborhoods have extended near the water to the north; but Tunis—because of the quasi-total flatness of the land—does not offer any panorama, only this stench from the lake; it doesn't bend in the lake's transparency, but at most in a miasma of weeds and rotten algae.[55]

During the Algerian anticolonial war, walking from one side of the city to the other reinscribed the Medinas as part of a historically contiguous space, despite the violent colonial fragmentation. A walk in the city is a form of *mise en relation*, a reparative movement from the Medina in Tunis to Rachid's native village:

> In the Medina, for me, the memory comes back: the white neighborhood of our native village, though its wild simplicity offers no resemblance to this bygone opulent city that kept ruined princes, the style of ease and a certain permissiveness. Maybe the quietness of comfort: its mosques always open, its ancient *medersas* with splendid doors and patios eroded by poverty, its merchants on the lookout, their gaze screened by immobility while beggars circulate, sing, curse, and breathe. [. . .] A *medina* not even comparable to our teenage neighborhoods, where there are brothels at the end of stairs climbing to the sky. Where the upper step, overlooking the seascape, is offered to the children and to the pensive poor. However, we walk like in the past in the streets of memories, and it is probably the only resemblance I want with the past.[56]

This walk in the city during the war is the only memory the protagonist wants to keep, "la seule ressemblance que je désire avec le passé." Tunis as the space of lived political experience informs this historical fiction, which drew on Djebar's and her husband's time with the FLN. In this experience of the city, the reader looking for historical records can follow the promeneur through the space: Tunis and Algiers are similar architecturally but different topographically. The quiet silence of the Medina in Rachid's Tunis, in *Les Alouettes naïves*, finds a contrasting equivalent in the Mediterranean landscape generously offered to all in the casbah in Dalila's Algiers in *Les Impatients*; the old traditional naming of the fortress, the casbah or the medina, both names pronounced in the specific regional accent (in colloquial Algerian and colloquial Tunisian), both names saying something different about the attributes of *ancient* spaces whose traces have been controlled and partly destroyed by the French colonial order.

Another passage in *Fantasia* narrates Djebar's memory of childhood in Césarée, the old coastal city, during summertime: "When I was a child, I spent every summer in the old coastal city, filled with Roman ruins that are such a tourist attraction. Girls and women of the family, of neighboring houses and those related by marriage, regularly visit some sanctuary or other. . . . Then gaggles of squealing females scatter over the surrounding countryside. One or two small boys keep watch while the little girls stay with the veiled women. Suddenly, the alarm is given: 'There's a man coming!'" (125).[57]

Outside the city is a space of potentially dangerous encounters with Arab men, while European men pose no danger. The outside becomes the theater of a hunt, a predatory space where the usually controlled interactions between genders are opened to possible transgressions. Seduction and sensual gazing can finally be practiced in the open:

> The women sitting under a fig or olive tree, or in the shade of a clump of lentisks, with their veils slipping onto their shoulders, hurriedly pull them back over their hair. One, who's uncovered her chest to display her jewelry, muffles herself up again; another stands up and tries to see without being seen, a third stifles her giggles in agitation at each male's approach.
>
> Sometimes it turns out to be a false alarm. "Oh!" says one, "it's only a Frenchman!"
>
> Normal modesty is no longer necessary. If the passer-by does look, since he's a Frenchman, a European, a Christian, can he really see anything? When the stranger is faced with all these women, whose life's mission, whose duty, whose most sacred inheritance is to preserve their image—when he's faced with all these women, my aunts, cousins, my equals, does he really see them, when he pauses, stares at them, thinking he's taken them by surprise? No, he imagines he sees them . . .

"Poor man," one of them comments, when the stranger close by glimpses the lustre of long, jet-black tresses, the glint of mocking, kohl-rimmed eyes. "Poor man, he's quite upset!"

For he does not know. His gaze, from the other side of the hedge, beyond the taboo, cannot touch them. There is no possible danger of being lured into any little flirtations; thus they can enjoy their secret walks without any need to hide.

So it was for me with the French language. Ever since I was a child, the foreign language was a casement opening on the spectacle of the world and all its riches. In certain circumstances it became a dagger threatening me. (*Fantasia* 125–26)[58]

Similarly, in *A Sister*, the experience of walking in Algiers is linked to the sensual experience of unveiling:

"Naked, I am Hajila, stripped naked!"

You throw back your head, like the woman yesterday in the little public garden.... You would like to find her again. Which way should you go? To find your way, you'd have to remember exactly.... What could you remember? You turn to the right, then to the left; you are still in a maze of narrow alley-ways. You avoid the boulevards, you're afraid of the cars, you recognize the [proximity of a] hospital. [. . .] You must have come here when you were small, when your father was ill.

"To go out naked!" you think. This is a return to childhood! O black rock of Mecca!

You feel you are going to suffocate! . . . It is only excitement. (*Sister* 32)[59]

In the passage just cited, Hajila is mutating. Her walk outside is the liberation of her body in the *urban* space, the only place that allows for this anonymous wandering; the promeneuse is alone, unknown, and free in her meandering in Algiers. The experiences of unveiling and exploring the city on foot is at once existential and political. She comes to term with the veil in an assumed deambulatory and liberatory movement ("'Naked, I am Hajila, stripped naked!' [. . .] 'To go out naked!' you think. This is a return to childhood! O black rock of Mecca! You feel you are going to suffocate! . . . It is only excitement"). Walking the city is not just gazing at the cityscape, it is discovering the resonances, sensations of her body in the light; it is moving without a cover on her head, it is feeling the sun on her body, it is being visible to herself in the space. Elsewhere, *A Sister* presents longer passages about this experience of urban wandering specific to Maghrebian cities. Before the independence of the Maghreb, the urban space was male dominated, the gender dynamic unbalanced. Women were more visible in the countryside, where they used to cultivate the fields and take care of the home. Women's visibility in the urban space was certainly accentuated by the Algerian war of liberation. The transformative experience affected both the space of Algiers and the character Hajila. Hajila becomes someone while discovering the space around her, just as Algiers reinvents itself as an independent city.

In *Oran*, the city waits between two wars, the end of the Algerian war for independence and the civil war in the 1990s. The narrator walks past characters who reveal the violence within the city. The text gives a rare, hidden glimpse of the Organisation de l'Armée Secrète / Organization of the Secret Army (OAS) period and its horrors in Oran, experienced as a dead city.[60] In the short story, street violence revives during the black decade, and the city is once again the theater of tragic violence. Likewise, *Les Nuits*—another text written during the urgency of civil war—does not contain the light, pleasant wanderings of the promeneur-se but the inquisitive presence of fear and unpredictable urban violence inscribed in its and Oran's history.[61] Thelja, *Les Nuits*'s protagonist, remembers the city's past, a faint echo of her recent confrontation with terrorist violence in Algeria in 1990s, as she walks in Strasbourg, thinking of the story of Harrad of Landsberg, a twelfth-century abbess whose *Hortus deliciarum* was destroyed by the 1870 Prussian bombing of Strasbourg's Dominican church:

> Thelja, this morning, does not wander across the city; she no longer feels the tourist's indolence. She holds a notebook in her hand; she asks for directions to the University Library. She lingers for a moment on the bridge that takes her to a square with the library's imposing double staircase. She hesitates, wants to have a coffee first. [. . .] Thelja starts to smoke a cigarette; she orders another coffee: Halim, head of an archival service in Algiers (as an architect he was passionate about the preservation of heritage), Halim had said to her:
>
> —Come with me this afternoon; I have a meeting, in a photography lab, with a French friend. Two of his colleagues, former soldiers from

the last war, took photographs at the heart of the Casbah, but by night. They took advantage of the curfew, and naturally of the impunity of their uniform, to capture, in empty spaces, images of the most beautiful old houses! I can't wait to see them! We can curate an exhibit to exactly evaluate the destruction that happened, all that we have neglected to preserve since then, to maintain! Would you come? I would love to have your insight on these traces.[62]

In *Les Nuits*, like in *Le Blanc*, other cities emerge; American cities that Djebar visited: Chicago and New York, as well as other European cities, mainly Padua, in *La Disparition de la langue française* (2003; The disappearance of the French language). Cosmopolitanism becomes not a posture but an escape, a vision outside of the political chaos: like the Paris of *Les Impatients*, where Dalila escapes both the war and her family to find her lover. Is all wandering in a city an escape from its present to its possible expression in literature?

Finally, it is important also to evoke Madina, the spiritual city and roots of Djebar's intimate Muslim being, in *Far from Madina*. Sacred and historical spaces found their way into Djebar's writing, producing prose at the intersection between genres and discourses. Madina is the city of mystic dreams in poetry, where Djebar revived, as a narrator and historian, stories of women in Islam and historical figures surrounding the Prophet Muhammad.[63] The narrative is not about the rigidity of religion, but its stories, its legends, and their potential to inspire transcendence. Madina is also the only place she did not visit to write about. The experience of Madina is mediated by oral narratives about historical women in the Islamic tradition. Madina is imagined and projected as a place where the characters lived, a mythical space in what can be read as historical short stories. Any Muslim reader will imagine this sacred space as one inhabited by stories. Like Jerusalem, its existence is narrative and imaginary before being experienced.

The urban palimpsest often accompanies wandering in Djebar's novels. The narrator meanders through the city as a reader of multiple superimposed texts, as if the complex Maghrebi landscape offers a series of hidden layers, past histories buried in the present. The world revealed in Djebar's literature is cosmopolitan per se, as the reader can understand from all the citations of texts from a world-literature library. Greek, Latin, Arabic, German, and French furnish the citations reinscribed in the walls of the cities; Djebar invited authors like Rilke, Baudelaire, and Dante to wander with her protagonists—and her readers.

The term "nomadic" is probably the most fitting way to describe the association between the wanderer of the city and the wanderer of languages and texts (Calle-Gruber, *Nomade entre les murs*). Each literary experience is grounded in space and time, cities and texts of survival. Strasbourg revives Algiers and Paris. Space becomes the *real* that resists the plasticity of the text always flirting with the dismembering, dislocation, and fragmentation of the self reunified in the language.

The nexus between places, texts, and their languages allows for a dynamic circulation of meaning. This connection between text and city shows the aesthetic process of Djebar's subjective transformation and repair through the dynamic plasticity of writing or *mise en écriture*. In the texts, she could produce the uncommon encounter of herself as an Algerian born under colonialism, a writer educated in Greek, Latin, and German, in addition to her mother tongue, Arabic, and her writing tongue, French. The "mise-en-récit" gives shape to the imprecision of memory, the "mise en écriture" to the imprecision of emotions.[64] The narrative, as a tool, locates the traumatic time of the Algerian war(s) that otherwise eternally haunts the present. Thus, to wander in the city is to ground words in a perceivable *reality*. It is almost the antidote to madness. The walls of the city give shape to the wandering imaginary of the space as a text, as if the movement between text and space were the same movement between the architecture of the self and its projection in the real (*le réel*). The subject of this modernity, in its postcolonial existence, needs to recapture the space of the city as a woman, which Djebar did by inscribing the city as part of her experience, through the characters she created as reflections of herself and her subjectivity: *as the only indexical reality of her French words*. It is the condition of postcolonial subjectivity to ultimately exist sensually in the urban space emptied of its haunting colonial presence. This excavation of time happens within the space of Djebar's cities and in the back-and-forth between her perceptions of historical, aspatial time, and the recapturing of the territory to feed historical representations. The experience of the body in space protects from the overwhelming burden of signs in all Djebar's languages, of voices besieging her. The word "architect" resonates with the actual meaning of a postcolonial double-consciousness subjectivity that discovers the making of space and its semiotics. Women's double consciousness lies in the discovery of the sensual body within a given space, the back-and-forth between the internal vision and its external existence. The body is as plastic as the consciousness that carries it. It is the perception of bilingual signs in the cityscape (i.e., Ottoman buildings and French buildings side by side on the same street), but not only that. As the subject's colonial experience extends to the landscape and the city, signs of translation are embodied in the experience of both space and language.

This dimension of translation is unique to Djebar's experience: she expressed the possibility of reading the city itself as a new dia-language into which she translated the sensations of her body, not just imagined, but the lived experiences of the space. "Space" is *lieu* in French, meaning not only a location but an extension with an emotional charge: the colonial cityscape that remains and surrounds the body of postcolonial subjectivity.

Just like in M. C. Escher's illustration of the tower of Babel, Djebar's *art poétique* was nurtured by the architecture of the spaces around her where language and reality are distinguished. The exploration of space is a way to actualize the indexical function of any language and its translation, as well as shown in Escher's drawing, its illusionary mimetic power. Space in the postcolonial context is also in translation and in different languages of architecture; the body thus experiences two simultaneous types of translation, one with *linguistic* signs, and the other with *architectural* signs, which inhabit the postcolonial space. The subject in translation has a *reversed semiotic experience*, as architectural signs enter into the process of translating forms that produces meaning while literary signs function as a space of both meaning's repair and its reindexation.

The subject in translation is thus also a body that performs in two different spatial languages. The space of translation is a space of circulation between *signs* and their indexical function, although the architectural sign is less plastic than the literary sign. In the colonial context, interpretation functions in the modality of translation. The body perceives everything as a language to be translated. Only a previously colonial space generates this permanent dynamic of translation-interpretation. Indeed, there are some architectural signs that can be ignored by the viewer when they do not represent a threat. In the case of European colonial urban architecture, the formalization of space, its divisions, and the way it shaped the landscape is also a trace of the "apartheid" that politically and civically defined the subject. Translation becomes, then, a part of everyday life in any (post)colonial society. Following independence, architectural signs keep their symbolic function but are never internalized as an indigenous language of the landscape. Therefore, the work of translating the language of architecture into text allows for the fluid circulation of signs between forms. For those citizens who have rejected the possibility of translating the language of the cityscape, colonial architecture stays foreign, present as a spattering of empty signs. But those who, like writers, accept their condition as subject in translation also accept the condition of this creolized landscape that requires the effort of deciphering and reinterpreting in several systems of meaning. Signs in literary discourse allow for a plasticity of interpretation that reinforms the everyday praxis of people in a postcolonial world.

Reading Djebar helps us to understand this complex legacy of colonialism and proposes a way to repair its formal presence in the landscape. Literary signs acknowledge the landscape's past and accept how it has transformed: colonial architectural signs are also interpreted in translation within literary space, which performs its indexical function to readjust, providing a renewed meaning to the viewer and repairing the absence of referentiality imposed by the colonial presence. Moving hermeneutically from literary interpretation of architectural signs to their reality (as forms in the actual Algerian landscape, where they remain in the middle of *real* life) is a way to encounter the aesthetic effect of architectural forms becoming open to interpretation; they become symbols, their effect is transferred in a text. Then they enter the circulation of meaning and dynamic encounters of the individual subjectivity. Literary discourse, like the spaces of encounters of other discourses and forms, absorbs the world of interpretation to invite subjectivity into the act of performing new meanings beyond the imposed ruptures of colonialism. Once inhabited within the text, landscape can be alive again. Its literary existence ensures its circulation in life outside of the text.

5

THE MAURITIAN BARD

Ananda Devi (1957–)

Being Creole

Along with other critics, Anjali Prabhu has thoroughly described how Creole in Mauritius is not thought of as a language, and how the repression of Creoleness is related to the ambiguous representation of the African component of the island. She makes an important statement about the position of Creole within Mauritian society: "Despite a tacit recognition of the reality of Creole and its universality on the Island, no official position exists on its usage. [. . .] The one language that is understood and spoken quasi universally, with perhaps different degrees of frequency, is unquestionably Creole. Yet Creole is the only language that no constituent wants to claim" (*Hybridity* 55–56). Mauritius is the fruit of several migratory waves (mainly from Africa and India) and a double colonial presence—the French until 1810, and the British until 1968. Mauritian people are still negotiating their cultural identity between the past, the present, and the cultures of Empire. The *créolité* occurring specifically in the Caribbean differs from the creolization process in Mauritius: "Mauritians of Indian origin [. . .] are a numerical majority in Mauritius. Among them, the urban educated elite speaks both French and English as well as Hindi or Tamil, whereas the rural Indians are generally bilingual in Bhojpuri and Creole. The white or mixed Mauritian minorities [to be read *mulâtres*], on the other hand, speak Creole, French, and English, and take pride in the fact that it is this very diversity of linguistic ability that makes Mauritius both unique and truly nonhegemonic" (Lionnet, "Créolité" 105). This controversy about Mauritian Creole—the fact that Creole "is the only language that no constituent wants to claim"—originates in an ideological and political speech given in the 1980s by the famous playwright Dev Virahsawmy, a cofounder of the Mouvement Militant Mauricien / Mauritian Militant Movement (MMM), which demanded more visibility and an official status for Mauritian Creole.[1]

In fact, Creole is a Mauritian universal but not officially accepted as such.[2] The Creole population (of African descent) is designated by the expression *population générale*, or "general population." The dilemma lies in the government's attitude regarding Creole's status; to recognize Creole as an official language would be to privilege that part of the population that identifies itself with the language. The hybrid linguistic case of Mauritius is remarkable because the creolized culture is simultaneously a part of the people of Mauritius, but also part of the island's more oppressed group; the Creole population comes from the former African slave population, which was displaced to work on sugar plantations. They were the only population forced to settle on the island against their will. In fact, although the Emancipation Act was passed in 1833, the official abolition of slavery did not come into effect in Mauritius until 1835. Great Britain encouraged Indian workers to immigrate, and "it was the first time that the introduction of coolie labour from India was made large scale" (Prabhu, *Hybridity* 54). In the Mauritian context, creolization also found an echo in the term *coolitude,* explained as hybridization in the Hindu Mauritian community, while "creolization" remained the generic term, even if the root, "creole," is still problematic since it carries the meaning of "segregated communities" in the Mauritian context and is the name of the shared language of the island.[3] Generally, critics note that Creole is not widely claimed and seems to represent "otherness" in a negative way.[4] Writers and artists (e.g., Devi, Shenaz Patel, Natasha Appanah, Barlen Pyamootoo, Yve Pitchen), are trying to change this repressed representation of Creole: some of them write in Creole, while the Francophone writers integrate Creole into the body of their texts.[5] In this context, how do Devi's texts induce a new configuration of cultural identity in Mauritius and a deeper understanding of the fundamental créolité of the Island?

Devi's novels are grounded in Mauritius's complex colonial experience. Though of Indian descent, she was born before independence; Devi's voice and her depiction of Mauritius are both Creole. Her prolific literary production has mostly been published in France.[6] This chapter focuses on a few texts that exemplify some of the arguments I develop later in this chapter: in the first section, these include *Ève de ses décombres* (2006; *Eve out of Her Ruins*, 2016);

Le Sari vert (2009; The green sari); and *Ceux du large* / *Afloat* (2017). The second part analyzes "La cathédrale," a short story from Devi's first published volume, *Solstices* (1977); the novel *Indian Tango* (2007; 2011); and a biographical essay, *Les Hommes qui me parlent* (2011; Men who talk to me).[7]

Since the beginning of Devi's career as an ethnographer and a professional translator, she has patiently crafted a complex, plastic vision of cultural identity in the Indian Ocean and in postcolonial contexts at large. She is in regular conversation with writers from other parts of the world. Her universe is multilingual, as are her characters and intertextual references, coming from Indian, French, English, and Creole literature, cinema, and visual arts. They coexist in her texts through the suffering voices of characters who represent ambiguous ties to the island and its diversity as expressed in violence and indifference to the seductive beauty of the landscape.[8]

In Devi's novels, Creole characters tend to embody the return of a repressed chaos, whereas, in a naive reading of postcolonial theory, one can think about the Creole character as a projected, positive third space. I would like to analyze the ambiguity of the political response to the diversity of ethnic and religious communities in literary representations. Though it seems that, in Mauritius, multiculturalism as a political model is the preferred system of bringing together different ethnic and religious groups (e.g., Chinese, Creole, European, African Muslim, Hindu, Catholic),[9] this model does not allow for the total cohesion of the nation but, rather, encourages communitarian conflicts and isolates ethnic groups.[10] Mauritian culture manifestly links the politics of diasporas with a recently established community's need to share the public sphere. If the aim of each nation is to avoid the violence that can lead to the implosion of a multiethnic society, the goal of political thought must be to establish a discourse that allows for harmony between the different entities within the larger society. This chapter highlights the question of *becoming* Creole, which Devi's fiction stages through the depiction of the violence precipitated by undesired ethnic plurality. Mauritian society suffers, as does any conservative postcolonial society, from an excess of differences and unexpressed paradoxes where the desire for purity is everywhere contradicted by a creolized reality.

Being Untranslatable

In *Eve* and *Le Sari vert*, Devi implicitly shapes a transethnic transgression through a homoerotic relationship, which is presented as the only way to fight attempts at preventing interethnic relationships on the inevitably plural island.[11] Often, being Creole is confounded with being "other." Moreover, ethnic otherness is highly associated with marginal sexualities, and, in conservative societies, with prostitution. Devi writes on and around the margins, where the grotesque body is feminine, disabled, animal, Creole.[12] Here, I question, as a leitmotif in two of her novels, the articulation of homoeroticism (lesbianism), animality, and Creoleness—in other words of ethnic cultural creolization and nonnormative sexualities perceived as the quintessential expression of marginalized difference. I will first explore this leitmotif as represented in *Eve*, then in *Le Sari vert*, with the intent to address the negotiation of difference in a highly normative society where creolization constitutes the rejected social narrative.

Mauritian society, like other conservative postcolonial societies, understands "identity" according to its literal definition, as coming from the Latin, *idem*, the quality of being identical, or the same, which, from a critical perspective, implies "murderous identities," to quote the famous title by Amin Maalouf.[13] Devi's novels stage the caricature, the figure of madness becoming a poetical tool to express the laughter of the Creole medusa within a repressed hybrid society.[14] In a society where identity must be the pure expression of being identical, homoerotism serves as a metaphor, or a trope, to represent the absurdity of sameness; it is used as both a sign of infertility and a positive difference to be added to all differences rejected by normative identity. Devi does more than thematically represent an object of dissension and repulsion in a conservative society; she clearly exhibits and pushes to its extreme the desire for a homogeneous social reality, the extent of its unproductiveness, while acknowledging, through the fragile voices of her characters, the creative beauty of a mixed-blood literary text.

Devi shows the Creole body, the mutilated body, destroyed by the limits imposed by a society sick with desire for sameness. Homoerotic relationships become the poetical and political nexus where the paradox of sameness explodes. I would argue that homoeroticism is a metaphor, a locus where social paradoxes show their absurdity, and, at the same time, a manifesto for better understanding difference. Devi's metaphor of homoeroticism works as a site of transfer, from social space to the intimacy of individual dramas, from the political space of the city to a poetical space of intimacy. It is almost a banality to remember that sexuality has always been an intimate space that is politically controlled to secure social reproduction, an intimate space to be understood as an ethnic and religious sameness and the pathway to an expression of society's purity.

Eve tells the story of four youngsters, Eve, Savita, Clélio, and Sad. Using the first person, each of them, in alternating accounts, narrates their life in an imaginary poor district, called Troumaron, which means literally "brown hole." These are terrible tales where verbal and physical violence permeate the everyday lives of the four characters. Savita is Indo-Mauritian and Eve's best friend. Eve is Creole, and probably Catholic; Sad and Clélio are Creole, too. Savita and Sad are both in love with Eve and try to help her avoid the drama that takes place. They all go to the same middle school, where their math professor tries to seduce Eve. At the end of the novel, he rapes her. Savita, who witnesses the rape, is murdered by the same professor. To end the circle of violence and misery, Eve murders her rapist. The reader is kept in the dark as to what happens to her afterward, but we can imagine that her life is ruined. The narrative is also about a form of urban violence tightly linked to ethnic diversity: "Port Louis, the dark one, the ugly one, Port Louis disfigured by all these grotesque shapes, Port Louis the impassible flood of bodies, I thought she was winking at me" (my translation).[15]

As a contrast to this ugliness, Savita says to Eve: "I kiss your mouse-shaped face. You're the beauty of the world, its light" (*Eve* 62).[16] Eve and Savita transgress two Mauritian taboos in this moment. They are two girls in love, and they belong to two different ethnic groups, which means two different religions that both condemn same-sex unions. Yet, against the ugliness and violence of the city, their sisterhood protects them. Their sameness as scattered, subaltern female subjects in a segregated society creates a certain closeness. They are Creole—that is, the name given to the subaltern language and body.

I cite a paradigmatic passage showing the differentiated use of each language of the island; each language has a specific social function. The principal of the middle school advises Eve in the three main languages of the island (the passage is difficult to translate if one wants to keep the visible interaction between the three coexisting languages of Mauritius): "Vous vous devez de réussir. You owe it to yourself. Pas gaspy u lavi" (78) ("You must succeed. You owe it to yourself. Don't waste your life" [67]). In fact, we can see that the sentence being repeated does not have the same meaning across the three languages.

Where French and English express responsibility, duty, and social image, Creole indicates responsibility to oneself. We see from this example that Creole is the language of intimacy, of feelings, of emotions, of life. This is probably how Mauritian people think of their shared language: as an inner space, one that is not only their intimate, untranslatable self but also the unconfessed one, the subaltern language. The school principal's trilingual utterance reminds us that each language has its place and function; there is no possible literal translation between them. Devi's writing contrasts the "embedded translation" analyzed in the writings cited in this book's other chapters. The languages *here* are kept away from each other. They appear in the same space by necessity, because each language can only express a limited range of ideas, emotions, and realities.[17] These statements by the school principal represent a broader reality: the repressed translation from one language to the other, perceived as a contamination of French by Creole. Both are so close, and the infamous Creole is seen as a kind of *petit nègre*.

The position of Creole as the repressed language in Mauritius parallels the position of colloquial Arabic in the Maghreb, where politics created a gap between the social reality of a culture and its official representation. The perception of Creole as the impure, chaotic part of the self, the *ça*, or "id," in English, resembles colloquial Arabic, or دارجة (*darija*), in the Maghreb, where colloquial Arabic is totally repressed by the politicians who condemn it as an impure language in comparison to the sacredness of classical Arabic, which is linked to the Quran. For example, in the Algerian Parliament, there is, still, a permanent debate around the use of colloquial or classical Arabic. Similarly, Mauritian Creole is surrounded by languages that have a strong literary tradition—French, English, and, as an Indian language, Hindi, which is culturally associated with Sanskrit. Once again, there is this recurrent paradox in postcolonial nations, where the social and political value of a language does not align with its actual social practice and visibility. Social violence, like the murder of the Sega singer Kaya in February 1999, which was followed by violent riots, finds its excuse in such a gap, between the reality of a cultural practice and its political representation.

As a contrast to this social violence, Devi presents Eve and Savita's love, which is mentioned early in the novel: "The poetry of women is when Savita and I walk together step by step to avoid the ruts. It's when we pretend to be twins because we look like each other. We wear the same clothes, the same perfume, as if we're dancing together. Our earrings chime. Her nose is pierced with a tiny jewel like a star. The poetry of women is laughter in this lost place, laughter that opens up a small part of paradise so we don't drown ourselves" (26).[18] Eve and Savita are visibly different: Eve is Creole, and Savita is Indo-Mauritian. Eve is Catholic, and Savita is Hindu. But Eve's gaze refuses ethnic and religious differences. Body language seals their friendship. They translate each other using not words but a sort of *performed* poetry, a "women's poetry." The body becomes the locus of this untranslatability: in their dance, the limits of what can be expressed in words morphs into a kind of *sensorial manifestation of the translation*.

Eve, written in a perfectly standard French, represses and controls the presence of Creole; in this, it exemplifies the rigidity of the *white tongue*. By contrast, Creole appears throughout Devi's recent trilingual volume of self-translated poetry, *Ceux du large / Afloat* (2017). On the first page of the book, she explains that the work is "librement traduit en anglais et en créole mauricien par l'auteure" ("freely translated in English and in Mauritian Creole by the authoress"). Similar to my observation about the middle school principal's exclamation in the three languages of the island (*Ève* 78; *Eve* 67), "librement"/"freely" implies something that cannot be *translated*, or, rather, that each language has its limits in what it can translate. The concept of the limits of translation takes our argument somewhere new vis-à-vis the territory explored by Emily Apter in *Against World Literature*.

Though I understand the thought-provoking first part of her title, I would like to expand on the second part, *On the Politics of Untranslatability*. I would like to ask, first, is the "untranslatability" claimed by Apter of the same nature as the "librement traduit" found in the subtitle to Devi's *Ceux du large*? In the case of *Ceux du large*, the reader comparing the three texts will perceive nuanced ways of articulating the migrant's crisis. Indeed, the reader sees how each language has shaped the uniqueness of the world for the author. That is, Devi has three lives: one in each language. The collection's three titles are *Ceux du large / Afloat / Bann nwaye,* and the first verse "L'océan est une vie offerte et refusée" / "The sea grants you a life then it takes it back" / "Losean donn twa lavi ek repran li" (9, 35, 61). Without making any assumption about the *true* meaning, the reader must read the texts as three ways of expressing the same experience, although, in Creole, the first verse is closer to the English version in its construction. "The sea" is the agent of a verb with a double object, which "grants you a life" / "donn twa lavi," but "L'Ocean" and "Losean" share the same acoustic image. Indeed, when put side by side, the words produce the same acoustic and visual effect for the reader as "BEAU DE L'AIR" / "Baudelaire" did in the mind of the young Assia Djebar when she first heard the name of the great French poet. The back-and-forth between the three versions, or ways of saying, explicates the position of the subject in translation. The wordplay of poetry active in both the work of translation and the back-and-forth between the three languages expresses three ways of *being* in relation to the world. The untranslatability is, therefore, to answer Apter, not *just* a resistance, but an *against*; it is the fluid, plural nature of each language that the intimate plastic space of the subject in translation performs. It is not the rigidity of a language that leads to its being untranslatable; rather, its untranslatability is due to the multiplicity and openness of the combinations formed by the *signifier* as an acoustic and visual image in a multilingual space, one that is *artificially* recreated in the work of a translation per se. Devi's free translations show the "ability to pass from one linguistic *register* to another" (Orlando, *Algerian New Novel* 4; my emphasis), and, I will add, to pass from one *sensation* of the world to another, without completely leaving any of them.

In *Eve*, Eve and Savita's sameness results from their relation to the place they exist in, "ce coin perdu" ("this lost corner of existence") (30; 26). Their solidarity is the only way to resist unhappiness and all the social violence surrounding the question of cultural identity. Explicit homoeroticism protects the protagonists from the dangers of rigid normative patterns, where male-female unions are solely responsible for the reproduction of normative identity. Eve and Savita's imagined sisterhood allows them to escape the gendered, cultural, and political violence associated with their divergent identity. Their sisterhood is interpreted as the creation of a common language that is the poetry of women, which Sad, as a male, cannot understand. This predominantly physical language (walking and dancing together) does not divide because it takes account of their differently colored skin. Eve and Savita's union transcends the divisive nature of language: their love declares the joyful essence of difference.

Apparently, Devi's decision to leave Creole visible comes later in her oeuvre, and, when it does, it is still under control. Is there an editorial choice behind not letting Creole inform her literary language? Indeed, in the everyday life in Mauritius, one cannot imagine Eve and Savita speaking to each other in any language other than Creole: the language of their intimate *sameness*. They certainly do not speak French, the language of schooling and administration. Their intimate selves are expressed in Creole.

In *Le Sari vert*, a misogynistic, homophobic, racist grandfather discovers that his granddaughter is a lesbian and part of an interethnic couple. The narrative is told from the first-person point of view of this sadistic Hindu-Mauritian man, who is dying from cancer. He was a doctor in his working years, called "le Dokter-Dieu" (God-Doctor) by the villagers—his only name in the novel. The entire narrative is overshadowed by the secret of his wife's death. She was burned alive in her green sari by her daughter, Kitty, still a child and unconsciously encouraged to commit the murder by her father, Dokter-Dieu. Kitty has repressed this memory, while Malika, Kitty's daughter, tries to discover the secret behind her grandmother's death. She is depicted as a form of revenge (43). The novel reflects Dokter-Dieu's denial of the reality of his society; the violence of his denial is murderous, as if only death could be the answer, which shows the strength of illusory national identity projections and constructions. The narrator seems to say, "With your desire for sameness, you will produce infertility, the impoverishment of our society, quite the opposite of your aim." *Le Sari vert* shows, on the one hand, the unproductiveness of such a desire for sameness, and, on the other, the Rabelaisian laughter condemning a highly conservative society.

The novel combines a number of subversive ideas, its main object the expression of two major marginalized subjectivities: being Creole-Mauritian, and being gay. Following this pattern, the love between Malika and Marie-Rose is the actualization of multiple repressed unions: Creole/Indian, Hindu/Catholic, and homosexual. What does homosexuality represent here?

The whole narrative is Dokter-Dieu's monologue expressing his hatred for women in general, and, particularly, for the lesbian couple his granddaughter is part of. From his perspective, this love between an Indo-Mauritian woman and a Creole-Mauritian is pornographic. The reader is thus exposed to the psychological and physical violence of normative Mauritian culture. This culture of violence results in a highly gendered society, as if the whole book ultimately expresses the hidden masculinity in the building of boundaries endemic to all spaces informing social life on the island. In response to the grandfather's violent desire for segregation, Malika describes the interface between interethnicity and homosexuality in the following provocative terms: "Look at the finger I am using to touch your food. Do you see it? I know that you're telling yourself, that's a big hand, that I have no grace, no elegance [. . .] and now, this pig's big index finger that's mixing your porridge and sweet cream, imagine it entered into a woman's sex, and not just any woman, you see, a very black one, my Marie-Rose, one of those you despise so much, a gorgeous Black woman, a large rose of flesh that gives you vertigo, my Marie-Rose."[19]

In *Le Sari vert*, the pornographic violence exhibited by Malika counterbalances Dokter-Dieu's powers of destruction. Malika's unique revenge against the violence of social norms manifests in unashamed acts of subversion. Malika's verbal violence is emphasized by the *monstration* of her homosexuality, both as a sexual performance and an act of resistance to the destructive paternalistic order, as in "Regarde ce doigt" (Look at this finger), "Tu le vois" (Do you see it?). She uses the deictic "cet index," knowing that, in French, as in English, it is the index finger that designates the world and actualizes the existence of an object. The repetition of "tu vois" (you see) and the insistence on Marie-Rose's skin color—"une bien Noire, une magnifique Noire" (a very Black one, a gorgeous Black woman)—implies that subversion here could be interpreted as imposition, as a forced internalization of difference through food (porridge, or "crème dessert"), which is similar in texture to "une vaste rose de chair" (a vast rose of flesh), Marie-Rose's soft and elastic sex.[20] As if touching his food with her lesbian finger will transform him through divine enlightenment, Malika compels her grandfather to ingest difference. This touch might make Dokter-Dieu accept and understand difference as an inherent component of one's humanity, one's body. It is no accident that the grandfather is a "Dokter" able to *normalize* bodies, to protect them from the difference of illness. Food contaminated by the lesbian index finger will transmit difference, just as the "hatred," transmitted through language, contaminates the imaginary, normalizes the world. By picturing the power of this finger, the novel, as a whole, represents contrastively how the hatred of difference functions in a highly normalized, segregated, heteronormative society, which imposes an inadequate ordering structure on a complex cultural reality.

In her depiction of ugliness, violence, and subversion, Devi's novels project the political reality produced as a reaction to a highly normative society, one where any resistance is expressed in violence. In other words, the novels obviously mirror not only normativity and rigidity in Mauritian society but also the performed reaction to such a society. Malika's speech responds pornographically to the symbolic violence of normativity and destructive authority, leaving the reader with the feeling that there is a compulsive process of violence and counterviolence, far from the idealized discourse of happy diversity. *Le Sari vert* is all about destructive interactions between normativity and subversion, giving birth versus giving death, between the life drive and the death drive, order and disorder. As if, finally, in such a context, accepting difference could kill as much as rejecting difference does, the grandfather resists, explaining in an internal monologue how Malika's words act upon him like a poison: "This disgust is giving me nausea. I can't vomit, too painful. I hold it and swallow my saliva, breathe through my nose, slowly."[21] In fact, Malika's speech inverts the usual power dynamic, making the oppressor feel what it is like to be oppressed. Fiction is the perfect safe space where this inversion of power can happen without tragic consequences. As a Black Creole woman, Marie-Rose's very existence testifies to past crossings of heteronormative boundaries fixed by social norms. Ethnic and religious segregation is meant to prevent creolization. At some point, Dokter-Dieu's monologue becomes disarticulated, muddled by parataxic construction, a logorrhoea without interruption (184–85). His hate speech induces self-destruction. The voice of Dokter-Dieu stands for the vox populi rejecting all forms of creolization, the sick Creole body seen as an abnormal body. Literary fiction serves as a receptacle to make the violence of oppressed creolization finally manifest, visible, and interpretable.

Being in Relation

Devi pushes the question of fixed identity to the extreme to show its limits, the psychological violence inflicted upon unacceptable differences. Devi portrays the body trapped, without any possible escape. In Muslim societies as well as in traditionally gendered societies, homoeroticism is paradoxically a lived social experience and a forbidden reality, which cannot be revealed and is condemned to invisibility. Fiction becomes the echo chamber of this reality. Moreover, though homoeroticism is not acknowledged and remains repressed, as a love that is kept hidden and silenced—which is another form of normative punishment—it offers a relatively innocuous way to love someone from another ethnic group without being suspected of an interethnic union.[22] The segregation of ethnic groups leads to an accumulation of prohibitions, which operate as walls between different areas on the island. Rigid heteronormative discourse supports the cult of motherhood and nationhood postindependence, responding to the urgent need to bolster and reaffirm the nation's desired population. Heteronormativity in a diverse and segregated society also aims to ensure the reproduction of purity (ethnoreligious) over creolization through the maintenance of distinct, fixed identities, as if creolization threatens to destroy the distinctiveness of those normative identities. Creolization is never forced and can never be prevented. In postcolonial societies, creolization is the unique expression of our relation to our own humanity. This relation cannot be measured or normalized by following certain rules to obtain an expected result or a society with predetermined colors and shapes.[23] The existence of Creole confirms the illusion of fixed and homogeneous cultural identities. In *Le Sari vert*, the fear of creolization becomes the fear of a blurred cultural territory, whereas heteronormative sexuality within same ethnic and religious groups ensures the reproduction of sameness and reinforces the contours of identity politics. The celebration of boundaries between ethnic groups prevents the circulation of meaning, representations, and texts: the segregation is translated from its symbolic existence in language to its reality in the city.[24] What Devi's novels tend to show is that increased segregation of ethnic groups increases the internal fear of otherness (Appiah, *Ethics of Identity* 65). To understand this hidden segregation specific to Mauritius, we need to understand more precisely how cultural identity functions.

Though Mauritian society presents itself as *multicultural* (e.g., through the politics of teaching multiple official languages at schools), its plurality of communities operates more as pseudonations separated by symbolic borders—which is quite explosive in such a small territory with such a small population—than as a unified nation. Idealistically speaking, the population benefits enormously from accepting "creolization" as a part of the social fabric, but the Mauritian case exemplifies how "being" Creole is not a desired posture, particularly in recent Mauritian history.

In fact, the internal social divisions produced by the accumulation of religious prohibitions should in theory prevent any mixed unions. Prohibitions are never creolized but simply accumulated in each group regarding its interactions to the others. In this sense, multiculturalism designates societies where the concept of identity deliberately serves to divide rather than unify and where creolization is implicitly repressed, while it is paradoxically the site of the making-of identity.

In Mauritius's highly conservative, multiethnic society without any discernibly dominant group, everyone is responsible toward the community they belong to and must respect each component of their identity (i.e., language-ethnicity-religion), reproducing at community level the homogeneity of a uniform national cultural model. But when one sees only the straightforward aspects of identity, such as religion or language, the other parts are hidden and forgotten. Each community is then closed off to the rest of the society, except when they speak in Creole. Will Kymlicka claims rightfully: "It is quite possible for a state not to have an established church. But the state cannot help but give at least partial establishment to a culture when it decides which language is to be used in public schooling, or in the provision of state services" (*Multicultural Citizenship* 111). Creole, then, could become a tool to help with the "partial establishment [of] a culture," the element that brings people together, particularly in the spaces of everyday life, such as markets. Clearly defined identities are the submerged parts of the iceberg, given that the creolized parts act internally, at the level of intimacy suggested by Devi's novels.

To make this complexity visible, the Mauritian bard, among other authors, represents the violence of everyday life in a so-called multicultural society, where distinct parts of an identity are pitted against each other, which causes identity to become a point of contention. The easy political and social reaction is to go back to the position of communitarianism to avoid the domination of one ethnic group over the rest of the population. So, how, then, does one truly become Creole?

To establish the transcendence of Creole culture is not an easy resolution for the Mauritian situation: praise of Creole culture must come from *above*, from the part of the population that is not *ethnically* interpreted as Creole. It is the paradoxical and unexpected act, against a homogenous model of cohesion that, in effect, reconfigures a new social order beyond "murderous identities."[25] India, France, England, and even Africa are spectrums of faraway homelands, an argument developed by Srilata Ravi (*Rainbow Colors* 2007), which invites Mauritius to decolonize the discourse of nationhood and invent its own national Creole model without allegiance to old ties. The multiethnic society in Mauritius, which is itself an expression of a specific multiculturalism, raises questions about the politics of difference, or how we can build a unity that is not exclusive and respects differences in religion and languages. Mauritian people suffer internal division due to their several layers of identities and traditional heritage. A Mauritian identity includes a religious and cultural recomposition of the former homeland as well as a Mauritian ethos that reflects a Creole layer common to a recent history on the island. The ghost homeland (be it Africa, France, Great Britain, or India) is revealed to be a spectral community that no longer has any relation to the present reality of the Mauritian community. I think that, to establish common ground, politicians could praise the Creole language, as well as the process of cultural creolization, as a solution to the communitarian violence. Creole language should serve as the cement of the nation. Mauritius's multiethnic society should also rethink the major division between sacred and secular. Political leaders in a multiethnic society have a duty to prevent conflict and to work to encourage a common space for the people, which can only be found in the secular creolization process. Creole culture, as a process, can then be perceived as a universal Mauritian culture in progress. Politicians need to find a way beyond the realm of small differences that always divide, because it is easy to incite conflict between communities. In other words, the task of politics, today, in postcolonial contexts—always multilingual and ethnically, culturally, and often religiously diverse—is to invent new discourses for plural, postcolonial nations (here, the countermodel is French republicanism) to foster a transcendent *Creole* culture, a secular space that would allow for the circulation of texts, representations, and meanings and encourage the formation of a shared imaginary. The best tool for creating this new, shared imaginary is a collective narrative praising Creole and recognizing creolization as inherent to the existence and nationhood of Mauritius, becoming the paradigm to joyful pluralism in this postcolonial nation.

In the nineteenth century, the family unit, language, and territory were key components in the formation of a shared national identity. Why not, in postcolonial contexts, reverse this process by building imagined, plural communities, where the main goal is to allow the circulation of representations and values that are imported from elsewhere, or even to think about cultural identity as fluid, as in recent conceptions of sexual identity?[26] Appiah claims a strong association between "identification and narrative dimension": "By way of my identity I fit my life story into a certain pattern [...] and I also fit that story to larger stories; for example, of a people, a religious tradition, or a race" (*Ethics of Identity* 68). To undo the formation of fixed identities, maybe we should think about investigating counternarrative imagination. Writers (as activists) can offer narratives that build dream communities, undoing how *imagined fixed national communities* (mainly following the German and French model of the nation) have affected the order of the world. Mauritian literature portrays the increase of violence responding to the inadequacy of such a monolithic model for the diverse society on such a small island.

In her writings, Devi shows how Creole identity simultaneously divides and, paradoxically, brings Mauritian people together. Her novels exhibit the reality that there is no *multiculturalism*, only a culture in the permanent shock of creolization as defined by Glissant: "What took place in the Caribbean, which could be summed up in the word *creolization*, approximates the idea of Relation for us as nearly as possible. It is not merely an encounter, a shock (in Segalen's sense), a *métissage*, but a new and original dimension allowing each person to be there and elsewhere, rooted and open, lost in the mountains and free beneath the sea, in harmony and in errantry" (*Poetics of Relation* 34).[27]

Through the beauty of homoerotic love, Devi's novels also celebrate femininity and creolization together, whereas, oversimplistically, masculinity and motherhood represent violence and division. The body and the island are comparable territories of meaning with visible boundaries.[28] But these boundaries are not only there to delimit space—they also regulate what can enter and what cannot; like a cell membrane, they filter which meanings and representations make it in. Sexuality, on the contrary, permits transgression and *relation*, which amount to an act of crossing the body's boundaries and entering an intimate space, usually only accessible through speech. Both sexuality and textuality share the same level of intimacy. Devi uses the more intimate locus of representation in the form of sexuality to represent an internal communitarian process, and the only way to act on this process is by means of *words*. Sexuality and creolization (both cultural and as visible in literary production) become sites where the return of the repressed is actualized, where exclusion can be healed. Sexuality and creolization are processes of relationality that cannot truly be controlled.

Moreover, the major, pragmatic problem faced by postcolonial societies is the confusion between religious identity (specific) and cultural identity (collective and creolized). A nation's diversity can be represented in terms of its languages, as long as they are no longer associated with religious practices. The greater the number of languages recognized as a part of the national culture, the more convivial a nation can be to its diversity. A symbolic way to start the conversation in Mauritius might be to recognize "Creole" as an official language and to officially advocate for multilingualism generally and Creole specifically to be reframed as valuable to the nation as a whole. Like in other postcolonial societies, it is time to recognize the language of the people as a valuable language in its own right, not just as the subaltern shared language, which in a way reproduces the hierarchies of colonial values. It is time to stop the perpetuation of division that arises from isolating Creole as the language of the poor. A language has a momentous reality. If this reality is not acknowledged, an entire part of the Mauritius's reality is made invisible, its intimate creolization a skeleton in the nation's closet.

From Urbanitas to Cosmopolitanism

Port Louis is the laboratory of creolization by all aesthetic measures: linguistic, poetic, musical, and architectural.[29] In Devi's novels, the city is always metaphorical and goes beyond the mere depiction of public space; rather, it becomes a recurring narrative character. In *Les Hommes qui me parlent* (2011), Devi explains her love for Toni Morrison's *Jazz*:

> *I'm crazy about this City.*
> Only this, like Virginia's sentence, the same jump in five words, the same internal landscape and external discovery like when, all of a sudden, we open the curtain. Yet, I have never been in love with a city (or maybe, yes, Port Louis?)[30]

Reading in between the lines, one recognizes the omnipresence of Port Louis, where several of Devi's novels are set: *Rue la poudrière* (1989; Street la Poudrière); *Moi, l'interdite* (2000; Me the forbidden); *Eve: La Vie de Joséphin le fou* (2003; Eve: The life of Joséphin the mad); and *Le Sari vert* (2011), to name only a few. Port Louis is accordingly what makes the "écrivain-sensoriel" / "sensory-writer" or "écriture-sensorielle" / "sensory-writing" (*Les Hommes* 56) a part of her poetics. With this expression, "écriture-sensorielle," Devi transforms her writing into a skin that collects the sensations around her.

Although rooted in Ferney-Voltaire, she is a traveler and a nomad; the roots of her works are forever the sensorial experiences of her island, Mauritius, her landscape, a cityscape and a seascape.[31] Port Louis is the laboratory of her perceptions, the place of creolization of languages and smells, cooking and colors, the place of vivid imagery that triggers the need to write, observe, and translate into words. More than ever, writing in the postcolonial context is a sensorial, urban drive to repair loss: "But, in the Beetle, other images came contradicting the nice tale. In Port Louis, we could see everything else. The true, the uncompromising, the unavoidable reality of an underdeveloped country, or like we used to say at the time, without fear of the politically incorrect, the reality of those who had to struggle for each breath, each complaint, each gasp. What became clear to me was their silence."[32] Port Louis is seen in all its monstrous paradoxes. This teratological approach nurtures most of Devi's novels, starting with *Rue la poudrière* (1989), and is particularly explored as a theme in *Moi, l'interdite*:

> Now it is time to see me. I must show you my face. They say I wear the sign of Shehtan. They look away or they pronounce words of exorcism. Give me the name you want, Rakshas, Shehtan, Satan or another.
>
> I was born with a harelip. In the villages, they don't call it a deformity; they call it a malediction.³³

This passage, like many others in *Moi, l'interdite*, presents recurrent themes in Devi's writings. The character (called La Mouna, or the female monkey) represents the invisible, the unwanted, the marginal, the monstrous that her society excludes because the monstrous has no life in conservative Mauritian societies.

In *Indian Tango* (2007), the opposition between the ancient city and the colonial city is essentially represented by the Francophone novel with a title in English. New Delhi, portrayed as an older version of Port Louis, seems to replicate this tension between the norm and the margins. In all cases, the city is a space where the unexpressed body finds a way to reveal its sensorial existence in the middle of misery, dirt, violence, perversity, and a space of transgression. In *Indian Tango*, the city appears regularly in the inner monologue of one of the main characters, Subhadra Misra. Bimala, the other main character, is an obvious intertextual reference to Tagore's *The Home and the World*. In Tagore's novel, Bimala will express the opposition between the home and the world in terms that remind us of Devi's Bimala, whose world seemed limited to the walls of her home in New Delhi for a long time: "My sight and my mind, my hopes and desires became red with the passion of this new age. Though, up to this time, the walls of the home—which was the ultimate world to my mind—remained unbroken, yet I stood looking over into the distance, and I heard a voice from the far horizon, whose meaning was not perfectly clear to me, but whose call went straight to my ear" (26).

In *Indian Tango*, Devi evokes an invisible genealogy for the Francophone reader, one she was nurtured by as a Indo-Mauritian writer. The masterpiece by Tagore recalls the patriarchal division between intimate spaces and the outside. In *Indian Tango*, like in Djebar's novels, inner life is expressed in transgressions, on the streets of the city, not in the "home." Old Delhi is the space where Misra the writer encounters Bimala in front of the musical instrument shop, where they feel a shared desire of the flesh: "That's how I go, on a whim, into the old fortified city, although it's a rabbit warren where strangers never go alone. [...] An hour later, I didn't know where I was. I went down stinking alley after stinking alley, hoping to come out on a main street; but in a completely inexplicable way I kept ending up in people's houses. The streets seemed to lead directly into the open doors of home-owners" (80).[34] The characters walk in New Delhi and in Old Delhi, both implicit avatars of Port Louis. The city reveals its deep existence, only captured and interpreted in the space of literary expression.

The literary text captures the changing world in the city, with all its voices and noises, without the filter of a social discourse that analyzes the city only through certain lenses. Devi's fictional works are defined by her methods of observation and the way her narrators capture the emotion on the street. Some protagonists wander without purpose, for the simple experience of the streets as a space forbidden to women of a certain class or strangers, who might be assaulted. Port Louis also has its "dédale dans lequel les étrangers ne se risquent jamais seuls" ("rabbit warren where strangers never go alone"), as if the purpose of the walk is to be lost and to lose track of space and time; to discover elements of reality that are hidden by reclusive lives and controlled discourses.

With Devi's references to Tagore's major work, *Indian Tango* rewrites the world outside of the home. *Indian Tango* represents the popular world of Delhi, the carnivalesque, the excessive: "A little girl, underlined by three hoops, takes the color of vertigo. She moves so quickly through her space that I can see only a burning streak of light" (77).[35] The characters in Devi's *Indian Tango* are witness to a sensorial life guided by their experiences of the city. Paradoxically, the little girl operates a feminization of the city through these sensorial triggers. For any dominated social group, this experience cannot happen but in fiction: "[Subha] has in any case never been able to put things into words, neither her opinions nor her wishes. A child shut up in her timidity as in a fortress, she became aware very early of the dust of humility that settled on her and thickened every year, as she emerged from childhood and became the 'burden' her parents were anxious to be rid of. Her only chance to shine, even faintly, was lost forever when her sitar lessons were cut off without warning" (69).[36] Devi also captures modern women's own capacities to see and accept the monsters produced by *mahanagar*, the big city, with its floating violence poised to act on anyone:

> Under the sun disguised in layers of sediment from this city that never sleeps, I escape and go in search of new obsessions. Obsessions? No, of

course not. She's not an obsession *but* an accompaniment, a melancholy siren song that seems to meld so well with the atmosphere of Delhi that I sometimes tell myself Bimala isn't real, just an incarnation of the city's sulfurous breath, the ghostly form become flesh, of something deeply rooted; flexible and fragile, earthy and capricious. [...]

If I were a predator, I'd drive her into a corner, drag her into a dead end, back her up against a wall. Then, very deliberately, right in the middle of this garbage-strewn alleyway, I'd move in for the kill, teeth bared, tongue thrusting, devouring everything in her that's waiting to be devoured, revealing everything that's waiting to be revealed. My senses on full alert, I would hear the sighs hidden beneath her sobs and feel her body's dark and bloody response. She'd be blind to the filth that surrounds her. She wouldn't hear the rats scuttling along the wall anymore, nor the dogs lapping at rotting leftovers. Her body would wallow with delight in all this grime and she wouldn't be aware of anything but me. And the fact that I said her name: Bimala. (62–64)[37]

The *I* experiments with the city, pushing the boundaries of strangeness; she, as a woman and a stranger, learns the territory as if it were a body she desired. It is as if Devi needs the city to be captured by female eyes, through a woman's sensations: a feminine cartography of the urban space, as if the existence of the masculine city could be undone and transformed by the female gaze. Like Djebar's Dalila in *Les Impatients,* Misra and Bimala experience space outside of the *home,* far from the family gaze, in mixed-gender crowds. In their inexperienced perceptions of the urban space, Devi's characters share the dirt, the crime, the sexual predators, the sensual, and the erotic with men who have been accustomed to these features of the city for centuries.

In the repetition of "mais"/"but" (my emphasis in the quote) and the "Si j'étais un prédateur" / "If I were a predator" following close on its heels, the conditional mode but short affirmative sentences accelerating the tempo, the series of assertive sentences implicitly teach the reader about the short distance between the *phantasm* of a sexual assault and its possible actualization in the *real violence of the city.* The traces, emotions, and sensations related to the urban space were in the past dominated by a masculine gaze, to which the female characters are now tentatively adding their perceptions of the world. As women, bearing witness to the urban space is their only way to survive the passage of time and its erasure of their traces in space.

Devi's Bimala becomes both the home and the world, inverting the genealogy of Mother India, like the postcolonial filiation to Mauritius: "[Bimala is] not an obsession *but* an accompaniment, a melancholy siren song that seems to meld so well with the atmosphere of Delhi that I sometimes tell myself Bimala isn't real, just an incarnation of the city's sulfurous breath, the ghostly form become flesh, of something deeply rooted; flexible and fragile, earthy and capricious" (62). Devi as Bimala is no longer the daughter of Tagore but herself a mother of modern Mauritius.

Delhi and Port Louis both have the same function in Devi's works: to offer a way to explore the world, to understand it from an anthropological and historical perspective. But it is not just any vision of the world. Her teratological view of the city implies that any postcolonial urban space has monsters buried within and underneath it.

In colonial times, India as depicted by the colonial gaze was mysterious and sensual, an encounter of both nature and culture in its gorgeous flora, as in *A Passage to India* (1924), by E. M. Forster, and *The River* (1946), by Rumer Godden, immortalized in Jean Renoir's movie of the same name (1951). By contrast, *nature* disappears in the film *Mahanagar* (1963), by Satyajit Ray, to which Devi refers in a subtle intertextuality between European and Indian traditions of depicting urban spaces in film and novels. Another of Devi's obvious intertextual references is *Untouchable* (1935), the masterpiece by Mulk Raj Anand that depicts a day in the life of an outcast. Devi's novels seem to follow this vein of realism in Indian literature that has developed beautifully in twentieth-century writing.[38] Devi thus claims her Indian genealogy openly, probably more than any other writer from Mauritius. This genealogy is not obvious to the majority of Francophone readers, who do not have the necessary knowledge to see that heritage active in her intertextual references. It becomes visible to the comparatist scholar and reader trained in reading world literature without national and linguistic borders. Devi, like Dutt, Djebar, and Ziyadah before her, exemplifies cultural itinerary of empires, in which maps are not always visible but hidden by national ideologies.

The city in reality and in literature represents the paradigmatic space of colonial transformation and anticolonial reappropriation. Indeed, mainstream discourse about colonial cities was imposed by the colonial experience and then modified by a masculine decolonial gaze. How is the city seen and experienced by women in postcolonial spaces? The world depicted by female characters is ethereal and plastic, as revealed in Devi's novels: "The city darkens as if expecting rain, but it isn't the season yet. When the monsoons come, the whole countryside will turn to water. There'll be no solid surfaces left. This is what dreams are like. They seem tangible, but you can put your hand right through them. Delhi in the rain, Bimala to see again, the little hoop girl briefly twirling: my thoughts pass right through and inhabit them, give them life, absorb them. They are me" (36).[39] The figure of the writer in *Indian Tango* is "a voyeur," an entomologist observing the city's movements and transformation, as if it were an ecosystem. The familiar is both what holds the world together and what destroys it. Characters are seen as part of their environment, back to their organic state; like in *Moi, l'interdite* or *La Vie de Joséphin le fou*, in *Indian Tango*, the characters fuse with their environment and the narrator's voice: "My thoughts pass right through and inhabit them, give them life, absorb them. They are me." Delhi is the ecosystem in which Bimala develops, in the company of "la petite au cerceau" ("the little hoop girl").

In *Eve*, the first sentence of the novel situates the main character in the turmoil of the city, Port Louis, as both an allegory and a reality: "Walking is hard. I limp, I hobble along on the steaming asphalt. With each step a monster rises, fully formed. The urban night swells, elastic, around me. The salty air from the Caudan waterfront scrapes my wounds and my skin, but I go on" (7).[40] Eve's vision is almost a deconstruction of the idealized, projected, colonial exoticism of the island. The text highlights what usually goes unseen, the undesired ugliness not romanticized, just bold and exacerbated in its abnormality: "The urban night swells, elastic, around me." The city is an ecosystem enveloping its inhabitants and crafting their lives. Like in Algiers, New Delhi, Calcutta, or Port Louis, the postcolonial city attracts the rural population, which is not yet urbanized. After gaining independence, the urban space becomes the space of adaptation and reinvention of the self in yet another instance of urban violence guided by social norms. The postcolonial self is then finally able to inhabit the urban space and to internalize it, to play with its sounds and images to produce new meanings and new decolonized myths of the city from within both the *home* and the *world*.

The colonial experience was once famous for controlling the circulation of the body; for the former colonized subject, the urban space and perceptions of it are filtered through fear. Like when Eve can feel the "salty air from the Caudan waterfront scrapes my wounds and my skin": the porosity between the inside and the outside is only regulated now by social norms keeping alive a form of domination, which fixed the urban space's meaning in the past. In all Devi's writings, urban experience is reinformed by female characters, remapped through their sensations, emotions, their perceptions of space and its violence. To go back to *Indian Tango*, Subhadra and Bimala are two aspects of the same character, the home and the world. The circulation between the two informs the novel. The gaze of the narrator, a stand-in for the writer, allows for this circulation between the different spaces—the free movement of a body that has been subject to the multiple prisons of social and religious norms still active on the small island, and their numerous, rhizomatic connections.

The visualized colonial experience captured in photographs, paintings, and commercial flyers is mainly an urban one. The conjunction between modernity, industrialization, and the development of urban spaces in Europe and its colonies centered the colonial project around the urban. The imperial project developed new cities in remote places, and colonial cities became parts of the gigantic, modern, imperial web. The postcolonial experience has witnessed additional growth of these urban spaces and the proliferation of the population through migration from rural areas. How is literature part of this performance of space and its rewriting? Similar to the vein of European realism grounded in urbanity as the expression of both the melancholic power of modernity and imperialism, Devi unveils the city as her major ally in fiction.[41] What Devi offers to her reader is a glance at the interactions between internal and external spaces: a new postcolonial urban configuration. The modern colonial urban space has always been a transformation of the native social fabric. Devi and other writers have decided it is time to decolonize the emotional social fabric of the city.

By circulating in an urban space, Eve, Bimala, and other characters are producing different types of knowledge—namely, they reveal the creolized urban space that is the result of the expressed sensorial experiences of postcolonial subjectivities. The buildings in a colonial city only exist because of the subjectivities that inhabit them, and postcolonial cities still need their populations to decolonize former colonial buildings, to truly possess them. The possibility of exploration is the complex product of independence and liberation. In walking these spaces, Devi's characters impose a new *semiotics* of the city. They tie texts from the world to this projected vision of space where, hand in hand, Renoir, Tagore, Godden, Ray, and Devi write the new cosmopolitan city with all its heritage of planned violence.

Fanon's reflections on the colonial Algerian urban space stated that cities are the center of the colonial apparatus, its expression of domination, and the space of its deconstruction. Fanon explained how a colonized individual needs to transgress several spatial boundaries, how the colonized city is divided in two:

> When colonized people undertake an action against the oppressor, and when this oppression is exercised in the form of exacerbated and continuous violence as in Algeria, they must overcome a considerable number of taboos. The European city is not the prolongation of the native city. The colonizers have not settled in the midst of the natives. They have surrounded the native city; they have laid siege to it. Every exit from the Kasbah of Algiers opens on enemy territory. And so it is in Constantine, in Oran, in Blida, in Bone.
>
> The native cities are deliberately caught in the conqueror's vice. [. . .] Apart from the charwomen employed in the conquerors' homes, those whom the colonizer indiscriminately calls the "Fatmas," the Algerian women, especially the young Algerian women, rarely venture into the European city. Their movements are almost entirely limited to the Arab city. [. . .] Each time she ventures into the European city, the Algerian woman must achieve a victory over herself, over her childish fears. She must consider the image of the occupier lodged somewhere in her mind and in her body, remodel it, initiate the essential work of eroding it, make it inessential, remove something of the shame that is attached to it, devalidate it. (*Dying Colonialism* 51–52)[42]

There are no similar accounts about Delhi or New Delhi, but it is easy to imagine, already in the toponymy (New Delhi/Old Delhi), the division between two spaces: the precolonial (Old Delhi) and the colonial (New Delhi), affecting the urban structure and people's circulation within it. Only servants circulate between European and native spaces. In Devi's novels, only characters from the middle and upper classes aimlessly explore the open urban areas of the former colonial cities of Port Louis and New Delhi. Their walks transfigure the space, as they see its disorder and irregularity instead of its normativity and organization. In *Indian Tango*, the reader experiences two organizations of space and society, Old Delhi and New Delhi, medieval and modern, the old, sinuous streets designed to prevent invasion and the straight, planned division of space, which all amount to the opposition between the casbah and the European city. Urban space is as creolized as the society that lives in it. They mirror each other, mutually transform each other. Society and the urban environment are an ecosystem in *perpetual* creolization. The feminine gaze witnesses the sensual existence of space beyond its fixedness.

Indian Tango unexpectedly brought New Delhi to the discussion about Port Louis and the contrast between the experience of different urban fabrics, shedding light on another axis of comparison far from European centers. Devi exposes the reader to new forms of comparisons between cities that are not European—that is, she departs from Dutt's vision of Calcutta as *quite* a European city to suggest another comparison between former colonized cities. Instead of comparing Port Louis to Paris or London, Devi offers the space to compare Port Louis to New Delhi. The novel explicitly engages with sound, smell, and imagery, revealing the invisible parts of the city that disturb social norms. Alternating between the city and the home, the city and the sensitive skin of the walker, through the characters' wanderings informs the transfiguration of these characters and their inherent, internal conflicts. The back-and-forth becomes a trope that structures the novel. For example, walking from the large avenues of New Delhi around Connaught Place to reach narrow medieval streets to go to Jamal Masjid is a transformative social experience of space. This vision of urban space as a new, creolized sphere changes the social experience of Port Louis and New Delhi: it accepts their ugliness and their irregularities as a part of reality, a postcolonial Baudelairean vision of the world. Colonial powers imposed a certain order to oppose what was interpreted as the chaos and disorder of the uncivilized native population. Unfortunately, this colonial gaze has been internalized by the colonized. In Devi's novels, the decolonial feminine gaze absorbs the chaos and the ugliness and reinterprets what it sees to include women in the social fabric and render them visible. Literature is uniquely suited to discover new interpretations and reveal what is yet hidden in and by a society's margins, as Devi accomplishes once more in her latest novel, set in Uttar Pradesh, *Le Rire des déesses* (2021), which follows the lives of Veena, the prostitute, and her daughter, Chinti, who are liberated by an army of women.

The social fabric and urban structure of the postcolonial city are, in the end, seen in their dynamic transformation through marginalized subjectivities. The female characters in Devi's novels are "agents de liaison" (liaison agents) who actualize the circulation between worlds translated into words, enabling the transformation of postcolonial subjectivities. They make visible the *signs* still imprisoned in the fixedness of binaries that affect the perception of space and body language. Indeed, transgressing the colonial-era boundaries separating communities and spaces starts by fictionalizing the possibility of free circulation within and between them. Transgression of boundaries in space translates into decolonizing the imaginaries of this formerly colonial urban fabric. Transgression in fiction, through the written word, gives visibility to the unseen in the real world. Fictional textual experiences orient readers' sensorial attentiveness to what was once hidden and marginalized in their own spaces.

Of course, there is the assumption in this statement that fiction informs the sensorial perception of the real and vice versa; it is as if the bodies of Devi's characters allow the potential reader to see what was—before the experience of the text—forbidden to their gaze. By naming the ugly and the monster in the fiction, Devi invites the marginalized, urban body to be seen as a new center that transforms signs into wonders.

6

BEING A SUBJECT IN TRANSLATION

The essence of relation is easy transition.
—GILLES DELEUZE, *Empirisme et subjectivité*

Moreover, the great Western languages were supposedly vehicular langages, which often took the place of an actual metropolis. The telling of Relation, in contrast, is multilingual. Going beyond the impositions of economic forces and cultural pressures, Relation rightfully opposes the totalitarianism of any monolingual intent.
—ÉDOUARD GLISSANT, *Poétique de la relation*

This chapter aims to synthesize and theorize what has been analyzed in this book. It offers a new understanding of the nature of language in a postcolonial context. Indeed, the entire point of the book is to show that the very essence of language as a tool to index the world is affected by the colonial language. It is not just a simple translation, but a deep transformation of the most intimate part of our existence as social beings: language as a system. The chapters of this book have demonstrated how we need to think of a differentiated semiotics when we analyze artifacts and texts from multilingual postcolonial regions. As we have seen, the subject in translation reveals the work of the *dia-language*, as the interaction between more than two languages; such is the case for writers like Dutt, Ziyadah, Djebar, and Devi. The binary political discourse of opposition between the colonial language and the native language(s) does not recognize the complex linguistic interactions visible within the text at linguistic, poetic, and symbolic levels. Through the encounter between languages and aesthetic forms, the subject journeys from a native, familiar space to a creolized existence, where the world and the word are in contact, transforming each other. This complex linguistic and symbolic transformation occurs at the level of the signifier and its acoustic and visual representations.[1] New sounds, core to the writing of poetry, will be attributed to the designation of the world.

As several colonized Francophone writers have described regarding their first encounter with the French, their world will be twice indexed: one in the voice of the mother tongue and a second time while learning the colonial language at school. The sound of the new language creates a new indexation, where terms in the native language and in the colonial language describe different realities. The world becomes multiple through the simultaneous use of these languages. The home language designates the world, mainly orally, without an immediate equivalence in writing, at least at first. The colonial language acquired at school overwrites the world already named by the native language, be it Bengali, Arabic, Tamazight, or Creole. These specific encounters between languages will have tremendous implications for a new semiotics. Indeed, for the young learner, words in the powerful colonial language will have no immediate referent in the world; eventually, the native language will be condemned to be used exclusively in the familiar, intimate sphere of the home. This specific practice of languages in a colonial context transforms the usual Saussurian model of the sign from *sign = signifier* (acoustic image and visual image) + *signified + referent* into *sign = signifier* (acoustic image / visual images in native language + acoustic / visual in colonial language) + *signified in native language and colonial language + double referentiation or indexation* (in the known world and in the inaccessible world of the imperial metropole). Comparing authors from different postcolonial contexts was central to understanding the systematic nature of the multilingual experience for postcolonial subjectivity.

Toru Dutt was raised in Bengali and in English. Her knowledge of French was a passion she developed during a trip to Europe between 1869 and 1873. She subsequently decided to write a novel in the language. Her writing in both English and in French reflects the translation of her endogenous imaginary, and the complicated obedience to colonial languages. The situation is very similar with Mayy Ziyadah, whose cosmopolitanism informed her relationship to the languages of Arabic, French, English, and German. As a Christian, she improved her Arabic by reading the Quran as advised by her intellectual friends; French was the language of the educated elite in Cairo. In the case of Assia

Djebar, Arabic (in both oral and written forms) and Tamazight were the inner languages that haunted her exile in France in the 1980s and in the United States in the 1990s. Colloquial Arabic, *darija*, became the language of family archives, the family memories surviving through songs, poetry, and folktales. Finally, Ananda Devi was born and raised in Mauritius, which has been a multilingual island for centuries, where Mauritius Creole is the common language shared among the people who have less political recognition and power. Devi was also raised multilingual, speaking Hindi, English, and French in addition to Creole, and she works as a professional translator.

All of these writers experienced the addition of at least one new language in which they were educated under colonial domination. The new language(s) opened the world up to their exploration: this precondition resulted in their being inherently translators and necessarily cosmopolitan. Their situation is therefore *ambiguous* vis-à-vis colonial powers, as they are perceived as unfaithful to the project of their native nation. Their invisible *être en traduction / being in translation* is puzzling as they observe themselves writing and adapting expectations of colonial cultures.

Translation in this sense has several functions. It is a tool of adaptation that accommodates the writer's inner self, a way to preserve who the writers are in their native languages. These writers develop strategies of preservation of women's cultural memory within the language that becomes a *living or emotional archive*. Languages perpetuate memory, and, in the case of these writers, translation forces them into this specific *reflexive* experience. The inner process of translation accompanies the *subjective* consciousness. Its reflexive nature is the manifestation between the back-and-forth movement between the two parts of the self, moved by sensations generated by two or more systems of languages. While the cogito ergo sum encapsulates the modern self-reflexive subject, the *being in translation* encapsulates the colonized woman subject translating between languages, divided under the power of coercion.

The *signifier* of the colonial language comprises the core of these experiences of languages and differentiation—that is, not only their differences, but their different uses and levels of social and political power. Languages become sites of *domestic wars* that start with the *sounds* of French or English (the signifier's acoustic image) perceived as empty, frightening bombshells contrasting with the comforting sounds of the mother tongue at home.

Being in translation also offers a way to envision the changing cityscape, the relation to a colonial urban identity that leads to an experience of guilty cosmopolitanism. Colonization in India, Egypt, Algeria, and Mauritius translated the cityscape both acoustically and visually. The landscape's visual transformation was part of the process of an inner experience of differentiation, and the impressions of being in translation. This inner urban experience of the native and the colonial manifests in these writers' poetic and literary production at large.

The hearts of this essential translation for the postcolonial subject is the need to maintain unity, to survive the scattered nature of colonial invasion. The only positive and optimistic answer is translation, which makes difference familiar and dynamic (because of the inherent back and forth movements between languages). The cityscape is not just an easy metaphor but the locus of differentiated sensorial experience of the body, be it in the hybrid architecture of the city, the sounds, music, languages, or smells, all felt as *new* in that same, no longer familiar space. Urban centers in former colonies exemplify this process in their monuments and colonial buildings, and vice versa in French and in British cities (in Paris and London, aesthetic details coming from the edges of the empire shaped architectural forms). The oriental as a sign becomes the signature of the expanded empire. Cosmopolitanism, as a concept, becomes the expression of this urban culture in translation, where today the obvious presence of signs in different languages asserts the existence of citizens of the world.

This process takes place in the *flesh* of the city, in the visible translation of endogenous architectures into Europeanized forms (e.g., the Hausmannization of Algiers and Cairo and the modernization of Calcutta, Port Louis, etc.), just as it does in the flesh of these women's texts. What results are signs of *creolization*.[2]

The Pleasure of the Plural

The essence of translation is, per se, two languages being in relation. The *enjoyment* of being plural and in relation within a plurality of roots, traditions, and languages defines the nature of creolized writers during and after colonial times. The "I" enunciator of a multilingual text recognizes colonialism as a toxic relation from which colonial language should be extracted and transformed, similar to the extraction of medicine from venom. The enjoyment comes from a reversed relation to language. Writers in postcolonial contexts reinvent their relation to the dominant language: they act on it. Thus, in the experience of writing in the language of the colonizer, postcolonial women writers experience otherness from within not only as a conflict, but also as a jouissance/enjoyment of the plural and the appraisal of literature as the space for such plastic encounters, as an open, metamorphic space.[3]

The situation is quite different for writers like Samuel Beckett, Eugène Ionesco, Nathalie Sarraute, Julia Kristeva, and other European intellectuals of the twentieth century. The latter adopted French as a literary language as the result of their condition as migrant, but not colonized, writers:

> If we take account of history as it is told in newspapers, there are two solutions for facing up to, and perhaps even putting an end to, Sarajevo and Chechnya: on one side, encourage the flourishing of national languages and cultures [...], but, on the other side, favor those species that, while on the way to proliferation, are still rare, protect those hybrid monsters that we are, migrant writers who risk what we know neither here nor there; and why should we do so, I ask you? Well, so as to generate new beings or blood, diplomats of the dictionary, genetic negotiators, wandering Jews of Being who challenge authentic, and hence military, citizens of all kinds in favor of a nomadic humanity that is no longer willing to sit quietly. (*Crisis of the European Subject* 169)

In his introduction to Kristeva's *Crisis of the European Subject*, Samir Dayal argues: "It is well to step back from this line of argument to see how fundamental the emphasis on plurality is for all of Kristeva's work. Her preoccupation with pluralization, or plurality, is as vital to her argument in this book as her argument for 'polymorphism,' difference, and 'openness' has been throughout her career. And the argument for plurality appears throughout a variety of theoretical registers in support of the theory of the constitution of the subject" (15). In a nationalist context, as shown by Kristeva's words, "plurality" is understood as the refusal to belong to one single community and the claim for an (unsustainable) cosmopolitanism in a world made rigid by oppositional binarism produced by a narrow definition of nationhood.[4]

In my perspective, plurality inspires new national narratives, without any naive belief in a better world. The subject in translation transforms melancholia into enjoyment, providing a constructive answer to the trauma of colonial experience. The enjoyment of the plurality of languages is not a simple answer to the historical split of the postcolonial subject, but an attempt to repair and be in relation beyond the schizophrenia and anger of the postcolonial situation.[5]

Through her practice of literature, Toru Dutt reinformed her perception of "the native." The practice of translation from French poetry to English triggered the desire to translate from Sanskrit to English as well. The actualization of the analogy between East and West in her literary practice bridges her imagination as a reader exposed to several languages. This subject is nurtured by texts from different eras and spaces of encounter. This multilingual writer defines herself in the in-betweenness. This subject born out of colonial experience puts in relation the *black skin* and the *white masks* in a work of language. For example, certain of Dutt's letters denounce the unfairness of the Anglo-Indian sahibs toward her countrymen, whom she calls "natives," yet, in the same letter, she mentions heroes and heroines of the *Ramayana* and the need to recognize them as a part of the Indian present, not just as a philological, forgotten past.[6] Dutt's remark does not have to be read as a betrayal, but as the metaphorical expression of relationality shared through literary and aesthetic experience. The complex enjoyment of the language as a space of reconciliation and agency, particularly for women, was experienced as shameful by the male intellectuals leading the anticolonial debate, who therefore silenced their female cohort.

Critics who condemned Dutt, as well as Ziyadah and Djebar, imagined a literal meaning, a transparent reading of ethics through poetics, without the work of interpretation. Dutt, Ziyadah, Djebar, and Devi represent a complex link between ethics and poetics fully expressed in the work of reading and interpreting their texts. Their relationality lies in the ability to bring different elements together and mold them into a new object whose existence can only happen in a literary text. Its plasticity allows for the soft encounter between differences; it is the space where conflicts are metaphorized and then discharged from their real violence. This complex ethics of the poetics is reparative as soon as the work of reading and interpretation are seen as an inner transformative action.[7]

In fact, an ethics of the poetics is possible only if the process is interpretative, giving room to nonoppositional terms. The poetics of the multilingual subject will then be an attempt to replace a divisive symbolic order à la Fanon with a relational, and therefore dynamic, metaphoric order, à la Glissant, allowing for the existence of plurality instead of reproducing a cycle of oppositional binarism. This poetics is thus a return to literature as such, as a space of plasticity and joyful interpretation in order to produce a complex ethical answer, to avoid the return of real violence. Within literary texts, interpretation, magnified through a work of invisible translation, is a moment of differentiation that welcomes transformative otherness.

The claim for enjoyment of the plural is not an idealistic position; on the contrary, it is the most pragmatic, relying on the complex analysis of the interconnectedness between multiple languages, the necessity of remembering these postcolonial territories as informed by a plural past. The claim for fluidity in the politics of language is to acknowledge the circulating plurality inherent to the postcolonial subject, without denying the struggle for independence; it can also be read as the final overthrowing of the colonizer. This perspective on the subject redefines the roots of postcolonial subjectivity not only as a failed expression of European humanism, but, on the contrary, as the hidden, complex history of an anticolonialism that is neither Western nor Eastern, but rather the location of a true cosmopolitan culture emerging from an abusive relationship.

Cosmopolitanism within Empires

Why are colonial experiences never seen as forced cosmopolitan experiences? This change in perspective repositions the colonial experience in terms of both multilingualism and cosmopolitanism. In their writings, Dutt, Ziyadah, Djebar, and Devi all perform a specific claim of a "vernacular" cosmopolitan ethos.[8] Our writers experience their cities as an expression of multiplicity and the attempt to encapsulate a decentered vision of the imperial world. Their cosmopolitanism is the result of their experience of the power of empire transforming the cityscape with a new sonorous and architectural language. The urban colonial space is the space of relationality, a space of circulation.

The new cosmopolitan cityscape appears in many parts in their writings. Their texts are like the chameleon's skin reflecting their changing world. The urban space is read and interpreted as a plural space, containing the world, expressed in architectural forms and designs, new acoustics, visual and tactile sensations and smells (e.g., around the lake in Tunis or on the street in Old Delhi). The sensations of colonial urban life carry with them the toxic climax of enjoyment and decadence as rendered in movies like *Mahanagar*, by Satyajit Ray, or, later, *The Battle of Algiers*, where the viewer can see in the intersections between modern European and native traditional spaces the change in body language, the back-and-forth movement between two segregated worlds.

The world, in the polis, is comparable to the world within the text. The space of comparison, of transmission, of circulation and construction, is similar to the inner space of the subject: it is plural, in-relation, as visible in the poetics of Dutt's writings. Dutt connects, weblike, different important female figures of Indian heritage and culture: Sita, Sakuntala, and Lakshmi share a convivial textual space with Shakespeare, Byron, and Baudelaire. Mentioning Sita and Leconte de Lisle, Hugo and Kalidasa, creates a new geopoetics, allowing for new models of cultural development, bringing people together through the medium of literary experimentation. The political nature of our subjectivities in translation is cosmopolitanism, the world in the city.

The postcolonial North African subject at the center of Fanon's theory of the postcolonial psyche is still caught in a double-bind structure of power relations: oppositional discourses produced by the dominant, postindependence violence of anticolonialism. Therefore cosmopolitanism is not only an expressed elitism of the colonized, but its visible locus of cultural creolization, in Glissant's terms, as an aesthetic phenomenon in its process, its speed, its cultural and linguistic manifestations. The material nature of this subject is a plasticity that allows for fluidity and circulation.[9]

The Return to Literature as Aesthetics

Literature as aesthetics means a form that provokes sensations and emotions. Colonial experiences have too often been considered as exclusively historical and political experiences, but not as aesthetic experiences, which they profoundly are through their relations to languages both oral and visual. A poetics of the subject in translation is based on the exposure to a variety of aesthetic experiences due to the colonial transformation of the writer's world. This aesthetic experience starts with the presence of a new spoken language, followed swiftly by new architectural forms in the colonized city, where native and colonial buildings coexist in a strange relation of simultaneously imposed power over the landscape and mimicry of native architecture, remnants of former empires whose traces are visibly decayed buildings in the cityscape.[10]

The expression of aesthetic differentiation is to be understood etymologically as cognitive sensations and affects linked to the experience of different sounds, smells, and visual artefacts traceable in the literary production of our writers. These authors, who had been exposed to European literature, express the differences between their cultures, the filiations of their languages in their works. Their selves were and are animated by multiple languages resonating in the colonial urban space. This fragile "I" is located within a literary aesthetic, in the realm of sensations and affects given shape within literary forms. As a literary subject, they are born out of the womb of an infanticidal mother. The resilience developed by women writers under colonial and postcolonial conditions reveals the ambiguous ties to systems of domination that are systems of signs.

CONCLUSION

The emergence of the subject is not always and only the result of the cogito. The carthesian cogito, in Anthony J. Cascardi's *The Subject of Modernity* (1992), is here interpreted as the "modern concept of reason, understood as a subjective self-consciousness and formulated in terms of quasi-mathematical representations of the world" (25). In contrast to Cascardi's cogito, the subject in translation arises from the aesthetic experiences and practices of life in several languages, during colonial domination, from their sounds, words, plastic experiences, and organization of speech. It arises as an inner world, an organization of space, and, finally, as the projected, inner creolized self, "I feel therefore I am," which is a conclusive variation of the introductory "I feel the language in the city therefore I am." Toru Dutt, Mayy Ziyadah, Assia Djebar, and Ananda Devi decided to act on hegemonic discourses instead of being acted on by them. Their works magnify the experience of difference instead of rejecting it.

Why is this subjectivity feminine? For many writers, the colonial language (French and/or English) enabled them to transgress the boundaries of a controlling, paternalistic space. Being a colonized woman informs the emergence of a plastic answer to two power structures: colonialism and nationalism. Moreover, being a woman born into the upper or middle class intensifies the ambiguous response to colonialization. This feminine subject is defined by the paradigm of multiplicity and hybridity. She is opposed to the uniformity and purity desired by the hegemonic powers, who, at the turn of the century, employed literature and language as sites of domination (e.g., colonial, anticolonial, religious). An explicit desire for multiplicity opposes the uniformizing discourse of nationalist figures for whom plurality, with its resulting hybridity, are the unclassified leftovers that do not fit in national narratives. The ambiguous discourse of all four writers is a sign of these conflicting powers. A fluid relationality, and new gender positionality become obvious when summarizing the political nature of this creolized subjectivity. I wish to conclude with a few paragraphs about the establishment of a new semiotics leading to a new semiosis and on cosmopolitanism and creolization as visible signs of the work of this new semiotics.

New Balance, Fluid Relationality, Positionality

Colonial relations impose a top-down direction on influential cultural exchanges, as suggested by Fanon and Memmi's theorization of the dominant/dominated configuration of the postcolonial subject. The configuration suggested by our writers is instead a more equal flow of cultural exchanges, a liberated circulation forming a constellation without a dominant center, reestablishing a healthy balance for the individual subject vis-à-vis the colonial power instead of those power structures inherited by the movement of colonial mimicry. Dutt, Ziyadah, Djebar, Devi, and many more do not presuppose power or authority of their own, but recalibrate the relation of margin to center. It is not an idealized perspective, but the attempt to produce a new configuration of colonized/colonizer interactions.

Dutt, Ziyadah, Djebar, and Devi see, feel, and think of the world as a relationality: if the world is seen as a text, it is not due to the supposedly transcendent value of literature, nor is it a sign of an elitist, cosmopolitan position. Rather, this vision of the world results from the interconnection of the text and subject through their experience of the other language(s). The self-reflexive vision of the world derives from this exposure to the colonial episteme and linguistic violence. These creolized cosmopolitan writers redefined the nature of colonialism as an imposed relationship. In essence, the postcolonial subject internalizes *with* through the forced experience of the language of the other. Our writers expressed this inherently hybrid and plural nature of the postcolonial self through their dia-language writings, becoming the paradigm of postcolonial ontology. Their common desire was the constitution of *un monde-avec* / a world-with in which subjectivity is essentially actualizing the relationality of the world. For our purposes, the movement of this *with* is rationalized and internalized in textual spaces. If Dutt's, Ziyadah's, Djebar's, and Devi's worlds are different, it is because their constitution is the *with* and not exclusively the *we*, as it might appear in nationalist discourses produced when each woman was writing. Focusing on the *with* instead of the *we* means looking at the process of colonial transformation on both sides of the mirror; looking at the process of creolization as dynamic.

By imposing a constellation that shifted the focus from the center to the periphery, these colonized writers led to an equalization of paradigms of the West/East and, at the same time, conserved their own authority as keepers of an important ancient literary tradition (Tamazight, Sanskrit, and Arabic). Each of them did this by following their own personal journey. The plasticity and hospitality of poetry allows for a fluid experience of the self and its in-betweenness. Instead of a "third space" as defined by Bhabha, all the cultural and linguistic spaces are in fluid contact with each other. Literature exists in the space of flowing languages, as a *with* instead of just an *et* (and). The emotional experience of the text blossoms first and foremost from the essence of its language, where words as images and sounds, in relation, repair the gaps of colonial loss and offer the healing power of interpretation and new meanings, as well as the possibility to read and hear BEAU-DE-L'AIR as a part of *Baudelaire*.

After reading and analyzing the works of Dutt, Ziyadah, Djebar, and Devi, there is no longer a pyramidal structure of power, expressed in postcolonial discourses since Fanon, Memmi, Said, and Bhabha, from the empire at the center to the dominated colonies on the margins. Rather, the world gets reconfigured through the reading and writing lens of our postcolonial women writers. This reconfiguration is not really an inversion (like in the expression "upside-down"), but it is more accurately a reconfiguration of a constellation of centers. Looking at the world as it was during the colonial era, but from the perspective of the other, also means relocating our theoretical tools and practices to see the world from the landscape of its production, from the experience of its languages, reducing the imperialist perspective that was part of the blind spot of the Orientalist interest in the other. In fact, the newness of the creolized world is not related to the accumulation of authors and their texts (texts by Byron, Shakespeare, Alphonse de Lamartine, Hugo, Kalidasa, Imru al-Qais, Tagore, and Morrison). Instead, it is the specific historical encounter formed by space, texts, and time. The world changes because of the position of the reader: a young Syrian woman reading Byron and al Quran in the sweet Lebanese forest in 1911, or a young Bengali woman reading Kalidasa and Charlotte Brontë in Calcutta in 1876, or a young Algerian girl reading Baudelaire and Imru al-Qais in Algiers in 1950s, or a young Mauritian girl reading Tagore and Toni Morrison in Port Louis in 1970s. It is not the accumulative process of world literature that makes the world new, but the constellations formed by the relation between space, time, and text.

From a New Semiotics to a New Semiosis

In colonial contexts, the experience of the sign as both an acoustic and a visual signifier comprises the core of this multilingual semiotics. The colonized learns to index the world both in the language spoken in the family, and in the colonial language that is first and foremost transmitted at school. Everything starts with the sounds of the colonial language imposed on and over the mother tongue. As such, the young learner is forced to fill in the gaps of the colonial language, whose world of reference is not aligned with the familiar reality of the colonized young learner. The colonial language (be it English or French) articulates a reality that the speaker cannot see or feel directly. I am referring to the words absent from the reality of Djebar or Dutt: How can a young Bengali girl intimately adopt a language which names birds and plants that do not belong to her reality but are imposed as the reality of the language she learns and reads in novels by Charlotte Brontë? In Djebar's words: "I write and speak French outside: the words I use convey no flesh-and-blood reality. I learn the names of birds I've never seen, trees I shall take ten years or more to identify, lists of flowers and plants that I shall never smell until I travel north of the Mediterranean" (*Fantasia* 185).[1]

As colonized learners, they associate each sign to two signifiers representing two realities: the "bouquet" becomes for Dutt both a "bouquet" and a "garland." As developed in chapter 6, this double indexation transforms the usual Saussurian model of the sign: *sign = signifier* (acoustic image and visual image) + *signified* + *referent* in a monolingual context becomes *sign = signifier* (acoustic/visual images in native language + acoustic/visual images in colonial language) + *signified* (in the native language and in the colonial language) + *double indexation* (in the known world and in the inaccessible world of the imperial metropole) in a plurilingual colonial context. What is a "bouquet" for Dutt? It is first a "garland" to which is added the signifier and the signified "bouquet" without the immediate experience of its referent in Bengal. The function of the sign is transformed in plurilingual colonial contexts; it fosters new interpretations and wordplay. The mother tongue transforms the experience of indexing the world and the referentiality of the language is doubled. This is why this specific function of the sign calls for new hermeneutic tools.[2]

Finally, on Cosmopolitanism and Creolization ...

"Cosmopolitanism" evokes in its pronunciation the joyful presence of the plural, urban experience. In postcolonial contexts, it is not just a form of indigenous imperialism. It is the experience of the complex landscape at the core of the subject in translation, interpreting a new semiotics of the space. Cosmopolitanism in this context provokes the subject to perform the ambiguous conception of cultural circulation.

I insist on the urban and the cosmopolitan because they both describe specific colonial experiences grounded first and foremost in bodily *sensations*: sounds, smells, colors, and the touch of the crowd.[3] Reading Calcutta, Cairo, Algiers, and Port Louis as cosmopolitan cities, through the experience of women writers and the "poetry of women," is a way to demasculinize and decolonize the city and the world. The political pressure known as "colonialism" induces a plastic response to the subject's early encounter with sensations carried by the *new* language (i.e., the colonial language) in an ancient landscape shaped by so many other encounters with languages. French or English with Arabic, English or French with Bengali provide an added source of sensations, sounds, and images sustained by the transformative power of a colonial presence in the native landscape. Changing a cityscape to almost resemble a European city mirrors the changes experienced by individual colonized subjects through the learning of the colonial language. The refusal and denial of such an experience is not an easy process. For these women writers, performing their voice in the colonial language empowered them. The translation of their native landscape brought ambiguous newness to their lives. The mitigation of the guilt associated with using the colonial language forged a way outside of the unbearable contradictions of being under colonial rule. These women writers synthesized the encounters between sounds and images from different languages; the space of the poem became the space of creolized expression—as in chemistry, its visualization and existence, a miscellaneous product.

This subject in translation is necessarily textual, and the space of the poem is its full expression. Indeed, poems like "Baugmaree" or "The Lotus" are texts that can embrace contradictions without harming the integrity of the writer's psyche. The symptomatic split imposed on postcolonial subjectivities is but the denial of the possibility of an easy transition (a Deleuzian *plie*, or "fold"), the bridge between words from different languages. The encounter between the "garland" and the "bouquet" in Dutt's poetry, the natural presence of the "minaret" in Ziyadah's French poem, Djebar's "Beau-de-l'air" all produce a new, creolized space of interpretation, and advance this interpretation beyond the walls imposed by both colonial and anticolonial (i.e., hypernationalist) ideologies. They are the new words of the fallen tribe. Their dia-language permits the fluid circulation of words, sounds, and images, the sensations and experiences of a subject surrounded by a violent, transformative experience of the world (i.e., the cityscape), which is what colonialism is all about.

The landscape is reshaped: architectural forms, spatial organization, meaning, symbols all become part of the dominant power, to give birth one day to a new semiotics.[4] By expressing the reality of this complex, plural experience of the world, the "self" captures this transformation within the plasticity of poetic language. Shame and guilt are cast back on those who ignore the fact that colonialism is a fundamentally ambiguous experience of a deep creolization triggered by a new language imposed on the world outside and within. In this context, *being* is translating; the response plays out through the practice of literature as a mediator between the *home* and the *world*.

Literature as architecture is the art of space and time, the only art able to build complex worlds within our words; it intimately invades the self, becoming part of its DNA. It is an everyday tool in the language we use from day to day; in poetry, it expands into a bridge, the Deleuzian "fold," that connects disparate parts of the psyche and the world. Like the air we breathe, literary language links both the inside and the outside, acting as the permanent mediator of how we are transformed. Poetic language has a power that no other art has: it is simultaneously familiar, intimate, elaborate, yet external. Writing in dia-language invites the reader to acknowledge the existence of a new semiotics applied to the multilingual text that reflects the inner creolized (post)colonial experience of the world. This is the way to *a decolonial language*.

The return to the literary text (as a text, not as a manifesto) is an acknowledgment of the power of the inner voice as the *via sensia / voie sensible*: literature as a space for the reinterpretation of the world and its resymbolization. The decolonial enterprise resides in resymbolization through writing in translation.

Therefore, being a subject in translation is the permanent burden of the postcolonial experience. That burden is not only transferred to literature, but it becomes a new hermeneutic of space and of the text. *Re-dire le monde* (Speak the world anew) seems to be the mantra of our creolized women writers. They have all accepted the fact that *to translate is to reinform the languages of their world*. Based on this last sentence, translation is not a loss, as so many have stated before, but the unfolding of new, hidden meanings. This resymbolization of the sign was described in Dutt's translations and in her own poetry, as well as in Ziyadah's citations from *Fleurs de rêve*. It took another turn with Djebar and Devi, who developed the practice of urban exploration in their novels. The *effet texte* represents the depth of the resymbolization process triggered by the act of reading and interpreting multiple languages. At a deep level of meaning, the process of the effet texte creolizes new modes of feeling in the host language. If we were to think about the crisis of modern subjectivity and its resolution (in the Mallarméen sense), our creolized writers found its resolution in dia-language: their crisis is differed (*différée*). The Baudelairean spleen ends in the celebration and joy of the *plural*, opening the door to interpretation and transcendence. The beautifully creolized subjectivities of Toru Dutt, Mayy Ziyadah, Assia Djebar, and Ananda Devi leave us, as critics and readers, with an urgent need to develop genealogies of multilingualism in all postcolonial contexts. Our tomorrow hinges on finding a political balance that includes more difference, a balance that will oppose the two major uniformizing processes of colonial inevitability: nationalism and capitalism. If the world is to reject the violence and the domination of a singular model of subjecthood, it can only do so by developing a multilingual semiotics (i.e., a multilingual modality of reading and interpreting texts and aesthetic forms). In its inherent plurality, this multilingual modality is our antidote to the colonial virus of a uniformizing identity.

NOTES

INTRODUCTION

1. The name Ziyadah has several transliterated spellings in English, including Ziyade and Ziyada.
2. Djebar's year of birth (1935, instead of the commonly thought 1936) is based on Calle-Gruber, *Assia Djebar* (2021).
3. Lionnet, *Autobiographical Voices;* Cascardi, *The Subject of Modernity;* Braidotti, *Nomadic Subjects;* Orlando, *Nomadic Voices of Exile;* Malabou, *Changer de différence.*
4. In reference to Georges Herbert Mead's linguistic theory of intersubjectivity and the distinction between "me" and "I"; see note 11.
5. Translation studies have always been an intrinsic part of comparative literature as a discipline and a field of inquiry. Already, in 2005, Sandra Bermann announced: "The essays in this collection afford an opportunity to rethink national, subnational, and international connections and conflicts, their histories and their futures, from the specific standpoint of language and translation. [. . .] Translation's distinctive ability to offer insight into the language process itself aligns it with ethics and the question of the foreign in a different, though not unrelated, way. As is frequently noted, translation's etymology—*trans* (across) and *latus,* the past participle of *ferre* (to carry)—suggests a transportation of meaning, a physical displacement" (*Nation, Language, and the Ethics of Translation* 2–5).
6. See Gauvin, "La surconscience linguistique de l'écrivain francophone."
7. It is important to acknowledge two recent publications on multilingual literature: Natalie Edwards, *Multilingual Life Writing by French and Francophone Women: Translingual Selves* (2019) and the edited volume by Jane Hiddleston and Wen-chin Ouyang, *Multilingual Literature as World Literature* (2021).
8. Pratt, "Planetarity," 29 (emphasis added).
9. Bertacco, *Language and Translation.*
10. In *Multilingualism and Nation Building,* Mansour explains how multilingual societies have always existed in a long-term transitory situation. Her

sociolinguistic and historical approach to African multilingualism is important to understanding how the remnants of colonial empires do not create a new linguistic situation. She also warns us about the simplistic approach to multilingualism in postcolonial contexts: "Many studies which admirably deal with the formal aspects of communication—who speaks what language to whom and when—are unnecessarily limited in scope, because they do not fully take into account the dialectical nature of the relationship between language and society. Even when multilingualism is placed in its social context this is often done in an ahistorical and unsystematic fashion" (5).

11. One of Mead's major contributions is the distinction between the "I" and the "me": "The self that arises in relationship to a specific generalized other is referred to as the 'Me.' The 'Me' is a cognitive object, which is only known retrospectively, that is, on reflection. When we act in habitual ways we are not typically self-conscious. We are engaged in actions at a non-reflective level. However, when we take the perspective of the generalized other, we are both 'watching' and forming a self in relationship to the system of behaviors that constitute this generalized other." Mitchell Aboulafia and Scott Taylor, "George Herbert Mead," *Stanford Encyclopedia of Philosophy*, accessed December 12, 2022, https://plato.stanford.edu/entries/mead/#IMe. In *White Tongue, Brown Skin*, the core of the theory of the subject is based on experience and emotions; literary texts are the receptacles of the traces of this empirical subjectivity.

12. I am freely using "relation" in this book with the meaning developed by Glissant in his work *Poétique de la relation* (*Poetics of Relation*), in mind. "Relating" will be closer to the English translation.

13. *Maghreb pluriel*.

14. Tant que la théorie de la traduction, de la bi-langue et de la pluri-langue n'aura pas avancé, certains textes maghrébins resteront imprenables selon une approche formelle et fonctionnelle. La langue "maternelle" est à l'œuvre dans la langue étrangère. De l'une à l'autre se déroulent une traduction permanente et un entretien en abyme, extrêmement difficile à mettre au jour. (Khatibi, *Maghreb pluriel* 179)

15. Bennabi develops the notion of the "signifier" and the body in his chapter "Bilinguisme et psychanalyse," in Bennani, *Du Bilinguisme*, 91–92.

16. See Ochs, *Religion without Violence*.

17. See Harrison, *Our Civilizing Mission*; and, more recently, Reynaud-Paligot, *L'École aux colonies*.

18. I am not using "decolonial" following Mignolo's *The Politics of Decolonial Investigations*. I would add that my use of "decolonial" exemplifies thoughtful

methodologies and *processes* of decolonization of epistemologies, discourses, and forms that are still informed by the system of signification and meaning produced by colonialism.
19. Gunew and Mahyuddin, *Beyond the Echo*; Derrida, *Le Monolinguisme de l'autre*.
20. See Ramazani, *Transnational Poetics*: "Because of the interconnecting cultural traces wound into the DNA of poetic forms and poetic language, poetry's cross-national molecular structure betrays the national imaginary on behalf of which it is sometimes made to speak. [. . .] But under modernity, even a 'national poet' turns out, on closer inspection, to also be a transnational poet" (13–14).
21. Calvet, *Les Voix de la ville*, 10.
22. See *L'An V* 288–89; *Dying Colonialism* 51–52.
23. See Gunew, "Estrangement as Pedagogy."
24. I am thinking of the recent book by Mortimer, *Women Fight, Women Write*, where the reader can see several instances of the confluence between the figure of the author and the narrator: "As we follow Djebar, who uses her triple role as historian, writer, and filmmaker to retrace Zoulikha's life, we find her developing the themes of memory and mourning in both *La nouba* and *La femme sans sépulture*. In this regard, these creative works may be considered meditations on collective and individual memory of the Algerian War, as both propose a dual narrative: a search for Algeria's vanished sisters and a quest for a vanished self" (190).

1. WHO IS THE SUBJECT IN TRANSLATION?

1. See, as an example, *Commentarii de Bello Gallico* (*The Gallic Wars*) by Julius Caesar (100–144).
2. As a reminder, "Tamazight" is the feminine form of "Amazigh"; it means both "free woman" and the language spoken by the Amazigh people, indigenous population of North Africa and the Sahel region.
3. See Tamalet Talbayev, *Transcontinental Maghreb*; and elhariry, *Pacific Invasions*. Both works foster remarquably a comparative and translinguistic approach to Maghrebi literature.
4. In *Plural Maghreb*, Khatibi elaborates on the need to invent methods to read texts written in French in the Maghreb, to decipher the subterranean work of the "mother tongue."
5. This literary couple exemplifies the length and complexity of the dynamic involved between languages as a site of plastic conflict resolution.
6. See Glissant's *Poétique de la relation* (*Poetics of Relation*); and Nancy's *Être singulier pluriel* (*Being Singular Plural*).

7. Language, in singular, is to be understood in a broad semiotic way: as a system of signs inducing interpretation; I will use the expression "language" not only for texts but also for architectural forms, acoustic experiences, and visual arts.
8. See Beauvoir, *Pour une morale de l'ambiguïté* (*The Ethics of Ambiguity*).
9. For studies on postcolonial women's subjectivity in the Francophone world, see the following pioneering works on which my own approach is based: Lionnet, *Autobiographical Voices*; Orlando, *Nomadic Voices of Exile*; and Donadey, *Recasting Postcolonialism*.
10. It is important to remember Du Bois's *Souls of Black Folk* as a first attempt to reveal the complexity of Black subjectivity. He was the first to use the expression "double consciousness" to describe the perception of the world from a subaltern perspective.
11. Lionnet, "Créolité in the Indian Ocean."
12. See Rancière, *Malaise dans l'esthétique* (*The Politics of Aesthetics*).
13. La Malinche was a Nahuatl interpreter and advisor for the Spanish conquistador Hernán Cortès during the conquest of Mexico between 1519 and 1521. She became his wife. See the remarkable account by Prescott, *History of the Conquest of Mexico*.
14. See Irigaray, *Speculum de l'autre femme* (*Speculum of the Other Woman*) on gender differences between men and women in the resolution of the Oedipus complex, where femininity and masculinity emerge as the first differentiation in the relationship to the parent figure.
15. See the concept of plasticity redeveloped by Malabou, "Plasticity and Elasticity in Freud's *Beyond the Pleasure Principle*": "Let's first point out two distinguishing features of the Freudian concept of plasticity. First of all, plasticity characterizes for Freud the fact that psychic life is indestructible. Second plasticity designates the fluidity of the libido. [. . .] We must remember that 'plasticity' generally describes the nature of that which is plastic, being at once capable of receiving and giving form. The psyche is plastic to the extent that it can receive the imprint and impose this earlier form upon recent developments" (80).
16. I use "aesthetics" to refer to the branch of philosophy of forms and their effect on the subject, a reflection on our sensations in the experience of forms (broadly speaking); its development by Hume (1711–1776) in *An Enquiry Concerning Human Understanding* (1748), Kant (1724–1804) in his *Critique of Judgment* (1790) and, later, Schiller, *On the Aesthetic Education of Man* (1795) highly oriented my approach in this book.
17. Indeed, there is an important body of texts that are related to this question from a neuropsychiatric perspective. See Nathan, *La Folie des autres*.

18. *Esprit* 2, no. 187 (Février 1952): 237–48. The magistral work by Khalfa and Young *Alienation and Freedom* sheds new light on Fanon's work regarding subjectivity and language as a tool of alienation in a postcolonial context.
19. La science psychanalytique tient l'expatriement pour un phénomène morbide. Ce en quoi elle a parfaitement raison. (*Oeuvres* 702)
20. Nous attachons une importance fondamentale au phénomène du langage. [. . .] Tout peuple colonisé—c'est-à-dire tout peuple au sein duquel a pris naissance un complexe d'infériorité, du fait de la mise au tombeau de l'originalité culturelle locale—se situe vis-à-vis du langage de la nation civilisatrice, c'est-à-dire de la culture métropolitaine. Le colonisé se sera d'autant plus échappé de sa brousse qu'il aura fait siennes les valeurs culturelles de la métropole. Il sera d'autant plus blanc qu'il aura rejeté sa noirceur, sa brousse. (*Oeuvres* 71–72)
21. I first articulated this concept in French, "le sujet en traduction," in an earlier publication, "Le style en arabesque d'Assia Djebar." I also used it in English in "Writing in *bi-langue*."
22. See Boutaghou, "Au-delà du miroir," 29.
23. Nous voudrions, nous référant à d'autres travaux et à nos observations personnelles, essayer de montrer pourquoi le Noir se situe de façon caractéristique en face du langage européen. Nous rappelons encore une fois que les conclusions auxquelles nous aboutirons valent pour les Antilles françaises; nous n'ignorons pas toutefois que ces mêmes comportements se retrouvent au sein de toute race ayant été colonisée. (*Oeuvres* 77)
24. Djebar describes French as a "stepmother tongue": "Le français m'est langue marâtre" (*Amour* 298; *Fantasia* 214).
25. Gates, "Critical Fanonism," 459.
26. Le malheur et l'inhumanité du Blanc sont d'avoir tué l'homme quelque part. [. . .]

    C'est par un effort de reprise sur soi et de dépouillement, c'est par une tension permanente de leur liberté que les hommes peuvent créer les conditions d'existence idéales d'un monde humain. Supériorité? Infériorité?

    Pourquoi tout simplement ne pas essayer de trouver l'autre, de sentir l'autre, de me révéler l'autre? [. . .]

    À la fin de cet ouvrage, nous aimerions que l'on sente comme nous la dimension ouverte de toute conscience.

    Mon ultime prière:

    Ô mon corps, fais de moi toujours un homme qui interroge! (*Oeuvres* 239)
27. Le Noir a deux dimensions. L'une avec son congénère, l'autre avec le Blanc. Un Noir se comporte différemment avec un Blanc et avec un autre Noir.

[...] Le Noir Antillais sera d'autant plus blanc, c'est-à-dire se rapprochera d'autant plus du véritable homme qu'il aura fait sienne la langue française. (*Oeuvres* 71)

28. The terms "split," "fragmentation," and "division" can also be used interchangeably in place of "schism."
29. Un enfant noir normal, ayant grandi au sein d'une famille normale, s'anormalisera au moindre contact avec le monde blanc. [...] Dans le cas du Noir, que voyons-nous? A moins d'utiliser cette donnée vertigineuse—tant elle nous désaxe—de *l'inconscient* collectif de Jung, on ne comprend absolument rien. [...] Fréquemment, le nègre qui s'anormalise n'a jamais eu de relation avec le Blanc. Y a-t-il eu expérience ancienne et refoulement dans l'inconscient? Le jeune enfant noir a-t-il vu son père frappé ou lynché par le Blanc? Y a-t-il eu traumatisme effectif? À tout cela, nous répondons: non. Alors? Si nous voulons répondre correctement, nous sommes obligés de faire appel à la notion de *catharsis collective*. (*Oeuvres* 181–82)
30. There is an implicit hierarchy imposed by the analysis of the postcolonial condition. The black woman represents the more oppressed position by virtue of the intersectionality of her blackness and her femaleness. See Crenshaw, "Demarginalizing the Intersection."
31. See Westphal, *La Géocritique*.
32. "Writers such as Maryse Condé, from Guadeloupe, Assia Djebar, from Algeria, and Leïla Sebbar, a Franco-Algerian, are part of an increasing number of astute interpreters of the postcolonial condition whose works, published in 1970s and 1980s, have been redefining Francophone history and literature. They create new paradigms that represent, through innovative and self-reflexive literary techniques, both linguistic and geographic exile, displacements from the margins to a metropolitan center, and intercultural exchanges." Lionnet, "Logiques métisses," 101.
33. Lionnet and Shih, *Minor Transnationalism*; Flax, "Multiples."
34. Samir Dayal's introduction to *Crisis of the European Subject*: "If jouissance is invariably a kind of suffering, as psychoanalysis reminds us, then perhaps suffering can engender or be the route to *jouissance*, an enjoyment that requires as new subjectification. What does it mean? Just as she had revealed that Arendt envisions a resubjectivation that passes through melancholia, Kristeva believes that precisely the suffering of Bulgaria [...] can become through *metanoia* the road to an approach to the Real of the European crisis" (41).
35. Cultural history and postcolonial discussions ignored their voices, because they did not fit the mainstream anticolonial ideology. The reaction from

conservative male intellectuals of both the Nahda and the Bengali Renaissance was to condemn general education for women, women's access to the press, and the constitution of a feminist voice as the pervasive effect of the West, the imitation of colonizer models of society. The debate is still present today in Egypt, India, Algeria, and Mauritius, about whether using a Western language in former colonized countries is considered *mimicry* of the West. Plurality was not useful for the promotion of nationalist discourse, which at the time was considered to be the only cohesive answer to the anticolonial cause.

36. Theorizing on postcolonial subjectivity in the field of psychiatry, Nathan (*La Folie des autres*) expresses the need to develop ethnopsychiatric approaches in understanding plurality as inherent to the subject. Perhaps this is the beginning of another moment in history where plurality and diversity become the norm, or the recognition, of the constitutive reality of the subject as a reader.
37. See Schiller, *On the Aesthetic Education of Man*.
38. For Khatibi, mainly in *La Blessure du nom propre* (The wound of the name, 1974); *La Mémoire tatouée* (Tattooed memory, 1971); *Amour bilingue* (Love in Two Languages, 1982); and *Maghreb pluriel* (Plural Maghreb, 1983). For Glissant, in the series *Poétiques I à V* (Poetics 1 to 5) includes, in order of publication: *Soleil de la conscience* (Sun of consciousness, 1956); *L'Intention poétique* (Poetical intention, 1969); *Poétique de la relation* (Poetics of Relation, 1990); *Traité du tout-monde* (Treaty of the all-world, 1997); and *La Cohée du Lamentin* (The manatee's cohey, 2005). I will also draw on *Le Discours antillais* (West Indian discourse, 1997); *Introduction à une poétique du divers* (Introduction to a poetics of diversity, 1996); and, last but not least, the interviews with Gauvin, *L'Imaginaire des langues* (The imaginary of languages, 2010).
39. See the discussion of "bi-language" in the introduction. Other expressions in French have been used to refer to similar phenomena: Naget Khadda uses the French term "bi-vocal" to describe Mohammed Dib's literary language. See Khadda, *Mohammed Dib*, 7.
40. I draw from Gauvin, *La Fabrique de la langue*.
41. See also the earlier note on Mead.
42. The anecdote inspiring this idea came from the first time Assia Djebar heard about Baudelaire at school; see *Ces voix qui m'assiègent* (1999). In her mind, the first time she heard the name, it was literally transcribed BEAU-DE-L'AIR; in English, this would be NICE-OF-THE AIR. Lionnet was the first to notice this important remark by Djebar; see Lionnet, "Ces voix au fil de soi(e)." Another anecdote is shared by Khatibi in "La langue de l'autre," in *Surimpositions d'identité*, where he talks about his passion for Baudelaire.

43. I am referring here also to Marcuse, *Aesthetic Dimension*.
44. See Baron, *Women's Awakening in Egypt*, to understand the role of European education in the *Nahda el-nissaiyat* in Egypt.
45. During the second half of nineteenth century, in colonized regions, readers had access to representations of transgressive female characters in novels written by men. See Boutaghou, *Occidentalismes*.
46. Agency is not only granted by education and writing; women in these specific precolonial societies also had agency in certain sectors of life, such as child-rearing, domesticity, and work in the fields (in some regions of the world); some women in Islamic societies could own property, but their voices were only rarely heard in the public sphere. Being granted a European education encouraged women to be present both in the domestic and public spheres.
47. In the bibliography, see critical pioneering works on Djebar by Lionnet, *Autobiographical Voices*; Chikhi, *Les Romans d'Assia Djebar*; Donadey, *Recasting Postcolonialism*; Mortimer, *Assia Djebar*; and Orlando, *Nomadic Voices of Exile*, among others.
48. In past published works, I have used the expression in French, *dia-langue*, or "dia-language," to expand the notion of "bi-language" to the plurality of languages informing the text, although I still wonder if "bi" is the essential movement. Are the authors only always writing in between two languages even if they practice more than two languages?
49. Gauvin, "La surconscience linguistique."

2. BEING COSMOPOLITAN IN NINETEENTH-CENTURY CALCUTTA: TORU DUTT

1. The first reference to Toru Dutt (spelt Tora Dutt) in postcolonial studies is by Edward Said in *Culture and Imperialism*, 218.
2. "Transculturation" was first coined by Fernando Ortiz (1881–1969) about Afro-Cuban culture in *Contrapunteo cubano del tabaco y el azúcar*; see Rama, *Transculturación narrativa en América Latina*.
3. See Ramazani, *Transnational Poetics*: "Walcott, like many other modern and contemporary poets, conceives the poetic imagination as translational, a nation-crossing force that exceeds the limits of the territorial and juridical norm" (2).
4. See Smith, *Cultural Foundations of Nations*: "Ethnic groups may be a 'fixture of history', found in every period, but existing nations are modern and really quite recent" (2).
5. Throughout this book, I use both meanings for "cosmopolitan": citizen of the world, and the world within the city.

6. Cette enfant du Bengale si admirablement et si étrangement douée, Hindoue de race et de tradition, Anglaise d'éducation, Française de cœur; poète en anglais, prosateur en français. (*Essais* 269–70)
7. The French language attracted several intellectual women of the nineteenth century such as Marie Bashkirtseff, the famous Ukrainian diarist (1858–1884), whom Dutt would have had the opportunity to meet in France.
8. This model of nationhood was somehow understood to conflict with the Muslim community. See Boutaghou, *Occidentalismes* 344.
9. In Edmund Gosse, "Introductory Memoir," in Toru Dutt's *Ancient Ballads and Legends of Hindustan* and in James Darmesteter's critical essay on Dutt ("Miss Toru Dutt") published in his *Essais de littérature anglaise* (Essays on British literature).
10. "Double nature" is an English expression used during the colonial period to describe Indians who had a double education in both Sanskrit and English.
11. "What in English concepts is known as the State was called in our country Sarkar or Government. This Government existed in ancient India in the form of kingly power, but there is a difference between the present English State and our ancient kingly power. England relegates to State care all the welfare services in the country; India did that only to a very limited extent" (Tagore, *Towards Universal Man* 50). It would be interesting to compare this discourse to Muslim nationalist discourse produced in the same historical period.
12. As in other contexts, the term "universal" is to be understood as European, even if Tagore revises this definition to a more balanced one. The term "cosmopolitan" is expressing this universalism, or, perhaps, a form of internationalism.
13. Tagore understands nationalism and the dangers coming from such cultural uniformity. Miyoshi, in "Borderless World?," also explains that India does not have tradition of the state, and this comprises India's primary difference from England as a power, as a state. India has a "social order," directed by the consciousness of each individual through the philosophy of dharma, or duty/destiny (*Towards Universal Man* 50).
14. A first version of this section was published as Maya Boutaghou, "What Book Do You Read? Imagining Francophone Intertextual Maps," *Contemporary French and Francophone Studies: Sites* 22, no. 2 (2018): 198–207.
15. This is the translation of the first verse of Hugo's poem "Sérénade": "L'aube naît et ta porte est close . . ."
16. Pondichéry was established as a French colony in 1674.
17. The Dutt family stayed in France for a few months between 1869 and spring of 1870. They visited Marseille, Nice, and Paris and then traveled to England.

On their way to England, they spent some time in Boulogne, a place that William Thackeray (1811–1863), born in Calcutta, often wrote about.
18. See *A Sheaf* (191). In *A Sheaf*, Dutt mentions *La Lyre française* by Gustave Masson (1898). She probably used the first edition (1867) while she was studying in France.
19. I have used this expression previously to explain how in a multilingual context the sign is open to new symbolic associations (*Occidentalismes*). It shows the plastic connections between unexpected signifiers.
20. "Le nid solitaire" (1860):

> Va, mon âme, au-dessus de la foule qui passe,
> Ainsi qu'un libre oiseau te baigner dans l'espace.
> Va voir! et ne reviens qu'après avoir touché.
> Le rêve... mon beau rêve à la terre caché.
>
> Moi, je veux du silence, il y va de ma vie;
> Et je m'enferme où rien, plus rien ne m'a suivie;
> Et de son nid étroit d'où nul sanglot ne sort,
> J'entends courir le siècle à côté de mon sort.
>
> Le siècle qui s'enfuit grondant devant nos portes,
> Entraînant dans son cours, comme des algues mortes,
> Les noms ensanglantés, les vœux, les vains serments,
> Les bouquets purs, noués de noms doux et charmants.
>
> Va, mon âme, au-dessus de la foule qui passe,
> Ainsi qu'un libre oiseau te baigner dans l'espace.
> Va voirg! et ne reviens qu'après avoir touché
> Le rêve... mon beau rêve à la terre caché! (*Poésies* 193)

21. Based on the Barthesian expression "effet de réel," the *effet texte* (text effect) represents the depth of the symbolization process activated by the act of reading and interpreting. Any reader is always first and foremost a reader of literary texts.
22. See Boutaghou, "Le testament soufi de Adbelwahab Meddeb."
23. In *Toru Dutt: Collected Prose and Poetry*, Lokugé takes a similar approach to Dutt's poetry. Her work helped the rediscovery of Dutt's writing in general.
24. Rahim, "Translation as Contemporary Qur'anic Exegesis."
25. J'ai visité la mère Grestine aujourd'hui; elle est la plus vieille femme du village; puis je suis allée chez les Corraine. J'ai trouvé Jeannette en train de faire bouillir une maigre soupe; j'y ai jeté un morceau de lard et un chou-fleur, que

j'avais dans ma boîte. J'ai fait cuire une douzaine de pommes de terre sous les cendres. (*Journal* 12)
26. Ce matin, papa et moi nous étions allés dans les bois; nous y avons rencontré le comte et son frère. J'étais en train de manger des mûres et des baies sauvages, dont le jus avait coloré mes lèvres. (*Journal* 9)
27. Just to give some context, this text was written a few years after Bankim Chandra Chatterjee's *Rajmohan's Wife* (1864).
28. "Do you love her?" "More than my life." "Will you make her happy?" "Yes, God be my witness." And a flush came over his pale face. "Then I give her to you, my son." Garcia's eyes were misty, and he turned aside to conceal his emotion. "Thank you!" said Lord Moore.
29. Lokugé, *Toru Dutt: Collected Prose and Poetry*: "Through her poetry then, Toru seems to break down cultural and literary boundaries for a challenging new space in which disparate worlds harmonize" (xliii).
30. The "Miscellaneous Poems" were found after her death and added to the *Ancient Ballads*.
31. Damrosh, *What Is World Literature?*: "Owen argued that third-world poets are increasingly running afoul of the literary hegemony of the major Western powers, with the result that they begin to write a 'world poetry' that is little more than watered-down Western modernism" (19).
32. See the Brahmo-Samaj nationalist movement: "Toru Dutt could well have been inspired by the nationalist reform movements that were developing within India during her time, as for instance the Brahmo Samaj (1828) whose special concern was the reform of the 'enslaved Indian woman'" (Lokugé, *Toru Dutt: Collected Prose and Poetry* xlv).
33. The creolized universalism contrasts with créolité as conceptualized by Patrick Chamoiseau. It is a way of thinking about our cultural identity as always already creolized. A creolized universalism is the consciousness of our making as cultural beings determined first by our shared humanity and our inner differentiation.
34. It is important to keep in mind that the Indian Renaissance was considered by some Indian intellectuals as "intellectually meaningless, mainly because they see it as an elite construct, an upper-middle-class invention that raises too many questions, and which, while identifying too closely with British ideas of 'progress,' was also an instrument of vague but voluble nationalist blarney" (Chaudhuri, *Clearing a Space* 64).
35. See Boutaghou, "Being Berber."
36. I also have in mind pictures of former colonized cities like Algiers and Port Louis, where the wanderer sees diversity performed everywhere, where

creolization is a living, organic process offered to the passerby through the languages on street signs, the smells of food, and the way people dress. Paradoxically, this modernity is not only the violent sense of encounters, but also its internalized boundaries and the oppositions between hegemonic discourses (nationalism, fundamentalisms, liberalism, imperialism).

37. Žižek, "Leftist Plea for 'Eurocentrism'": "The abstract universal is what hegemonic perspectives provide, be they neoliberal or neo-Marxist. The perspective from the colonial difference [. . .] instead opens the possibility of imagining border thinking as the necessary condition for a future critical and dialogic cosmopolitanism. Such a critical and dialogic cosmopolitanism itself leads toward 'diversality,' instead of towards a new universality grounded (again) 'on the potential of democratic politicization as the true European legacy from ancient Greece onward'" (1009). A new universalism recasting the democratic potential of the European legacy is not necessarily a solution to the vicious circle between (neo)liberal globalization and "regressive forms of fundamentalist hatred" (Mignolo, "Many Faces of Cosmo-polis," 743).

38. Are we saying with Benhabib that "every claim of universality are constituted by determinative exclusions; difference is constitutive of identity" (*Another Cosmopolitanism* 161)?

3. BEING COSMOPOLITAN IN NINETEENTH-CENTURY CAIRO: MAYY ZIYADAH

1. See Gunew, "Estrangement as Pedagogy." *Adab* is explained in more detail below.
2. See also al Joundi, *Prisonnière du Levant*.
3. Starr, *Remembering Cosmopolitan Egypt*: "Although many theorists have noted that a relationship exists between the cosmopolitan and empire, the nature of that relationship remains under-explored" (9).
4. Later republished in her book *bayna al-jazr wa al-madd* (Between the ebb and flow).
5. It is quoted from her work *bayna al-jazr wa al-madd*: "takalamu ma si'tum mina al lughat ya bani umi! wa lakin la tansu lughatakum" (465).
6. For more information on the historical context in which Ziyadah grew up and developed her approach as a critic, see Khoury, *Mayy Ziyada*, 226–27.
7. Khoury, 223. He explains how she was quite unique in terms of the diversity of languages and cultures she mastered.
8. For a discussion about *adab* in Salim Al-Bustani's writings, see Sheehi, *Foundations of Modern Arab Identity*, 46–75.

9. Hanley, "When Did Egyptians Stop Being Ottomans?," shows how the collapse of the Ottoman Empire did not erase the sense of an Ottoman culture in Egypt, particularly in Cairo at the end of World War I.
10. See Cheah and Robbins, *Cosmopolitics*.
11. Starr, *Remembering Cosmopolitan Egypt*; Singerman and Amar, *Cairo Cosmopolitan*; and Çelik, *Empire, Architecture, and the City*.
12. MacLean and Karmali Ahmed, *Cosmopolitanisms in Muslim Contexts*.
13. Malcomson, "Varieties of Cosmopolitan Experience."
14. Chaudhuri, *Clearing a Space*: "Intellectually meaningless, mainly because they see it as an elite construct, an upper-middle-class invention that raises too many questions, and which, while identifying too closely with British ideas of 'progress,' was also an instrument of vague but voluble nationalist blarney" (64).
15. The use here is quite different from the concept established by Kenneth White. While, in its first occurrence, it seeks to capture the interconnectedness between *poesis* and *geo* (earth) as an equivalent to geopolitics or how politics informs spatial relations, in this work "geopoetics" refers to how the construction of poetical discourse informs spatial relations between different cultural actors. It also refers to the intertextuality between Middle Eastern and European literatures, showing how new comparisons are displacing imaginary boundaries between them to inform a new interpretation of the relations between the two spaces. In other words, this new geopoetics can be translated into a new geopolitics of knowledge circulation.
16. In this passage, there is no attempt to propose a translation of the concept, but of discovering, with the acute consciousness of Apter in *Against World Literature*, that untranslatability does not denote dissimilarity and radical difference. The concepts in dialogue with one another are not synonymous but overlap, shining a kaleidoscopic light on any attempt at transcultural theorization and, ultimately, any comparison.
17. Gabrieli, "adab," in *Encyclopedia of Islam*, 175–76.
18. *Fleurs de rêve* is certainly an intertextual reference to Baudelaire's *Les Fleurs du mal*.
19. An interesting note about the use of French in Cairo can be found in Khaldi, *Egypt Awakening* (127): "In one of her salon sessions when her guests mentioned an Egyptian public figure (probably Sa'd Zaghlul), Ziyadah spoke appreciatively of him but criticized him for talking to her in French: 'When I was at the Egyptian University, Lutfi al-Sayyid introduced me to him. He praised my Arabic and French books. But this public figure forgot that I am an Arab and I write in Arabic and he chose to speak to me in French

instead and he insisted on doing so although all my answers to his questions were in Arabic.' When he left, Ziyadah said to Ahmad Lutfi al-Sayyid: 'Why was he talking to me in French?' Ahmad Lutfi al-Sayyid replied: 'Do you want him to talk to you in all the languages you know?' She said: 'No, but he should understand that I am not European. I am Arab. He should have spoken to me in Arabic only.'" In fact, a dichotomy existed between, on the one hand, Ziyadah's understanding of the historical and political context and, on the other hand, her desire to confront her own predicament, a tension that was mirrored in the cultural and political paradoxes of the Nahda.

20. Lamartine spent time in Antoura between 1832 and 1833. He narrated this experience in *Voyage en Orient*.
21. See the controversial article by Ziegler, "Late Rediscovery of Mayy Ziyadah's Works."
22. Pascal m'ennuie, c'était un neurasthénique, il n'a pour sa gloire que son discours sur les passions de l'amour. (*Fleurs de rêve* 134)
23. Il est dix heures et demie du matin, et je suis seule dans la forêt depuis plus de deux heures. Seule avec Byron, le poète sauvage et délicieux que les Anglais classent au quatrième rang de leurs poètes parce qu'il est trop bon rimeur, peut-être, et qui après Shakespeare, mériterait d'être le premier. [...] Savait-il, le malheureux Byron, pouvait-il savoir lorsqu'il écrivait ce triste et charmant poème, qu'une jeune fille Syrienne irait passer avec lui, avec ce qui reste de lui, de longues heures solitaires dans les douces forêts libanaises? (*Fleurs de rêve* 146)
24. This concept can be defined as the copresence of aesthetics that belong to different time periods—for example, the encounter between romanticism and symbolism or modernism within the same text or image.
25. See Zubaida, "Cosmopolitanism and the Middle East," 15–33; and Yerasimos *Cosmopolitanism, Identity, and Authenticity*, 35–39.
26. Among her works, there are several books published on Arab women writers such as Aisha Taymur (1840–1902); Malak Hafni Nasif, who used the pseudonym Bahithat al-Badiya (1886–1918); and Wardat al Yajizi (1838–1924). See Khoury, *Mayy Ziyadah*.
27. Mayy est tellement imbue de culture arabe et européenne, qu'elle arrive à puiser des souvenirs des parcours d'un nombre imposant de sources ce dont elle a besoin, pour donner au thème étudié, à l'idée examinée le contour de la solidité, de la citoyenneté du monde; n'a-t-elle pas dédié ses *Fleurs de Rêve* à Lamartine, [par qui] elle était fascinée, et qui, dans un grand cortège d'écrivains européens, allemands, français et autres, avait dit: "Je suis concitoyen de tout homme qui passe" (Khoury 30).

28. Sheehi, *Foundations of Modern Arab Identity*: "Ibrahim al-Yaziji, son of the famed Sheikh Nasif al-Yaziji, wrote a series of articles in various journals, including his own journals *al-bayan* and *al-diya*,' discussing the creation of this new language, which he called 'the language of the newspaper' (*lughat al-jaridah*). The creation of a language unencumbered by classical Ciceronisms and baroque embellishment is critical to the reform movement's desire for efficiency. It also accurately represents the epistemological foundation of the movement. That is, Arab reformers and modern literati needed a language that seemed to present objective, scientific knowledge in a way that was not self-conscious or opaque. Despite their reverence for the ancients, these reformers and literati were committed to creating a language that would not call attention to itself or demand the erudition of its reader, thereby interfering with the naturalness of the knowledge that it presents" (109).
29. Khaldi, *Egypt Awakening in the Early Twentieth Century*: "'Abbas Mahmud al-'Aqad mentions 30 regular attendees, who belong to different or even opposing cultural groups," among them "Ahmad Lutfi al-Sayid; the Egyptian politician, judge, and poet 'Abd al-'Aziz Fahmi (d. 1951); the Lebanese doctor and writer Shibli Shumayyil (d. 1917); the Syrian poet Sulayman al-Bustani (d. 1925); Ahmad Shawqi; Khalil Mutran; Antun al-Jumayyil; the Syrian editor of *al-Ahram*, Dawud Barakat (d. 1933); the Egyptian calligrapher of the king of Egypt and the lawyer Najib Hawawini (d.); the Egyptian journalist Tawfiq Habib (d. ?); Amin Wasif (d. ?); the Islamic philosopher and writer Mustafa 'Abd al'Raziq (d. 1946) [. . .]; the Egyptian woman activist Huda Sha'rawi (d. 1947); the Egyptian woman activist Ihsan al-Qusi (d. ?); the Syrian editor of *La Liberté* Edgar Jallad (d. ?); Salim Sarkis; the editor of *al-Muktataf* Ya'qub Sarruf (d. 1927); Hafiz Ibrahim; the Egyptian poet and reporter for Ziyadah's salon Isma'il Sabri Pasha (d. 1923); the governor of the province Qaliyubiyyah Idris Raghib (d. 1922); the Syrian doctor and journalist Fu'ad Sarruf (d. 1985); the editor of *al-Balagh* (Report), 'Abd al-Qadir Hamzah (1941); the Egyptian writer and scholar Mansur Fahmi (d. 1959); Taha Husayn; the Egyptian woman writer Malak Hifni Nasif; her brother Majd al-Din Hifni Nasif (d.); and her husband 'Abd al-Sattar al-Basil (d. ?). The list includes many others, as well as occasional visitors, Arabists, and Orientalists" (55).
30. As Sheehi explains about Beirut in his epilogue, "Towards an Aesthetic of the Colonial Self," the city of Cairo was, like Beirut, "*the* example of this hybridity and interconnectedness." This is a definition of "cosmopolitan Cairo," not as a superb multicultural center, but as a place of performed "hybridity and interconnectedness." This complex formation requires specific analysis and

demands that we pay attention to local production and interactions in order to recreate the sensibilities and debates of the time without putting forth an anachronistic or Eurocentric understanding of cosmopolitanism. The following quotation is particularly relevant to Cairo, from *Foundations of Modern Arab Identity:* "This concept of the cosmopolis corresponds to a new sense of vision, a new way of seeing society and space. It corresponds to a new aesthetic that framed the fiction, poetry and nonfiction of the day as well as the city's architecture and urban planning" (190). In his introduction to *Alexandrie, 1860–1960,* Ilbert explains how it is important to specifically analyse Alexandria's cosmopolitanism; it is not the mere reflection of the multiplicity of citizenships present at the same time in the same city or a cosmopolitanism that can be easily compared to that of New York, Paris, Brussels, or Vienna at the end of the nineteenth century.

31. Starr, *Remembering Cosmopolitan Egypt:* "To talk about cosmopolitanism, one must contend with its foundations in and indebtedness to empire" (9). The book addresses the question of cosmopolitan Egypt in the work of Ibrahim Abdel Meguid (1946–), Youssef Chahine (1926–2008), Edwar al-Kharrat (1926–), and Jewish writers Yitzhaq Gormezano Gorens (1941–) and Ronit Matalon (1959–). As the author states, the book is an attempt to "return to this past to explore the range of possibilities offered by the cosmopolitan" (27). Although Ziyadah's work was produced earlier than most of the writers and artists discussed in Starr's book, she is certainly representative of the potential that comes from imagining the future from the starting point of cosmopolitanism.

32. When it comes to Mayy Ziyadah, the notion of identity is similar to that defined in the introduction of Carter, Donald, and Squires, *Space and Place:* "The logics of universalism and, more recently, modernization and globalization have sought to represent localized identities as historical, regressive characteristics, and have worked to undermine the old allegiances of place and community" (ix).

33. Yarjaʻu ataru al sinaʻati wa al tijarati fi takwin al ʻalaʼiqi al ijtimaʻiyyati ila ʻahdin abʻada kathiran min yawmi wataʻa al finiqiyyun al satiʻa al ʻigriqiyya lil marrati al ʼawla, wa rubbama intaha bina ila fajr tarikh al ʻumran. Wa lawlaʼ tilka al ʻalaʼiq ma inkhalatati al aqwamu, wa la tamazajati al ʼajnasu, wa la takawwunnati al madaniyyatu, wa ladhallati al jamaʻatu fi wahdatiha al ʼithnughrafiyya, wa inkitaʻiha al hayawii, baʻidatan baʻduha ʻan baʻdin. ("fadlu al-adab" 76)

34. innama al suʻub kalʼafradi, la yatafahamun illa biltaʼalifi al fiqriyy, wa la yatawahhadun bighayri al tamazuj al ruhi. Mataʻu al masaniʻ wa nataju

al ma'amil yahfadhu 'abadan tabi' al sa'bi al ladi ibtakarahu 'aw 'alajahu. Wa lakinn 'ahlu al fikri wa al 'abqariyyati la yusabakun fi kalibin wa la yahmalun tabi'an, bal yakhussuna al insaniyyati biasriha, wa yakhdamuna al-jami'a bila hasrin, wa la istitna.' Yatakalamuna, wa ya'maluna, wa yaktubuna, wa siwa hum 'afsahu 'an nadaratihim wa masa'irihim bil yunaniyya wa al latiniyya aw al'arabiyya wa al hindiyya, fa'innama hum yatarjamuna 'an hajat basariyyat, wa raghabatin insaniyyatin, tajamharat fi nufusihim al kabirati al hassasati. ("fadlu al-adab" 77)

35. See Zaydan, *tarikh al-tamaddun al-islami*.
36. ma gharadu al adabi wa 'lbayani siwa 'alta'biri 'an al fikri wa al'atifati kalaman wa kitabatan, wa naqli suwarin dihniyyatin khafiyyatin ila 'alami al'atla' wa listi'radi. Yafdi kula sa'bin bisara'ir damirihi 'ala uslubin khassin, wa yatlaku si'ran wa nathran ma kamana fihi min kaabatin wa haniinin [. . .] bilqalami 'ladi huwa 'adatu al bayan, wa bilqalami wahdihi, yabrazu kulla sa'bin adabihi, ay 'asir ruhihi, wa huwa 'asir juz'in min ruhi al 'insaniyyat. ("fadlu al-adab" 77-78)
37. In *nussus kharij al-majmou'a*, 234-56.
38. On the same topic, see Tageldin, "One Comparative Literature?"
39. Peled, "Creative Translation," 128-50.
40. See Booth, *Migrating Texts*.
41. Mayy Ziyadah, *al-a'mal al-kamilat*, 2:438.
42. Walter Benjamin, "Task of the Translator": "Translation thus ultimately serves the purpose of expressing the central reciprocal relationship between languages. It cannot possibly reveal or establish this hidden relationship itself; but it can represent it by realizing it in embryonic or intensive form. [. . .] As for the posited central kinship of languages, it is marked by a distinctive convergence. Languages are not strangers to one another, but are, *a priori* and apart from all historical relationships, interrelated in what they want to express" (73).
43. I think the expression "littérature monde" covers the context and Mayy Ziyadah's ambition.
44. Even-Zohar, "Position of Translated Literature": "Moreover, in such a state when new literary models are emerging, translation is likely to become one of the means of elaborating the new repertoire. Through the foreign works, features (both principles and elements) are introduced into the home literature which did not exist there before" (47).
45. Ethnocentrique signifiera ici: qui ramène tout à sa propre culture, à ses normes et valeurs, et considère ce qui est situé en dehors de celle-ci—l'Etranger—comme négatif ou tout juste bon à être annexé, adapté, pour accroître la richesse de cette culture. (*La Traduction* 29)

46. I am referring here to McCarthy's "On Reconciling Cosmopolitan Unity and National Diversity," which is a rereading of Kant's "Idea for a Universal History with a Cosmopolitan Purpose," among other of his works.
47. First defined by Deleuze and Guattari as literatures that are written in a major language (in the case of *Fleurs de rêve*, French) from "a marginalized position," minor literatures also involve a "political nature" and indicate that language is "no longer [obviously] designatory," meaning that the language is challenged with representing an unfamiliar reality. My previous example of the "minaret" illustrates this point. See Deleuze and Guattari, *Kafka*.
48. Even-Zohar, "Polysystem Theory": "Therefore, on the one hand a system consists of both synchrony and diachrony; on the other, each of these separately is obviously also a system. Secondly, if the idea of structuredness and systemicity need no longer be identified with homogeneity, a semiotic system can be conceived of as a heterogeneous, open structure. It is, therefore, very rarely a uni-system but is, necessarily, a polysystem—a multiple system, a system of various systems which intersect with each other and partly overlap, using concurrently different options, yet functioning as one structured whole, whose members are interdependent" (11).
49. Here I quote from McCarthy, "On Reconciling Cosmopolitan Unity": "The Enlightenment universalism underlying Kant's construction of the cosmopolitan ideal has to be replaced by a multicultural universalism more sensitive to the dialectic of the general and the particular" (216).
50. Hanley, "Grieving Cosmopolitanism."

4. THE MAGHREBI BARD: ASSIA DJEBAR

1. This important new information about her birth comes from Calle-Gruber, *Assia Djebar*.
2. Several articles and books have addressed the political question of Djebar's languages, very often by scholars who perceived the "palimpsestic" process in her writings: Zimra in her afterword to *Women of Algiers*; Chikhi, *Les Romans d'Assia Djebar*; Tlatli, "L'Ambivalence linguistique"; Donadey in her seminal works on Djebar, "Multilingual Strategies of Postcolonial Literature," *Recasting Postcolonialism*, and *Approaches to Teaching the Works of Assia Djebar*; Boutaghou, "Le Style en arabesque"; Michel, "Pour une lecture polyphonique"; Gauvin, "Assia au pays du langage"; Thiel, *Assia Djebar, la Polyphonie comme principe générateur de ses textes* (2005); Lionnet, "Ces voix au fil de soi(e)"; Dobie, "Assia Djebar"; and Ali-Benali, *Assia Djebar*.

3. This relation between "sounds" and "images" is first developed in her movies and in her postface, "Regard interdit, son coupé," in *Femmes d'Alger dans leur appartement / Women of Algiers in Their Apartment*.
4. The palimpsest, as an object that has been written on, erased, and overwritten, is the closest metaphor to explain the way languages are not hidden but coexist in the same internal space, where the reader is invited to understand this strange linguistic situation. Djebar's multilingualism aligned with that of other multilingual authors writing in a dominant language. Indeed, anyone who practices several languages can feel the need to code-switch. In the case of Djebar's style, the alternately hidden and open translation from Arabic into French allowed her to code-switch without disturbing her reader. What makes the process interesting is the double bind imposed upon the writer: on the one hand, the need to hide Arabic (dialectal and classical) and, on the other hand, the internal impossibility of preventing Arabic from being intimately linked to French. It is as if the reader were bearing witness to the powerful internalization of the rule taught by French schools, where students were only allowed to speak French. The strategies Djebar developed were a way to include all of her languages in one literary language.
5. About the gendered dimension of Djebar's languages, see Kouchkar Ferchouli, "Emergence du parler féminin arabe."
6. Femme, berbérophone par les grands-parents, arabophone par les parents, elle écrit dans la langue française qui fut celle de la colonisation au Maghreb, celle du père instituteur de la France dans un village du Sahel algérien. (Assia Djebar 17)
7. La langue étrangère me servait, dès l'enfance, d'embrasure pour le spectacle du monde et de ses richesses. Voici qu'en certaines circonstances, elle devenait dard pointé sur ma personne. (*Amour* 180)
8. I borrow this image of the thread unveiling her languages from Lionnet, "Ces voix au fil de soi(e)." The expression "multivocal" is an extension of Naget Khadda's "bi-vocale," used in *Mohammed Dib*, to describe similar phenomena. The dimension of the "voice" is to be differentiated from that of "language"; the term "voice" comes from narratology (i.e., "narrative voice"). In Djebar's writing, the two dimensions coexist: the multivocal narrative and their multilingualism. This difference is important in thinking about the plurality of the subject in translation.
9. See Shafik, *Arab Cinema*. She offers the very first detailed analysis of the work of languages and genres in *The Nouba*.
10. During Djebar's time, Arabic was the language of the Quran, and writing in general was a sacred practice from which women were banned once they

reached a certain age. This was particularly the case in the Maghreb, which had a very discreet practice of Islam.

11. Laghouati shows how diglossia functions in four novels by Djebar. He analyzes Djebar's French-language imitations of Arabic poetical forms that use alliteration and poetical games in *L'Amour* (105).
12. The early postcolonial studies works by Mortimer, Donadey, and Lionnet cited above reveal the gendered dimension in Djebar's writings. They are pioneers in the field of postcolonial studies and feminism, and their dialog with the author when she was alive was a turning point in the studies of her writings. See also Ringrose, *Assia Djebar*.
13. See Tlatli, "L'Ambivalence linguistique."
14. See Calle-Grueber, *Assia Djebar*. As stated in *Le Blanc de l'Algérie* (*Algerian White*), during this time Djebar was with Fanon, Alice Cherki, and other intellectuals who wrote in *El Moudjahid*, the FLN's newspaper.
15. See Donadey, *Approaches*, 3.
16. In January 1957, the year of the Battle of Algiers, she was in Paris. After three consecutive years of strikes during the examination period (May–June 1956, March 1957, and March 1958), she was forced to leave her prestigious institution for women, the ENS Sèvres.
17. See Mortimer's chapter on Djebar as a writer whose production as a novelist paralleled the liberation of the Algerian nation, "Herstory Is the War Story," in *Women Fight, Women Write* (49–76). Djebar indeed focused "primarily [on] Algerian women's struggle against both French colonialism and indigenous patriarchy" (50).
18. Boutaghou, "History and Untold Memories."
19. See Shafik, *Arab Cinema*, 119.
20. Car ce silence a été non vraiment d'écriture, mais fait de tentatives d'écritures diverses, de nature différente, de disciplines multiples—théâtre, enquêtes sociologiques en terrain rural algérien, tournage de cinéma . . .

Ces dix années de non-publication littéraire ont donc servi à cela: chercher, sinon à sortir de mon français, langue d'écriture, du moins à élargir, et pour finir à y revenir dans un total libre arbitre, consciente enfin de la nécessité d'inscrire dans la pâte même de ma langue française, ainsi que dans la structure romanesque, tous les tenants de mon identité personnelle. [. . .]

Les allers et retours entre la littérature et le travail cinématographique m'ont influencée. Le cinéma m'amena à la confrontation avec le corps même de la langue maternelle, en usage, jusque-là en moi, presque exclusivement familial: le dialecte maternel me permettait, il est vrai, la jouissance surtout musicale (poésie ancienne chantée avec la musique traditionnelle savante,

dite andalouse, mais aussi le chant bédouin du Sud et d'autres régions maghrébines). (*Ces voix* 35–36)
21. En 1975 et 1976, durant des repérages dans ma tribu maternelle, je fus sensible à un "arabe des femmes," de telle sorte que la diglossie de départ (dialecte utilisé familialement d'une part, arabe littéraire d'autre part, dont je voudrais le rapprocher), cette diglossie que je dirais "verticale," se trouve doublée par une séparation qui me semble "horizontale," une véritable fissure secrète correspond à la ségrégation sexuelle du quotidien.

    Il s'agit d'une "langue des femmes" à usage parallèle, le plus souvent clandestin et occulte, par rapport à l'arabe ordinaire, celui de la communauté (pour ne pas dire la "langue des hommes"). (36)
22. Dire aussi, maintenant, tant de décennie après, ces trois mots: BEAU DE L'AIR.

    Lentement, après la première syllabe, l'image se lève: de longs doigts aux ongles si longs eux aussi, mais d'un rouge écarlate, deux mains de femmes réunies en un geste . . . de prière? d'offrande? Je regarde, n'ayant jamais vu d'ongles écarlates, longs, si longs au bout de doigts si effilés, et c'est une voix qui revient, traversant tant de décennies, précautionneuse et grave, avec un accent qu'alors je ne sais reconnaître, disons un accent provençal chez cette femme longue et mince. [. . .] C'est la voix qui fixe en moi pour toujours, comme la première fois son image, elle qui m'a donné, oui, la première à m'avoir donné à boire le tout premier vers français, prononcé comme j'étais auparavant habituée à recevoir seulement les versets du Coran: avec une lenteur quasi majestueuse, une gravité à peine marquée, une fluidité tranquille, presque fervente dans la chute. (*Nulle part* 101–2)
23. See Boutaghou, "Au-delà du miroir," 34.
24. J'écris et je parle le français au-dehors: mes mots ne se chargent pas de réalité charnelle. J'apprends des noms d'oiseaux que je n'ai jamais vus, des noms d'arbres que je mettrai dix ans ou avantage à identifier ensuite, des glossaires de fleurs et de plantes que je ne humerai jamais avant de voyager au nord de la Méditerranée. En ce sens, tout vocabulaire me devient absence, exotisme sans mystère, avec comme une mortification de l'oeil qu'il ne sied pas d'avouer. . . . Les scènes des livres d'enfant, leurs situations me sont purs scénarios; dans la famille française, la mère vient chercher sa fille ou son fils à l'école; dans la rue française, les parents marchent tout naturellement côte à côte. . . . Ainsi, le monde de l'école est expurgé du quotidien de ma ville natale tout comme de celui de ma famille. A ce dernier est dénié tout rôle référentiel. (*Amour* 261)
25. Dans mon écoute d'alors, je me mis à repérer quelques-unes de ces réticences, de ces retenues, ou de ces litotes du parler des femmes—y compris la

résurgence, par instants, de la langue berbère qui réapparaît spontanément aux forts moments d'émotion, pour ainsi dire presque comme une langue du refoulé (parfois dans la bande-son de mon film: *La Nouba des femmes du mont Chenoua*). [...]

De tout ce matériel sonore, apparemment non utilisé, je me suis nourrie les années suivantes: autant pour élaborer la fin de mon roman *L'Amour, la fantasia* que surtout pour prendre enfin conscience vivacement de mon horizon d'écrivain! [...]

Ce particularisme féminin de mes langues d'origine (celle que je parle couramment: le dialecte arabe de ma région et le berbère perdu mais pourtant non effacé) me fut comme une mémoire sonore ancienne qui resurgissait en moi et autour de moi, qui me redonnait force—voix âpres, livrant si souvent la peine, le chagrin, la perte, et pourtant rendant présente, à mon oreille, une telle tendresse maternelle, une solidarité si profondes, qu'elles m'empêchent de vaciller, encore maintenant. (*Ces voix* 36–37)

26. Comment traduire ce "hannouni," par un "tendre," un "tendrelou"? Ni "mon chéri," ni "mon coeur." Pour dire "mon coeur," nous, les femmes, nous préférons "mon petit foie," ou "pupille de mon oeil." . . . Ce "tendrelou" semble un cœur de laitue caché et frais. (*Amour* 117; ellipsis in original)

27. [...] Ma mère tenait surtout [...] à ses cahiers de musique: elle qui n'écrivait pas le français [...] elle ouvrait ces feuillets où, adolescente, elle avait noté la poésie des *noubas* andalouses. Elle en savait par cœur les couplets, mais relire les vers inscrits en arabe la préservait, dans notre cercle, du statut d'analphabète qui aurait pu être le sien. (*Vaste est la prison* 170–71)

28. See Kashani-Sabet, "Swinging Pendulum"; and Tatli, "Ambivalence."

29. The recent movie by Tarik Saleh, *La Conspiration du Caire* (2022), takes place inside of al-Azhar, the prestigious university and mosque of the Sunni world. The movie shows how the transformation and departure from meaning into its pure sensual acoustic experience is perceived as unorthodox by some Islamist students.

30. See Boutaghou, "History and Untold Memories," 222.

31. A first version of this section was published as "Writing in *bi-langue*: Assia Djebar's Veiled Arabic," in Donadey, *Approaches to Teaching the Works of Assia Djebar*.

32. See Donadey, "Multilingual Strategies"; Kouchkar Ferchouli, "Emergence du parler féminin arabe"; Thiel, *Assia Djebar*; and Boutaghou, "Le style en arabesque."

33. It is particularly striking in the titles *La Disparition de la langue française* and *Oran, langue morte*.

34. Les multiples voix qui m'assiègent—celles de mes personnages dans mes textes de fiction—, je les entends, pour la plupart, en arabe, un arabe dialectal, ou même un berbère que je comprends mal, mais dont la respiration rauque et le souffle m'habitent d'une façon immémoriale. (*Ces voix* 29)
35. See Kashani-Sabet, "Swinging Pendulum," for a deeper understanding of the intricate history of languages and politics in Algeria: "Before the French conquest, the educational system consisted of Islamic institutions of learning such as the *kataba*, or elementary schools, the *madrasa*, or secondary schools, and the *zawiya*, or schools of higher education. The French, however, altered the existing education [sic] institutions to accommodate the needs of the *colons*, or settlers. In the meantime, the education of indigenous Algerians was largely excluded until 1895, when a school was founded for the offspring of the workers of the French colonial bureaucracy" (266).
36. Passionnée, étais-je à vingt ans, par la stature d'Averroes [. . .] mais alors que j'avais appris au collège l'anglais, le latin et le grec, comme je demandais en vain à perfectionner mon arabe classique, j'ai dû restreindre mon ambition en me résignant à devenir historienne. (Asholt, *Assia Djebar: littérature et transmission* 413)
37. In Algeria, Arabic is the official language. Algeria is a multilingual country where different Amazigh languages coexist alongside Arabic—both the rich and popular dialectal version and the classical Arabic that is now mainly associated with the state. It must be understood that dialectal Arabic is a language and not just a colloquial version of classical Arabic. The syntax is similar to classical Arabic, but with a specific vocabulary that mixes Arabic with other Mediterranean languages. There exist different dictionaries of dialectal Algerian Arabic. Finally, there is a traditional culture in dialectal Arabic that includes songs, literature, and proverbs.
38. Kashani-Sabet reminds us how Ibn Badis and the Ulama gathered in 1936 for the Islamic Congress in Algiers ("Swinging Pendulum," 268). Ibn Badis "requested further reforms such as the recognition of Arabic, in addition to French, as the Algerian national language." The same went for members of the FLN who did not impose a specific language and for whom "language was not the overarching concern [. . .] during the years of revolt that led to Algerian independence." She explains the position of one of the "neuf historiques" (nine recognized leaders of the Algerian independence movement), Hocine Aït Ahmed, who wrote in his memoirs that "the French language has been the principal, if not, exclusive vehicle, on a certain level of abstraction, of communication, oral or written, in the hearts of the leading organs of our district and of the party" (268).

39. Thiel suggests that, in the case of dialogues and first-person narratives, there are translations from Arabic and transpositions of Arabic syntactic structures into French (*Assia Djebar: la polyphonie* 54).
40. "Greek: 'carrying back'. In discourse, the meaning of some linguistic forms can only be with reference to another form somewhere in the surrounding text (or co-text), since they have no fixed meaning of their own. For example in the sentence *She quickly pulled it in and shoved it through the slot*, we have no idea who and what the pronoun *she* and *it* refer to without access to the co-text. If the relevant co-text precedes these empty forms, this is an example of *anaphoric* reference. If it follows these forms, it is known as *cataphoric* reference" (Pearce, *Routledge Dictionary*, 15).
41. Paronomasia is classified as a "figure de mot" [word figure] and defined as the repetition of words with similar sounds but different meanings. (Ducrot and Schaeffer, *Nouveau Dictionnaire* 480–81).
42. The published English translation of this sentence reinstates the missing verb, so I have modified it here to facilitate comprehension.
43. "Il" s'est éloigné. Ses souliers crissent régulièrement sur les dalles. "Il" tousse; "il" ouvre des portes; "il" est parti.
44. Toi au soleil désormais exposée, moi tentée de m'enfoncer dans la nuit resurgie. [. . .] Ton rire désespéré à l'aube, ô Hajila, après que ma fillette t'a hélée, par-dessus la rampe. Sur la ligne d'horizon noyée, l'oeil de l'aurore darde sur nous sa menace. (*Ombre* 11)
45. Word play frequently features in the titles of articles on Djebar's work. Here are just a few examples: Gauvin, "Assia au pays du langage"; Rice, "Algerrance: envois et envols"; and Lionnet, "Ces voix au fil de soi(e)."
46. See Boutaghou, "New History and Untold Memories," 228.
47. See Zimra, "Mapping Memory," as the first who worked on this important dimension of Djebar's writing.
48. Cette langue que j'apprends nécessite un corps en posture, une mémoire qui y prend appui. [. . .] Quand j'étudie ainsi, mon corps s'enroule, retrouve quelle secrète architecture de la cité et jusqu'à sa durée. (*Amour* 260)
49. Je me remis à marcher. Comme j'avais chaud, je pris un sentier qui s'engageait sous les arbres. La ville n'était pas loin. À un détour, Alger m'apparut étalée, paresseuse; je la contemplai longuement. Le soleil lui-même essayait de l'épargner: il l'auréolait. Arrêtée au bord du spectacle, je me laissai tomber sur l'herbe rase. Après un regard aux alentours, je me renversai sur le dos. Je soupirai. Transpercée du froid de la terre, je me suis abandonnée à la somnolence, les yeux à demi fermés, remplis du ciel large comme un ventre de bête. (*Les Impatients* 13)

50. Cet été, je retrouvai avec une indifférence morne à la fois le soleil éclatant de M***, et les estivants habituels, agglutinés par parquets et par familles nombreuses, pour parader dans le bruit, la chaleur et la nudité. [...]
   Je n'aimais pourtant pas la tristesse, ni le vague à l'âme. Et je venais d'avoir vingt-ans.... Cette dernière année avait glissé comme les autres: le rythme léger des sorties en groupe dans les cinémas et les casinos d'Alger, les surprise-parties, les dimanches pluvieux, les courses folles au vent dans des voitures nerveuses comme de jeunes chevaux racés. (*La Soif* 11–12)
51. Dans le vieux quartier arabe, au pied de la montagne, les maisons à façade blanche crépie à la chaux se ressemblent. Dans ces lieux où s'étendait autrefois, de la ville maintenant agrandie, le seul faubourg—celui où les familles aisées de l'époque aimaient venir, dès la fin du printemps, pour y trouver, près des sources et des vergers proches, un peu de fraîcheur—chaque demeure est le fond d'une impasse où l'on fait halte après qu'on s'est perdu dans un dédale de ruelles, de silence qui ne se troublent à présent que des chuchotements, coupés soudain de cris stridents, des enfants que les mères voudraient en vain retenir chez elles. (*Les Enfants* 13)
52. Je m'enfuis. [...] Des larmes coulaient sur mon visage. Le vent, qui me fouettait les joues, les séchait rapidement. Je marchais avec un sentiment de libération. Heureuse de sentir mes cheveux sur mon cou, dans mon dos, heureuse du grand air, je courais droit devant moi.... Maintenant, la ville à mes pieds, je dors, tranquille comme une reine.
   Bientôt le soleil sauta au-dessus de ma tête. Les yeux fermés, éblouie, j'enlevai le boléro de ma robe qui voilait mes épaules. Le soleil tapa sur ma peau; avec délices, je le laissai me mordre. Pour la première fois de ma vie, je dormais seule ainsi, en pleine nature. J'allais penser que c'était imprudent. Mais que pouvait-il exister d'autre que moi, et le ciel, à cette heure? Pendant dix-huit ans, on m'avait empêché d'aimer le soleil rouge, le ciel plein et rond comme une coupe fraîche. J'étais enfin dans la lumière. Je m'endormis.
   Ce fut sur un visage que j'ouvris les yeux. Un visage d'homme où je remarquai d'abord les yeux étroits qui riaient. [...]
   Pendant le retour dans l'autobus, je ne pensais à rien. La nuit allait s'étendre sur la ville; elle approchait peu à peu de l'horizon, pour encercler cette débauche de lumière qui ne savait où disparaître. Seule au milieu des citadins qui ramenaient leur dimanche en poussière, j'éprouvais un bonheur aigu, nerveux. Dans la paix du soir d'été, j'écoutais le cœur du monde battre lentement dans une infinie clarté. (*Les Impatients* 15–17)
53. De Tunis me restera surtout en mémoire l'odeur de pourriture du lac. Chaque année, paraît-il on parle de plans d'assèchement. Mais le lac est toujours là.

> Lorsque je dois sortir de la ville et que je prends le petit train—le "treno," disent les habitants qui imitent la minorité italienne–, je ne regrette pas sa présence: son sel miroite au soleil, des pique-bœufs volent au-dessus de sa surface d'argent, ou quelques élégants oiseaux aquatiques. La lagune est séparée de la mer par une mince languette de terre qu'occupe le chemin de fer sur plusieurs kilomètres: ainsi, que l'on s'éloigne ou que l'on approche de la capitale, pendant plus d'une demi-heure (le train est poussif), nous saisit la sensation de naviguer à l'instar des paquebots vieillots qui entrent chaque jour au port. J'aime cette blancheur de moire du lac, qui contraste avec la nappe glauque ou d'un vert infiniment triste de la Méditerranée. (*Alouettes* 221)

54. I refer here to Baudelaire, "Le peintre de la vie moderne," and his reading by Benjamin, "On Some Motifs in Baudelaire."
55. En ville, nulle trace d'eau: le port est installé loin et la cité, depuis sa naissance, s'est résolument accroupie en terrienne sur des collines de l'intérieur. Son cœur ancien sent l'ombre, le musc et l'ambre; j'y vais souvent chercher un rêve de silence. Depuis le début du siècle, les quartiers neufs qui se développent voisinent l'eau au nord; mais Tunis ne bénéficie, à cause de la platitude quasi-total du terrain, d'aucun panorama, seulement de cette puanteur du lac; elle ne se penche point dans la transparence lacustre, tout au plus dans un miasme d'herbes et d'algues pourries. (*Les Alouettes* 221–22)
56. En médina, pour moi, le souvenir remonte: quartier blanc de notre village natal, bien qu'il n'offre aucune ressemblance, dans sa simplicité agreste, avec cette ville autrefois opulente et qui conserve, comme les princes ruinés, le style de l'aisance et un certain laisser-aller. Une tranquillité du confort peut-être: ses mosquées toujours ouvertes, ses anciennes medersas aux portes splendides mais aux cours rongées par la pauvreté, ses marchands qui demeurent à l'affût, le regard tamisé d'immobilité tandis que les mendiants circulent, chantent, maudissent et soufflent. . . . Une médina même pas comparable à nos quartiers d'adolescence où les bordels sont la fin d'escaliers montant au ciel, où la marche supérieure, surplombant le paysage marin, est livrée aux enfants et aux miséreux pensifs. Nous marchons cependant comme autrefois dans les ruelles du souvenir et c'est peut-être la seule ressemblance que je désire avec le passé. (*Les Alouettes* 226–27)
57. J'ai passé chacun de mes étés d'enfance dans la vieille cité maritime, encombrée de ruines romaines qui attirent les touristes. Jeunes filles et femmes de la famille, des maisons voisines et alliées, rendent régulièrement visite à quelque sanctuaire. . . . Des groupes piailleurs se répandent, dès lors, dans la campagne proche. Un ou deux garçonnets font office de guetteurs vigilants, tandis

que nous, les fillettes, nous nous mêlons aux parentes voilées. Soudain, c'est l'alarme:

—Un homme approche! (*Amour* 179)

58. Sous le figuier ou l'olivier, ou contre le bosquet de lentisques, les voiles qui ont glissé sur l'épaule sont remontés vivement sur les chevelures. L'une se réemmitoufle, alors qu'elle arborait ses bijoux sur sa poitrine découverte, une autre se relève et veut voir sans être vue, une troisième étouffe ses rires, agacés à chaque approche d'un mâle.

Le danger se révèle quelquefois sans fondement:

—Voyons, remarque l'une, c'est un Français!

La pudeur habituelle n'est plus nécessaire. Le passant, puisqu'il est Français, Européen, chrétien, s'il regarde, a-t-il vraiment un regard? Face à elles, qui ont mission, leur vie entière, de préserver leur image, de considérer ce devoir comme le legs le plus sacré, face à elles toutes, mes tantes, mes cousines, mes semblables, l'étrange, en s'arrêtant, en les dévisageant, les voit-il lorsqu'il croit les surprendre? Non, il s'imagine les voir . . .

"Le pauvre," commente l'une, quand l'inconnu, tout près, a levé les yeux, a aperçu l'éclat de jais d'une tresse trop longue, la lueur d'yeux fardés et moqueurs:

—Le pauvre, il s'est troublé!

Car il ne sait pas. Son regard, de l'autre côté de la haie, au-delà de l'interdit, ne peut toucher. Aucune stratégie de séduction ne risque de s'exercer; dès lors, pour ces promeneuses d'un entracte furtif, pourquoi se cacher?

Ainsi de la parole française pour moi. La langue étrangère me servait, dès l'enfance, d'embrasure pour le spectacle du monde et de ses richesses. Voici qu'en certaines circonstances, elle devenait dard pointé sur ma personne. (*Amour* 179–80)

59. "Nue, je suis Hajila toute nue!" Tu renverses la tête, comme la femme du square, hier . . . Tu désirerais la retrouver. Comment te diriger? S'orienter, c'est se rappeler; tu te rappellerais quoi? . . . Tu tournes à droite, à gauche; toujours des ruelles. Tu évites les boulevards, tu as peur des voitures, tu reconnais l'abord d'un hôpital. Tu as dû y venir petite, lors de la maladie du père. "Sortir nue! songes-tu. Voilà que l'enfance revient! Ô pierre noire de la Mecque!" Pour un peu, tu te sentirais suffoquer! . . . C'est l'ivresse, tout simplement. (*Ombre* 49)

60. In 2022, historian Malika Rahal published *1962, une histoire Populaire* (1962, a popular history). This groundbreaking work reveals to the general public the violence committed in 1962 by the OAS and the FLN in Oran. Many witnesses have shared their experience; Rahal's exceptional work is a tribute to

these very often unheard voices. Djebar did not witness Oran's 1962s events personally, as she was in exile in Rabat. She came back to Algiers in July 1962 to write a report on the first days of Algerian independence. She was sent there by Françoise Giroud (Calle-Gruber, *Assia Djebar*).
61. Strasbourg was under Nazi domination between 1940 and 1944.
62. Thelja, ce matin, ne traverse pas la ville en promeneuse; non, elle ne manifeste plus d'indolence de touriste. Elle tient un cahier à la main; elle demande la direction de la bibliothèque universitaire. Elle s'attarde un instant sur un pont, débouche sur une place que la bibliothèque domine par une double rampe d'escalier imposante. Elle hésite, veut d'abord prendre un café. [. . .]

Thelja se met à fumer une cigarette; elle redemande un autre café: Halim, à la tête alors d'un service d'archives à Alger (comme architecte, il se passionnait pour la préservation du patrimoine), Halim lui avait proposé:

—Viens avec moi cet après-midi: j'ai rendez-vous, dans un laboratoire de photo, avec un ami français. Deux de ses collègues, des anciens soldats de la guerre d'hier, avaient pris alors des photos au cœur de la Casbah d'Alger, mais de nuit. Ils profitaient du couvre-feu, et naturellement de l'impunité de leur uniforme, pour, dans des lieux vides, saisir en images les plus belles maisons anciennes! Je suis impatient de les voir! On pourrait monter, chez nous, une exposition pour évaluer exactement les destructions survenues, tout ce qu'on a négligé de préserver depuis, d'entretenir! Viendras-tu? J'aimerais avoir ton avis sur ces traces. (*Nuits* 95–96)
63. See Bourget, *Coran et tradition islamique*.
64. On the notion of "mise-en-récit" / "put in narrative" in the Algerian literature context, see Boutaghou, "Introduction," in *Représentations* (12).

5. THE MAURITIAN BARD: ANANDA DEVI

1. See Boutaghou, "Défense et illustration," 453.
2. For further references about the sociolinguistic situation of Mauritius, see Hawkins, *Other Hybrid Archipelago*; Ravi, *Rainbow Colors*; and Baker and Kriegel, "Mauritian Creole."
3. The definition of a Mauritian "creolization" has been compared to other contexts, mainly the Caribbean (negritude): Torabully, "Créolité, coolitude, créolisation: les imaginaires de la relation" http://www.afrik.com/article 10880.html (accessed November 23, 2022). About the difference between coolie and creole, see Torabully, "Coolitude," in *Notre librairie* (59–61). He defines "coolitude" as the creolization of the Mauritian-Indian community in Mauritius and explains the link between marginalized identity in process and language. I define "creolization" as the consciousness of identities in

process or, in French, *la fabrique identitaire* (the making of identity) inspired by Gauvin's title *La Fabrique de la langue*.
4. Prabhu, *Hybridity*; Lionnet, "Ces voix au fil de soi(e)"; Jean-François, *Poétiques de la violence*.
5. Hawkins, *Other Hybrid Archipelago*: "The effective *lingua franca* of the Island is in fact Mauritian Creole, spoken by 95 percent of the population, used daily by most Mauritians. Paradoxically, it has no official recognition in the school system, although, since the 1970s, there has been a movement to use the language for literary expression, notably by the dramatist, Dev Virahsawmy. Most significant in oral culture: theatre and popular music, as in the neighbouring island of Réunion; but several novels in Creole have also been published, the first, René Asgarally's *Quand montagne prend difé* in 1977" (95).
6. At the time of this writing, Devi has published fourteen novels, five volumes of short stories, four volumes of poetry, and two essays. I had to make the difficult choice between exhaustivity and exemplarity. Obviously, my approach can be extended to her oeuvre, which, hopefully, future scholars will be inspired to pursue. Ananda Devi is the 2024 Winner of the Neustadt International Prize for Literature.
7. An adaptation directed by Harrikrisna Anenden came out in France in June 2007.
8. See Jean-François, *Poétiques de la violence*.
9. For example, the Indian community is Hindu or Muslim or secular (which is rare); its people can speak Hindi or Bhojpuri or Tamil, but also French, Creole, and English. The Creole group is mainly Catholic; they speak French, English, and Creole.
10. I am referring to the mysterious death of the Sega singer Kaya in February 1999, which was followed by violent riots in Mauritius.
11. A first version of this section was originally published as a book chapter, "Creolization as Subversion in Ananda Devi's Novels," in *Creoles, Diasporas, and Cosmopolitanisms*, ed. David Gallagher, 29–44 (Palo Alto, CA: Academica Press, 2012).
12. Kistnareddy, "Représenter l'altérité," 182.
13. See Ananda Devi, "Contre le culte de la différence: entretien de Boniface Mongo-Mboussa avec Ananda Devi," Africultures, http://www.africultures.com/php/index.php?nav=article&no=1734 (accessed August 8, 2011) in a new attempt to access this link, the article was changed [23 November 2022].
14. Kistnareddy, "Représenter l'altérité" (181): "Le grotesque peut donc être un processus d'aliénation, un moyen de donner libre cours à l'altérité, de le rejeter, de le mettre à l'écart par le simple fait que le corps différent ne doit pas

avoir d'allié" (The grotesque can be a process of alienation, a means to free otherness, to reject the different body, to put it aside for the simple reason that a different body should not have an ally).

15. Port Louis la noire, la vilaine, Port Louis défigurée par des formes grotesques, Port Louis l'infranchissable dans ses marées humaines, j'ai cru qu'elle me faisait de l'oeil. (*Ève* 67)
16. J'embrasse ta figure de souris. Tu es la beauté du monde, son illumination. (73)
17. In this way, Devi's novels are very similar in her use of French to Maghrebi writers of the first generation, who repressed the subjugated language, keeping the language from contaminating their French, like in Djebar's first cycle, between 1957 and 1980.
18. La poésie des femmes, c'est quand Savita et moi, on marche ensemble en synchronisant nos pas pour éviter les ornières. C'est quand on joue à être jumelles parce qu'on se ressemble. Nous portons les mêmes vêtements, le même parfum. Nous avons l'air de danser. Nos boucles d'oreilles tintent. Elle a une pierre minuscule à l'aile du nez, comme une étoile. La poésie des femmes, c'est le rire, dans ce coin perdu, qui ouvre un bout de paradis pour ne pas nous laisser nous noyer. (*Ève* 30)
19. Regarde ce doigt avec lequel je touche ta nourriture. Tu le vois? Je sais tu te dis que c'est une main épaisse, que je n'ai aucune grâce, aucune élégance [. . .] et maintenant, ce gros index de cochon qui touille ton porridge et ta crème dessert, imagine qu'il est entré, cet index, dans une autre femme, et pas n'importe quelle femme, tu vois, une bien noire, ma Marie-Rose, de ceux que tu méprises si fort, une magnifique Noire, une vaste rose de chair qui donne le vertige, ma Marie-Rose. (*Sari* 47)
20. The semantic proximity between food, sexuality, and literature is present in other of Devi's novels, particularly for female characters, as shown in Devi's novel titled *Manger l'autre* (Eating the other, 2018).
21. Le dégoût me donne des haut-le-coeur. Je ne dois pas vomir, c'est trop douloureux. Je me retiens et ravale ma salive, respire par le nez, lentement. (*Sari* 48)
22. In highly gendered societies, male-female relationships always have a sexual connotation—that is, they are always immediately suspected of being sexual.
23. See Glissant, *Poétique de la relation*.
24. See Kymlicka, *Multicultural Citizenship*.
25. Maalouf, *Les Identités meurtrières*; the literal translation is "murderous identities." The published English translation is titled *In the Name of Identity: Violence and the Need to Belong*.

26. See Ong, *Flexible Citizenship*. On the interface between self destruction and identity, see Bragard and Lindo, "Débris d'humanité" 245.
27. Le mot de créolisation [. . .] Non seulement une rencontre, un choc (au sens ségalénien), un métissage, mais une dimension inédite qui permet à un chacun d'être là et ailleurs, enraciné et ouvert, perdu dans la montagne et libre sous la mer, en accord et en errance. (*Poétique de la relation* 46)
28. See O'Flaherty, "Every Woman Is an Island?"
29. See Jauze, "La pluriethnicité dans les villes mauriciennes," 7–32.
30. "*I'm crazy about this City*" (emphasis in original).

    Rien que ça, comme la phrase de Virginia, même sursaut en cinq mots, même paysage intérieur et extérieur découvert comme lorsque, d'un seul coup, on écarte un rideau. Pourtant, je n'ai jamais été amoureuse d'une cité (ou peut-être si, Port-Louis?). (*Les Hommes* 186)
31. To read more about Devi's life and works, I highly recommend her page (http://ile-en-ile.org/devi/) on Thomas C. Spear's website, Ile en Ile (http://ile-en-ile.org/).
32. Mais, dans la Beetle, d'autres images sont venues contredire ce beau conte. À Port-Louis, on voyait tout le reste. Le vrai, l'intransigeant, l'incontournable réalité d'un pays sous-développée comme on le disait à l'époque sans crainte du politiquement incorrect, la réalité de ceux qui devaient lutter pour chaque souffle, chaque plainte, chaque ahanement. Ce qui m'est apparu le plus clairement, c'était leur silence. (*Les Hommes* 37)
33. À present, il est temps de me voir. Je dois vous montrer mon visage. Ils disent que je porte le signe de Shehtan. Ils détournent les yeux ou prononcent des mots d'exorcisme. Donnez-moi le nom que vous voulez, rakshas, Shehtan, Satan ou autre.

    Je suis née avec un bec-de-lièvre. Dans les villages, ils n'appellent pas cela une difformité; ils l'appellent une malédiction. (*Moi, l'interdite* 8–9)
34. C'est ainsi que sur un coup de tête, je me rends dans la vieille ville fortifiée, qui est pourtant un dédale dans lequel les étrangers ne se risquent jamais seuls. [. . .] Au bout d'une heure, je ne savais plus où j'étais. J'empruntais des enfilades de ruelles puantes, espérant que je finirais chaque fois dans les maisons des gens. Les rues semblaient mener tout droit chez des particuliers aux portes ouvertes. (*Indian Tango* 129)
35. Une petite fille, soulignée de trois cerceaux, prend couleur du vertige. Elle va si vite dans son espace que je ne vois plus qu'une fulgurance de lumière. (*Indian Tango* 70)
36. [Subha] n'a d'ailleurs jamais su formuler quoi que ce soit, ni ses opinions ni ses envies. Enfant fermée dans sa timidité comme dans une forteresse, elle

avait senti très tôt la poussière d'humilité qui se posait sur elle et s'épaississait chaque année, à mesure qu'elle sortait de l'enfance et devenait cette "charge" dont les parents avaient hâte de se débarrasser. Son unique chance de briller, même d'une lueur pâle, s'était envolée lorsqu'on avait interrompu sans la prévenir ses cours de sitar. (*Indian Tango* 111)

37. Sous le soleil dissimulé par les couches de sédiment de la ville qui ne dort jamais, je m'échappe et pars à la recherche d'obsessions nouvelles. D'obsessions? Non, certes. Elle n'est pas une obsession *mais* un accompagnement, un chant de sirène mélancolique qui semble se marier si parfaitement à l'atmosphère de Delhi que je me dis parfois que Bimala n'est pas réelle, *mais* seulement une incarnation du souffle sulfureux de la ville, la forme fantomatique, faite chair, de quelque chose d'enraciné; élastique et friable, terreux et versatile. [...]

 Si j'étais un prédateur, je la pousserais dans ses retranchements. Je l'entraînerais vers une impasse. Je l'acculerais à un mur. Puis, avec une grande délibération, au beau milieu de cette ruelle remplie d'ordures, je mènerais à bien ma curée, dents exposées, langue chercheuse, dévorant en elle tout ce qui attend d'être dévoré, révélant tout ce qui attend d'être révélé. Les sens aux aguets, j'entendrais les soupirs dissimulés sous ses sanglots et sentirais la réponse ténébreuse et sanglante de son corps. Elle ne verrait plus les souillures qui l'entourent. Elle n'entendrait plus la course des rats longeant le mur ni les chiens léchant les restes décomposés. Son corps se vautrerait dans toute cette crasse avec délectation et elle ne serait plus consciente que de moi. Et du fait que j'aie prononcé son nom: Bimala. (*Indian Tango* 105-7)

38. See as an example, Anita Desaï, *Clear Light of Day* (1980).
39. La ville s'assombrit comme en attente d'une pluie, mais ce n'est pas encore la saison. Quand la mousson viendra, tout le paysage se transformera en eau. Aucune surface ne restera solide. Les rêves sont ainsi faits. Ils semblent tangibles, mais la main passe au travers. Delhi sous la mousson, Bimala à l'horizon, la petite au cerceau dans son bref tourbillon: ma pensée passe au travers et les habite, les anime, les absorbe. Elles sont moi. (*Indian Tango* 62)
40. Marcher m'est difficile. Je claudique, je boitille en avant sur l'asphalte fumant.
 À chaque pas naît un monstre, pleinement formé.
 La nuit de la ville s'enfle, élastique, autour de moi. L'air salé venant du Caudan racle mes douleurs et ma peau, mais je continue. (*Ève* 9)
41. This is not the place to develop fully the implicit comparison with writers from the European realist tradition such as Charles Dickens, Victor Hugo and Honoré Balzac, Guy de Maupassant, or Stendhal. The city, be it London or Paris, is a major character in their novels.

42. Quand un colonisé entreprend une action contre l'oppresseur, et quand cette oppression s'est exercée sous les formes de la violence exacerbée et continue comme en Algérie, il doit vaincre un nombre important d'interdits. La ville européenne n'est pas le prolongement de la ville autochtone. Les colonisateurs ne se sont pas installés au milieu des indigènes. Ils ont cerné la ville autochtone, ils ont organisé le siège, Toute sortie de la Kasbah d'Alger débouche chez l'ennemi. De même à Constantine, à Oran, à Blida, à Bône.

Les villes indigènes sont, de façon concertée, prises dans l'étau du conquérant. [. . .] En dehors des femmes de ménage employées chez le conquérant, celles qu'indifféremment le colonisateur prénomme les "Fatmas," l'Algérienne, la jeune Algérienne surtout, s'aventure peu dans la ville européenne. Les déplacements ont presque tous lieu dans la ville arabe. [. . .] L'Algérienne, à chaque entrée dans la ville européenne, doit remporter une victoire sur elle-même, sur ses craintes infantiles. Elle doit reprendre l'image de l'occupant fichée quelque part dans son esprit et dans son corps, pour la remodeler, amorcer le travail capital d'érosion de cette image, la rendre inessentielle, lui enlever de sa vergogne, la désacraliser. (*Oeuvres* 288–89)

6. BEING A SUBJECT IN TRANSLATION

1. See Boutaghou, "Au-delà du miroir."
2. As defined by Glissant. Other scholars and theorists like Gauvin and Lionnet contributed to this reflection about the intersection between the creolization of forms and languages. See Gauvin, *La Fabrique de la langue* and *L'Écrivain francophone*.
3. Of course, one can think about other modalities of plurilingualism not resulting from colonial experiences but that is not the object of this book.
4. This is particularly the case in postcolonial subjectivities, which is, in a sense, similar to the Bulgarian subject that informs Kristeva's experience, even if the title of her book (*Crisis of the European Subject*) can be read as pertaining to the post-Soviet subject.
5. Peter Ochs, the Edgar M. Bronfman Professor of Modern Judaic Studies at the University of Virginia, introduced this expression and meaning as a philosopher and semiotician during our numerous discussions about bilingualism and postcolonial subjectivity. During our conversations around religion and conflict, and our coteaching a seminar in his cluster at UVA—Politics, Religion, and Conflict—in the spring of 2020, my reading of his works helped me understand the notion of "repair" as a function of signification in literary language. Only to inspire the reader, I mention the following: *Religion without Violence* and "Reparative Reasoning."

6. See Lokugé's introduction to *Toru Dutt: Collected Prose and Poetry*, xli.
7. See Ochs, *Religion without Violence*.
8. Gunew, "Estrangement as Pedagogy," 132–48.
9. See Malabou, *L'Avenir de Hegel*.
10. See Cohen, Oulebsir, and Kanoun, *Alger*.

CONCLUSION

1. J'écris et je parle le français au-dehors: mes mots ne se chargent pas de réalité charnelle. J'apprends des noms d'oiseaux que je n'ai jamais vu, des noms d'arbres que je mettrai dix ans ou davantage à identifier ensuite, des glossaires de fleurs et de plantes que je ne humerai jamais avant de voyager au nord de la Méditerranée. (*Amour* 261)
2. For further developments, see Boutaghou, "Au-delà du miroir."
3. The colonial experience in nonurban spaces will be addressed in another project.
4. See all the "Expositions universelles," as a sign of this appropriation of native architecture with a subtle Western touch.

BIBLIOGRAPHY

Alessandrini, Anthony C. *Frantz Fanon: Critical Perspectives.* New York: Routledge, 1999.
Agrawal, Krishna Avtar. *Toru Dutt: The Pioneer Spirit of Indian English Poetry, A Critical Study.* New Delhi: Atlantic, 2009.
Anand, Mulk Raj. *Untouchable.* London: Penguin, [1935] 1990.
Anenden, Harrikrisna, dir. *La Cathédrale.* 78 mins. Mauritius: Cine Qua Non, 2006.
Appadurai, Arjun. "Disjuncture and Difference in the Global Cultural Economy." *Public Culture* 2, no. 2 (1990): 1–24.
———. *Modernity at Large: Cultural Dimensions of Globalization.* Minneapolis: University of Minnesota Press, 1996.
Appiah, Kwame Anthony. *The Ethics of Identity.* Princeton, NJ: Princeton University Press, 2005.
Apter, Emily S. *Against World Literature: On the Politics of Untranslatability.* London: Verso, 2013.
Asholt, Wolfgang, Mireille Calle-Gruber and Dominique Combe, eds. *Assia Djebar, littérature et transmission.* Paris: Presses Sorbonne Nouvelle, 2010.
Augustine. *Les Confessions.* In *Oeuvres*, vol. 1. Edited by Lucien Jerphagnon. Paris: Bibliothèque de la Pléiade, 1998.
Badiou, Alain. *Theory of the Subject.* Translated by Bruno Bosteels. New York: Continuum, 2009.
Baker, Philip, Sibylle Kriegel. "Mauritian Creole." In *The Survey of Pidgin and Creole Languages, Vol. 2: Portuguese-based, Spanish-based and French-based Languages*, edited by Susanne Maria Michaelis, Philippe Maurer, Martin Haspelmath, and Magnus Huber, 250–60. Oxford: Oxford University Press, 2013.
Baron, Beth. *The Women's Awakening in Egypt: Culture, Society, and the Press.* New Haven, CT: Yale University Press, 1994.
Beauvoir, Simone de. *Pour une morale de l'ambiguïté; suivi de Pyrrhus et Cinéas.* Paris: Gallimard, 2003. Translated by Bernard Frechtman as *The Ethics of Ambiguity.* New York: Philosophical Library, 1948.
Beck, Ulrich. *The Cosmopolitan Vision.* Translated by Ciaran Cronin. Cambridge, MA: Polity, 2006.

Benhabib, Seyla. *Another Cosmopolitanism*. New York: Oxford University Press, 2006.

Benjamin, Walter. "On Some Motifs in Baudelaire." In *Illuminations*, edited and with an introduction by Hannah Arendt, translated by Harry Zorn, 155–200. London: Pimlico, 1999.

———. "The Task of the Translator." In *Illuminations*, edited and with an introduction by Hannah Arendt, translated by Harry Zorn, 69–82. London: Pimlico, 1999.

Bennani, Jalil, ed. *Du Bilinguisme*. Paris: Denoël, 1985.

Bensmaia, Réda. "Multilingualism and National 'Character' in Abdelkebir Khatibi's 'Bilanguage.'" In *Algeria in Others' Languages*, edited by Anne-Emmanuelle Berger, 161–83. Ithaca, NY: Cornell University Press, 2002.

Berger, Anne-Emmanuelle, ed. *Algeria in Others' Languages*. Ithaca, NY: Cornell University Press, 2002.

Bergner, Gwen. "Who Is That Masked Woman? Or, the Role of Gender in Fanon's *Black Skin, White Masks*." PMLA 110, no. 1 (1995): 75–88.

Berman, Antoine. *La Traduction et la lettre ou l'auberge du lointain*. Paris: Seuil, 1999.

Bermann, Sandra and Michael Wood, eds. *Nation, Language, and the Ethics of Translation*. Princeton, NJ: Princeton University Press, 2005.

Bernabé, Jean, Patrick Chamoiseau and Raphaël Confiant. *Éloge de la créolité, In Praise of Creoleness*. Translated by M. B. Taleb-Khyar. Paris: Gallimard, 1993.

Bertacco, Simona, ed. *Language and Translation in Postcolonial Literatures: Multilingual Contexts, Translational Texts*. New York: Routledge, 2014.

Bhabha, Homi K. *The Location of Culture*. New York: Routledge, 2004.

———. "What Does the Black Man Want?" *New Formations*, no. 1 (Spring 1987): 118–24.

Booth, Marilyn, ed. *Migrating Texts: Circulating Translations around the Ottoman Mediterranean*. Edinburgh: Edinburgh University Press, 2019.

Bourget, Carine. *Coran et tradition islamique dans la littérature maghrébine*. Paris: Karthala, 2002.

Boutaghou, Maya. "Au-delà du miroir: Signe, référentialité et interprétation dans le roman francophone." *Les Lettres romanes* 75, nos. 1–2, (2021): 29–53.

———. "Being Berber, or How to Be Condemned to Cosmopolitanism, Jean Amrouche (1906–1962)." In *Migrating Minds: Theories and Practices of Cultural Cosmopolitanism*, edited by Didier Coste, Kristina Kkona, and Nicoletta Pireddu, 105–16. Boca Raton, FL: Routledge, 2021.

———. "Creolization as Subversion in Ananda Devi's Novels." In *Creoles, Diasporas, and Cosmopolitanisms*, edited by David Gallagher, 29–44. Palo Alto, CA: Academica, 2012.

———. "'Défense et illustration' d'un universel mauricien." *International Journal of Francophone Studies* 13, no. 3 (2010): 451–69.

———. *Ernest Renan, "Qu'est-ce qu'une nation?" 1882, texte et présentation, suivi de Genèse et postérité: de l'empire à la nation*. Paris: Honoré Champion, 2020.

———. "History and Untold Memories: New Realism in Assia Djebar's films." In *Landscapes of Realism: Rethinking Literary Realism in Comparative Perspectives, Vol. 2: Pathways through Realism*, edited by Margaret Higonnet, Steen Bille Jørgensen, and Svend Erik Larsen, 217–29. Amsterdam: John Benjamins, 2022.

———. "Introduction." In *Représentations de la guerre algérienne d'indépendance*, edited by Maya Boutaghou with the collaboration of Anne Donadey, 7–20. Paris: Classiques Garnier, 2019.

———. *Occidentalismes, romans historiques postcoloniaux et identités nationales au dix-neuvième siècle, Juan Antonio Mateos, Bankim Chandra Chatterjee, Jurji Zaydan, Marcus Clarke*. Paris: Honoré Champion, 2016.

———. "Le style en arabesque d'Assia Djebar." *French Studies* 67, no. 2 (2013): 216–31.

———. "Le testament soufi de Adbelwahab Meddeb." *Expressions Maghrébines* 6, no. 2, (2017): 135–53.

———. "What Book Do You Read? Imagining Francophone Intertextual Maps." *Contemporary French and Francophone Studies: Sites* 22, no. 2 (2018): 198–207.

———. "Writing in *bi-langue*: Assia Djebar's Veiled Arabic." In *Approaches to Teaching the Works of Assia Djebar*, edited by Anne Donadey, 138–47. New York: MLA, 2017.

Bragard, Véronique, and Karen Lindo. "Débris d'humanité: altérité et autodestruction dans *Ève de ses décombres* d'Ananda Devi." In *Écritures mauriciennes au féminin: penser l'altérité*, edited by Véronique Bragard and Srilata Ravi, 239–48. Paris: l'Harmattan, 2011.

Bragard, Véronique, and Srilata Ravi, eds. *Écritures mauriciennes au féminin: penser l'altérité*. Paris: l'Harmattan, 2011.

Braidotti, Rosi. *Nomadic Subjects: Embodiment and Sexual Difference in Contemporary Feminist Theory*. New York: Columbia University Press, 1994.

Braidotti, Rosi, Patrick Hanafin, and Bolette Blaagaard, eds. *After Cosmopolitanism*. Oxon: Routledge, 2013.

Calle-Gruber, Mireille. *Assia Djebar, nomade entre les murs*. Paris: Maisonneuve et Larose, 2005.

Calle-Gruber, Mireille, ed. *Assia Djebar*. Paris: Association pour la diffusion de la pensée française, 2006.

Calle-Gruber, Mireille, and Anaïs Frantz, eds. *Assia Djebar: le manuscrit inachevé*. Paris: Presses Sorbonne Nouvelle, 2021.

Calvet, Louis-Jean. *Les Voix de la ville: Introduction à la sociolinguistique urbaine.* Paris: Payot, 1994.

Carter, Erica, James Donald, and Judith Squires, eds. *Space and Place: Theories of Identity and Location.* London: Lawrence & Wishart, 1993.

Cascardi, Anthony J. *The Subject of Modernity.* Cambridge: Cambridge University Press, 1992.

Çelik, Zeynep. *Empire, Architecture, and the City: French-Ottoman Encounters, 1830–1914.* Seattle: University of Washington Press, 2008.

Çelik, Zeynep, Julia Clancy-Smith, and Frances Terpak, eds. *Walls of Algiers: Narratives of the City through Text and Image.* Seattle: University of Washington Press, 2009.

Chatterjee, Bankim Chandra. *Rajmohan's Wife.* Edited by Meenakshi Mukherjee. Delhi: Ravi Dayal, 1996.

Chaudhuri, Amit. *Clearing a Space: Reflections on India, Literature, and Culture.* Oxford: Peter Lang, 2008.

Cheah, Pheng, and Bruce Robbins, eds. *Cosmopolitics: Thinking and Feeling beyond the Nation.* Minneapolis: University of Minnesota Press, 1998.

Chikhi, Beïda. *Les Romans d'Assia Djebar.* Alger: Office des publications universitaires, 1990.

Cohen, Jean-Louis, Nabila Oulebsir, and Youcef Kanoun, eds. *Alger paysage urbain et architectures, 1800–2000.* Besançon: Editions de l'Imprimeur, 2003.

Copia, Isis [Mayy Ziyadah]. *Fleurs de rêve.* Cairo: Boehme et Anderer, 1911.

Coste, Didier, Kristina Kkona, and Nicoletta Pireddu, eds. *Migrating Minds: Theories and Practices of Cultural Cosmopolitanism.* Boca Raton, FL: Routledge, 2021.

Crenshaw, Kimberlé. "Demarginalizing the Intersection of Race and Sex: Black Feminist Critique of Antidiscrimination Doctrine, Feminist Theory, and Antiracist Policies." *University of Chicago Legal Forum,* no. 1 (1989): 139–67.

Cuddon, J. A., and Claire Preston. *The Penguin Dictionary of Literary Terms and Literary Theory.* London: Penguin, 1998.

Damrosch, David. *What Is World Literature?* Princeton, NJ: Princeton University Press, 2003.

Darmesteter, James. *Essais de littérature anglaise.* Paris: Librairie Ch. Delagrave, 1883.

Das, Harihar. *Life and Letters of Toru Dutt.* London: Oxford University Press, 1921.

Dasgupta, Subha Chakraborty. "Structuring Forces in the Emergence of a Genre: The Novel in Bengal." *Jadavpur Journal of Comparative Literature* 29 (1990–91): 45–53.

Déjeux, Jean and Albert Memmi, ed. *La Poésie algérienne: de 1830 à nos jours (approches socio-historiques).* Paris: Mouton et Cie, 1963.

Deleuze, Gilles. *Empirisme et subjectivité: essai sur la nature humaine selon Hume.* Paris: Presses Universitaires de France, 1953.

———. *Le Pli: Leibniz et le baroque.* Paris: Éditions de Minuit, 1988.

Derrida, Jacques. *Le Monolinguisme de l'autre: ou la prothèse de l'origine.* Paris: Galilée, 1996. Translated by Patrick Mensah as *Monolingualism of the Other; or, The Prosthesis of Origin* (Stanford, CA: Stanford University Press, 1998).

Desbordes-Valmore, Marceline. *Poésies.* Paris: Gallimard, 1983.

Descartes, René. *Discours de la méthode.* Paris: Flammarion, 1966.

Devi, Ananda. *Ceux du large.* Paris: Éditions Bruno Doucey, 2017.

———. *Ève de ses décombres.* Paris: Éditions France Loisirs, 2006. Translated by Jeffrey Zuckerman as *Eve out of Her Ruins* (Dallas, TX: Deep Vellum, 2016).

———. *Les Hommes qui me parlent.* Paris: Gallimard, 2011.

———. *Indian Tango.* Paris: Gallimard, 2007. Translated by Jean Anderson as *Indian Tango* (Austin, TX: Host, 2011).

———. *Manger l'autre.* Paris: Grasset, 2018.

———. *Moi, l'interdite.* Paris: Dapper, 2000.

———. *Le Rire des déesses.* Paris: Grasset, 2021.

———. *Rue la poudrière.* Abidjan: Les Nouvelles éditions africaines, 1988.

———. *Le Sari vert.* Paris: Gallimard, 2009.

———. *Solstices: recueil de nouvelles.* Port-Louis: P. Mackay, 1976.

———. *La Vie de Joséphin le fou.* Paris: Gallimard, 2003.

Djebar, Assia. *Les Alouettes naïves.* Arles: Actes Sud, 1997.

———. *L'Amour, la fantasia.* Paris: Albin Michel / Librairie générale française (Livre de poche), 1995. Translated by Dorothy S. Blair as *Fantasia: An Algerian Cavalcade* (Portsmouth: Heinemann, 1993).

———. *Le Blanc de l'Algérie.* Paris: Albin Michel / Librairie générale française (Livre de Poche), 1995. Translated by Marjolijn de Jager and David Kelley as *Algerian White* (New York: Seven Stories, 2001).

———. "Discours d'entrée à l'Académie Française." In *Assia Djebar, littérature et transmission,* edited by Wolfgang Asholt, Mireille Calle-Gruber, and Dominique Combe, 403–18. Paris: Presses Sorbonne nouvelle, 2010.

———. *La Disparition de la langue française.* Paris: Albin Michel, 2003.

———. *Les Enfants du nouveau monde.* Paris: Julliard, 1962.

———. *Femmes d'Alger dans leur appartement.* Paris: Albin Michel / Librairie générale française (Livre de poche), 2002. Translated by Marjolijn de Jager and Clarisse Zimra as *Women of Algiers in Their Apartment* (Charlottesville: University of Virginia Press, 1992).

———. *Les Impatients.* Paris: René Juliard, 1958.

———. *Les Nuits de Strasbourg*. Arles: Actes Sud, 1997.
———. *Nulle part dans la maison de mon père*. Paris: Fayard, 2007.
———. *Ombre sultane*. Arles: Albin Michel / Librairie générale française (Livre de poche), 2006. Translated by Dorothy S. Blair as *A Sister to Scheherazade* (Portsmouth: Heinemann, 1993).
———. *Oran, langue morte*. Arles: Actes Sud, 1997. Translated by Tegan Raleigh as *The Tongue's Blood Does Not Run Dry: Algerian Stories* (New York: Seven Stories, 2006).
———. *La Soif*. Paris: René Julliard, 1957. Translated by Frances Frenaye as *The Mischief* (New York: Simon & Schuster, 1958).
———. *Vaste est la prison*. Paris: Albin Michel, 1995. Translated by Betsy Wing as *So Vast the Prison* (New York: Seven Stories, 2001).
———. *Ces voix qui m'assiègent: en marge de ma francophonie*. Paris: Albin Michel, 1999.
Djebar, Assia, dir. *La Nouba des femmes du Mont-Chenoua*. Women Make Movies, 1977.
———. *La Zerda et les chants de l'oubli*. Algeria: Radiodiffusion Télévision Algérienne (RTA), 1982.
Dobie, Madeleine. "Assia Djebar: Writing between Land and Language." *PMLA* 131, no. 1 (2016): 128–33.
Donadey, Anne. "The Multilingual Strategies of Postcolonial Literature: Assia Djebar's Algerian Palimpsest." *World Literature Today* 7, no. 1 (2000): 27–36.
———. *Recasting Postcolonialism: Women Writing between Worlds*. Portsmouth: Heinemann, 2001.
———. "Rekindling the Vividness of the Past: Assia Djebar's Films and Fiction." *World Literature Today* 70, no. 4 (1996): 885–92.
Donadey, Anne, ed. *Approaches to Teaching the Works of Assia Djebar*. New York: Modern Language Association of America, 2017.
Du Bois, W. E. B. *The Souls of Black Folk*. Chicago: A. C. McClug, 1903.
Ducrot, Oswald, and Jean-Marie Schaeffer. *Nouveau Dictionnaire encyclopédique des sciences du langage*. Paris: Seuil, 1995.
Dutt, Toru. *Ancient Ballads and Legends of Hindustan*. London: Kegan Paul, Trench, 1885.
———. *Bianca, or The Young Spanish Maiden*. New Delhi: Prachi Prakashan, 2001.
———. *Le Journal de Mlle d'Arvers*. Paris: Didier, 1879. Translated by N. Kamala as *The Diary of Mademoiselle D'Arvers* (New Delhi: Penguin, 2005).
———. *A Sheaf Gleaned in French Fields*. Bhowanipore: M. Bose, 1876.
———. *Toru Dutt: Collected Prose and Poetry*. Edited by Chandani Lokugé. New Delhi: Oxford University Press, 2006.

Dwivedi, A. N. *Toru Dutt: A Literary Profile*. New Delhi: BR, 1998.
Edwards, Natalie. *Multilingual Life Writing by French and Francophone Women: Translingual Selves*. New York: Routledge, 2019.
elhariry, yasser. *Pacific Invasions: Arabic, Translation, and the Postfrancophone Lyric*. Liverpool: Liverpool University Press, 2017.
Even-Zohar, Itamar. "The Position of Translated Literature within the Literary Polysystem." *Poetics Today* 11, no. 1 (Spring 1990): 45–51.
Fanon, Frantz. *Les Damnés de la terre*. Paris: Maspero, 1961.
———. *Écrits sur l'aliénation et la liberté*. Edited by Jean Khalfa and Robert James Craig Young. Paris: La Découverte, 2015. Translated by Steven Corcoran as *Alienation and Freedom* (New York: Bloomsbury, 2018).
———. *Peau noire, masques blancs*. Paris: Seuil, 1952. Translated by Richard Philox as *Black Skin, White Masks* (New York: Grove, 2008).
———. *Oeuvres: L'An V de la révolution algérienne*. With an introduction by Achille Mbembe. Paris: La Découverte, 2011. Translated by Haakon Chevalier as *A Dying Colonialism* (New York: Grove, 1965).
———. *Oeuvres: Peau noire, masques blancs / L'An V de la révolution algérienne / Les Damnés de la terre / Pour la révolution africaine*. With an introduction by Achille Mbembe. Paris: La Découverte, 2011.
———. *Oeuvres: Pour la révolution africaine*. With an introduction by Achille Mbembe. Paris: La Découverte, 2011. Translated by Haakon Chevalier as *Toward the African Revolution* (New York: Grove, 1967).
Flax, Jane. "Multiples: On the Contemporary Politics of Subjectivity." *Human Studies, Postmodernity, and the Question of the Other* 16, nos. 1–2 (1993): 33–49.
———. "What Is the Subject? Review Essay on Psychoanalysis and Feminism in Postcolonial Time." *Signs* 29, no. 3 (Spring 2004): 905–23.
Forster, E. M. *A Passage to India*. London: E. Arnold, 1978.
Fuhrmann, Malte. *Port Cities of the Eastern Mediterranean: Urban Culture in the Late Ottoman Empire*. Cambridge: Cambridge University Press, 2020.
Gabrieli, F. "adab." In *Encyclopedia of Islam*, vol. 1, 175–76. Leiden: Brill, 1960.
Gaha, Kamal. "al-tarjama fi al-'asr al'hadith: tarikhiha wa qadayaha." In *al-tarjama wa nadhariyatiha: Théories de la traduction*. Carthage: Beït al-Hikma, 1989.
Gallagher, Mary. *World Writing: Poetics, Ethics, Globalization*. Toronto: University of Toronto Press, 2008.
Gates, Henry Louis, Jr. "Critical Fanonism." *Critical Inquiry* 17, no. 3 (Spring 1991): 457–70.
Gauvin, Lise. "Assia au pays du langage." In *Assia Djebar, nomade entre les murs . . . pour une poétique transfrontalière*, edited by Mireille Calle-Gruber, 219–29. Paris: Maisonneuve & Larose, 2005.

———. *Écrire, pour qui? l'écrivain francophone et ses publics.* Paris: Karthala, 2007.

———. *L'Écrivain francophone à la croisée des langues.* Paris: Karthala, 1997.

———. *La Fabrique de la langue: de Françoise Rabelais à Réjean Ducharme.* Paris: Seuil, 2004.

———. *Le Roman comme atelier, la scène de l'écriture dans les romans francophones contemporains.* Paris: Karthala, 2019.

———. "Statut de la parole et traversée des langues chez Assia Djebar." *Carnets* 7 (2016): https.//doi.org/10.4000/carnets.908.

———. "La surconscience linguistique de l'écrivain francophone: Positions des revues québécoises." *Revue de L'Institut de Sociologie* 62 (1990–91): 83–101.

Gauvin, Lise, and Rainier Grutman. "Langues et littératures: éléments de bibliographie." *Littérature*, no. 101, (1996): 88–125.

———. "Penser/parler la langue ou des mille manières de décrire/d'écrire le réel." In *Langues choisies, langues sauvées: poétiques de la résistance*, edited by Christine Meyer and Paula Prescod, 37–58. Würzburg: Königshausen & Neumann, 2018.

Glissant, Edouard. *La Cohée du Lamentin, Poétique 5.* Paris: Gallimard, 2005.

———. *Le Discours antillais.* Paris: Gallimard, 1997.

———. *L'Intention poétique, Poétique 2.* Paris: Seuil, 1969.

———. *L'Imaginaire des langues: entretiens avec Lise Gauvin, 1991–2009.* Paris: Gallimard, 2010.

———. *Introduction à une poétique du divers.* Paris: Gallimard, 1996.

———. *Poétique de la relation, Poétique 3.* Paris: Gallimard, 1990. Translated by Betsy Wing as *Poetics of Relation* (Ann Arbor: University of Michigan Press, 1997).

———. *Soleil de la conscience, Poétique 1.* Paris: Falaize, 1956.

———. *Traité du tout-monde, Poétique 4.* Paris: Gallimard, 1997.

Godden, Rumer. *The River.* Boston: Little, Brown, 1946.

Gosse, Edmund. "Introductory Memoir." In *Toru Dutt's Ancient Ballads and Legends of Hindustan*, 7–27. London: Kegan Paul, Trench, 1885.

Gunew, Sneja. "Estrangement as Pedagogy: The Cosmopolitan Vernacular." In *After Cosmopolitanism*, edited by Rosi Braidotti, Patrick Hanafin, and Bolette Blaagaard, 132–48. Oxon: Routledge, 2013.

Gunew, Sneja, and Jan Mahyuddin, eds. *Beyond the Echo: Multicultural Women's Writing.* Saint Lucia: University of Queensland Press, 1988.

Hanley, Will. "Grieving Cosmopolitanism in Middle East Studies." *History Compass* 6, no. 5 (2008): 1346–67.

———. "When Did Egyptians Stop Being Ottomans? An Imperial Citizenship Case Study." In *Multilevel Citizenship*, edited by Willem Maas, 89–109. Pennsylvania: University of Pennsylvania Press, 2013.

Hannerz, Ulf. "The World in Creolization." *Africa: Journal of the International African Institute* 57, no. 4 (1987): 546–59.

Harrison, Nicholas. *Our Civilizing Mission: The Lessons of Colonial Education*. Liverpool: Liverpool University Press, 2019.

Hawkins, Peter. *The Other Hybrid Archipelago*. Lanham, MD: Lexington, 2007.

Hiddleston, Jane, and Wen-chin Ouyang, eds. *Multilingual Literature as World Literature*. London: Bloomsbury, 2021.

Hume, David. *An Enquiry Concerning Human Understanding*. Oxford: Oxford University Press, 1999.

Ilbert, Robert and Ilios Yannakakis. *Alexandrie 1860–1960, un modèle éphémère de convivialité: communauté et identité cosmopolite*. Paris: Editions Autrement, 1992.

Irigaray, Luce. *Speculum de l'autre femme*. Paris: Éditions de Minuit, 1974. Translated by Gillian Gill as *Speculum of the Other Woman*. Ithaca, NY: Cornell University Press, 1985.

Jauze, Jean-Michel. "La pluriethnicité dans les villes mauriciennes." *Les Cahiers d'Outre-Mer. Revue de géographie de Bordeaux* 225 (January–March 2004): 7–32.

Jean-François, Emmanuel Bruno. *Poétiques de la violence et récits francophones contemporains*. Leiden: Brill Rodopi, 2017.

Joundi, Darina al. *Prisonnière du Levant: la vie méconnue de May Ziadé*. Paris: Bernard Grasset, 2017.

Kant, Immanuel. *Critique of Judgment, Including the First Introduction*. Translated with an introduction by Werner S. Pluhar. Indianapolis: Hackett, 1987.

Kashani-Sabet, Firoozeh. "The Swinging Pendulum: Linguistic Controversy in Post-Colonial Algeria." *Middle Eastern Studies* 32, no. 4 (October 1996): 264–80.

Keller, Richard. *Colonial Madness: Psychiatry in French North Africa*. Chicago: University of Chicago Press, 2007.

Kellman, Steven G. *Switching Languages: Translingual Writers Reflect on Their Craft*. Lincoln: University of Nebraska Press, 2003.

———. *The Translingual Imagination*. Lincoln: University of Nebraska Press, 2000.

Kellman, Steven G., and Natachsa Lvovich, eds. *The Routledge Handbook of Literary Translingualism*. Abingdon: Routledge, 2022.

Khadda, Naget. *Mohammed Dib: cette intempestive voix recluse*. Aix-en-Provence: Édisud, 2003.

Khaldi, Boutheina. *Egypt Awakening in the Early Twentieth Century: Mayy Ziyadah's Intellectual Circles*. New York: Palgrave Macmillan, 2012.

Khanna, Ranjana. *Algeria Cuts: Women and Representation, 1830 to the Present*. Stanford, CA: Stanford University Press, 2008.

Khannous, Touria. "The Subaltern Speaks: Assia Djebar's *La Nouba*." *Film Criticism* 26, no. 2 (2001): 41–61.

Khatibi, Abdelkebir. *Amour bilingue*. Saint-Clément-de-la-Rivière: Fata Morgana, 1983. Translated by Richard Howard as *Love in Two Languages* (Minneapolis: University of Minnesota, 1990).

———. *La Blessure du nom propre*. Paris: Denoël, 1974.

———. *La Langue de l'autre*. Tunis: Les mains secrètes, 1999.

———. *Maghreb pluriel*. Paris: Denoël, 1983. Translated by P. Burcu Yalim as *Plural Maghreb: Writings on Postcolonialism* (New York: Bloomsbury, 2019).

———. *La Mémoire tatouée: autobiografie d'un décolonisé*. Paris: Denoël, 1971.

———. *Surimpositions d'identité*. In *Oeuvres de Abdelkébir Khatibi, Essais 3*. Paris: La Différence, 2008.

Khoury, Raif Georges. *Mayy Ziyada (1886–1941) entre la tradition et la modernité: ou le renouvellement des perspectives culturelles et sociales dans son œuvre, à l'image de l'Europe*. Neckarhausen: deux mondes, 2003.

Kistnareddy, Ashwiny O. "Représenter l'altérité: le corps grotesque dans l'œuvre Romanesque d'Ananda Devi." In *Écritures mauriciennes au féminin: penser l'altérité*, edited by Véronique Bragard and Srilata Ravi, 179–96. Paris: l'Harmattan, 2011.

Kouchkar Ferchouli, Fatma-Zohra. "Emergence du parler féminin arabe dans la langue française dans le roman d'Assia Djebar: *L'Amour, la fantasia*." In *Actes du colloque langues—cultures et traduction*, edited by Meriem Bedjaoui, 101–16. Alger: El-hikma, 2001.

Kristeva, Julia. *Crisis of the European Subject*. Translated by Susan Fairfield with an introduction by Samir Dayal. New York: Other Press, 2000.

Kumar, Nita, ed. *Women as Subject: South Asian Histories*. Charlottesville: University of Virginia Press, 1994.

Kymlicka, Will. *Multicultural Citizenship: A Liberal Theory of Minority Rights*. Oxford: Clarendon, 1995.

Laghouati, Sofiane. "Assia Djebar: Quand l'écriture est une route à ouvrir, un territoire entre les langues . . . : Prolégomènes pour une 'diglossie littéraire.'" In *Assia Djebar: entre littérature et transmission*, edited by Wolfgang Asholt, Mireille Calle-Gruber, and Dominique Combe, 97–118. Paris: Presses Sorbonne Nouvelle, 2010.

Laliótou, Ioánna. *Transatlantic Subjects: Acts of Migration and Cultures of Transnationalism between Greece and America*. Chicago: University of Chicago Press, 2004.

Lamartine, Alphonse de. *Voyage en Orient*. Paris: C. Gosselin, 1841.

Laredj, Waciny. *May Ziade: le vrai roman d'une femme atypique*. Casablanca: Centre culturel du livre, 2020.

Lionnet, Françoise. *Autobiographical Voices: Race, Gender, Self-Portraiture.* Ithaca, NY: Cornell University Press, 1989.

——. "Ces voix au fil de soi(e): le détour du poétique." *L'Esprit créateur* 4, no. 48 (2008): 104–16.

——. "Créolité in the Indian Ocean: Two Models of Cultural Diversity." *Yale French Studies* 82, no. 1 (1993): 101–12.

——. *Écritures féminines et dialogues critiques: subjectivité, genre et ironie.* Trou d'Eau Douce: l'Atelier d'écriture, 2012.

——. "Frantz Fanon (1925–61)." In *The Columbia History of Twentieth-Century French Thought*, edited by Lawrence D. Kritzman, 518–20. New York: Columbia University Press, 2006.

——. "'Logiques métisses': Cultural Appropriation and Postcolonial Representations." *Teaching Postcolonial and Commonwealth Literature* (October 1992–February 1993): 100–120.

——. *Postcolonial Representations: Women, Literature, Identity.* Ithaca, NY: Cornell University Press, 1995.

——. *Le Su et l'incertain: cosmopolitique créole de l'Océan Indien.* Trou d'Eau Douce: l'Atelier d'écriture, 2012.

Lionnet, Françoise, and Shu-mei Shih, eds. *The Creolization of Theory.* Durham, NC: Duke University Press, 2011.

——. *Minor Transnationalism.* Durham, NC: Duke University Press, 2005.

Lootens, Tricia. "Bengal, Britain, France: The Locations and Translations of Toru Dutt." *Victorian Literature and Culture* 34, no. 2 (2006): 573–90.

Maalouf, Amin. *Les Identités meurtrières.* Paris: Grasset, 1998. Translated by Barbara Bray as *In the Name of Identity: Violence and the Need to Belong* (New York: Penguin, 2003).

MacLean, Derryl N., and Sikeena Karmali Ahmed, eds. *Cosmopolitanisms in Muslim Contexts: Perspectives from the Past.* Edinburgh: Edinburgh University Press, 2012.

Malabou, Catherine. *L'Avenir de Hegel.* Paris: Vrin, 1996.

——. *Changer de différence: le féminin et la question philosophique.* Paris: Galilée, 2009.

——. "Plasticity and Elasticity in Freud's *Beyond the Pleasure Principle*." *Diacritics* 37, no. 4 (Winter 2007): 78–86.

Malcomson, Scott L. "The Varieties of Cosmopolitan Experience." In *Cosmopolitics: Thinking and Feeling beyond the Nation*, edited by Pheng Cheah and Bruce Robbins, 233–45. Minneapolis: University of Minnesota Press, 1998.

Mansour, Gerda. *Multilingualism and Nation Building.* Clevedon: Multilingual Matters, 1993.

Marcuse, Herbert. *The Aesthetic Dimension: Toward a Critique of Marxist Aesthetics.* Boston: Beacon, 1978.

Masson, Gustave. *La Lyre française.* London: Macmillan, 1898.

McCarthy, Thomas. "On Reconciling Cosmopolitan Unity and National Diversity." *Public Culture* 11, no. 1 (1999): 175–208.

Memmi, Albert. *Portrait du colonisé, précédé du Portrait du colonisateur.* Paris: Gallimard, 1985. Originally published in 1957. Translated by Howard Greenfeld as *The Colonizer and the Colonized.* New York: Orion Press, 1965.

Meyer, Christine, and Paula Prescod, eds. *Langues choisies, langues sauvées: poétiques de la résistance.* Würzburg: Königshausen & Neumann, 2018.

Michel, Raymond. "Pour une lecture polyphonique. Assia Djebar: langage tangage, langage tatouage." *Pratiques: linguistique, littérature, didactique,* nos. 123–24 (2004): 75–111.

Mignolo, Walter D. "The Many Faces of Cosmo-polis: Border Thinking and Critical Cosmopolitanism." *Public Culture* 12, no. 3 (2000): 721–48.

———. *The Politics of Decolonial Investigations.* Durham, NC: Duke University Press, 2021.

Miyoshi, Masao. "A Borderless World? From Colonialism to Transnationalism and the Decline of the Nation-State." *Critical Inquiry* 19, no. 4 (1993): 726–51.

Mongo-Mboussa, Boniface. "Contre le culte de la différence: entretien de Boniface Mongo-Mboussa avec Ananda Devi." *Africultures,* January 31, 2001. https://africultures.com/contre-le-culte-de-la-difference-1734/.

Mortimer, Mildred. *Assia Djebar.* Philadelphia: CELFAN Monographs, 1988.

———. *Women Fight, Women Write.* Charlottesville: University of Virginia Press, 2018.

Nancy, Jean-Luc. *Être singulier pluriel.* Paris: Galilée, 1996. Translated by Robert D. Richardson as *Being Singular Plural* (Stanford, CA: Stanford University Press, 2000).

Ngugi wa Thiong'o. *Moving the Centre: The Struggle for Cultural Freedoms.* Oxford: James Currey, 1993.

Nussbaum, Martha. *The Cosmopolitan Tradition: A Noble but Flawed Ideal.* Cambridge, MA: Belknap Press of Harvard University Press, 2019.

Ochs, Peter. *Religion without Violence: The Philosophy and Practice of Scriptural Reasoning.* Eugene, OR: Cascade Books, 2019.

———. "Reparative Reasoning: From Peirce's Pragmatism to Augustine's Scriptural Semiotic." *Modern Theology* 25, no. 2 (April 2009): 187–215.

O'Flaherty, Ailbhe. "Every Woman Is an Island? The Island as an Embodiment of Female Alterity in Mauritian Women's Writing." In *Écritures mauriciennes au féminin: penser l'altérité,* edited by Véronique Bragard and Srilata Ravi, 43–59. Paris: l'Harmattan, 2011.

Ong, Aihwa. *Flexible Citizenship: The Cultural Logics of Transnationality*. Durham, NC: Duke University Press, 1999.

Orlando, Valérie. *The Algerian New Novel: The Poetics of a Modern Nation, 1950–1979*. Charlottesville: University of Virginia Press, 2017.

———. *Nomadic Voices of Exile: Feminine Identity in Francophone Literature of the Maghreb*. Athens: Ohio University Press, 1999.

Ortiz, Fernando. *Contrapunteo cubano del tabaco y el azúcar: advertencia de sus contrastes agrarios, económicos, hisóricos y sociales, su etnografía y su transculturación*. La Habana: Jesús Montero, 1940. Translated by Jacques-François Bonaldi as *Controverse cubaine entre le tabac et le sucre: leurs contrastes agraires, économiques, historiques et sociaux, leur ethnographie et leur transculturation* (Montréal: Mémoire d'Encrier, 2011).

Parry, Benita. "The Postcolonial: Conceptual Category or Chimera?" *Yearbook of English Studies* 27 (1997): 3–21.

Pearce, Michael. *The Routledge Dictionary of English Language Studies*. New York: Routledge, 2007.

Peled, Mattityahu. "Creative Translation: Towards the Study of Arabic Translations of Western Literature since the Nineteenth Century." *Journal of Arabic Literature* 10 (1979): 128–50.

Penas Ibáñez, Beatriz, and M. Carmen López Sáenz, eds. *Interculturalism: Between Identity and Diversity*. Bern: Peter Lang, 2006.

Penman, Leigh. *The Lost History of Cosmopolitanism*. New York: Bloomsbury, 2021.

Piégay-Gros, Nathalie, ed. *Le Lecteur*. Paris: Flammarion, 2002.

Pireddu, Nicoletta, ed. *Reframing Critical, Literary, and Cultural Theories: Thought on the Edge*. Cham: Palgrave Macmillan, 2018.

Pontecorvo, Gillo, dir. *La Bataille d'Alger*. Paris: Créon Music, [1965] 2003.

Prabhu, Anjali. *Hybridity: Limits, Transformations, Prospects*. Albany: State University of New York Press, 2007.

Pratt, Mary Louise. *Imperial Eyes: Travel Writing and Transculturation*. New York: Routledge, 1992.

———. "Planetarity." In *Intercultural Dialogue: Mary Louise Pratt, Ron G. Manley, Susan Bassnett*, 10–31. London: British Council, 2004.

———. *Toward a Speech Act Theory of Literary Discourse*. Bloomington: Indiana University Press, 1977.

Prescott, William Hickling. *History of the Conquest of Mexico*. New York: Modern Library, 1936.

Rahal, Malika. *Algérie 1962: une histoire populaire*. Paris: La Découverte, 2022.

Rahim, Ahmed H. al-. "Translation as Contemporary Qur'anic Exegesis: Ahmed Ali and Muslim Modernism in India." In *The Two-Sided Canvas: Perspectives* on *Ahmed Ali*, edited by Mehr Afshan Farooqi, 136–50. New Delhi: Oxford University Press, 2013.

Rancière, Jacques. *Malaise dans l'esthétique*. Paris: Galilée, 2004. Translated by Gabriel Rockhill as *The Politics of Aesthetics* (New York: Continuum, 2004).

Rama, Angel. *Transculturación narrativa en América Latina*. México: Siglo veintiuno, 1987.

Ramazani, Jahan. *A Transnational Poetics*. Chicago: University of Chicago Press, 2009.

Ravi, Srilata. *The Rainbow Colors: Literary Ethno-topographies of Mauritius*. Lanham, MD: Lexington Books, 2007.

Ray, Satyajit, dir. *Mahanagar* Vernon: Ciné Vidéo film [1963] 1999.

———. *Jalsaghar / Le Salon de musique*. Paris: Films sans frontières, [1958] 2001.

Renoir, Jean, dir. *Le Fleuve*. Paris: Carlotta films, [1951] 2012.

Reynaud-Paligot, Carole. *L'École aux colonies: entre mission civilisatrice et racialisation, 1816–1940*. Paris: Champ Vallon, 2020.

Rice, Alison. "Algerrance: envois et envols." In *Assia Djebar, nomade entre les murs . . . pour une poétique transfrontalière*, edited by Mireille Calle-Gruber, 247–52. Paris: Maisonneuve & Larose, 2005.

Ringrose, Priscilla. *Assia Djebar: In Dialogue with Feminisms*. New York: Rodopi, 2006.

Said, Edward. *Culture and Imperialism*. New York: Knopf, 1993.

Sartre, Jean-Paul. *Les Mots*. Paris: Gallimard, 1964.

Schiller, Friedrich. *On the Aesthetic Education of Man*. Translated by Reginald Snell. Mineola: Dover, 2004.

Shafik, Viola. *Arab Cinema: History and Cultural Identity*. Cairo: American University in Cairo Press, 1998.

Sharpe, Mani. "Representations of Space in Assia Djebar's *La Nouba des femmes du Mont Chenoua*." *Studies in French Cinema* 13, no. 3 (2013): 215–25.

Sheehi, Stephen. *Foundations of Modern Arab Identity*. Gainesville: University Press of Florida, 2004.

Singerman, Diane and Paul Amar, eds. *Cairo Cosmopolitan: Politics, Culture, and Urban Space in the New Globalized Middle East*. Cairo: American University of Cairo Press, 2006.

Smith, Anthony D. *The Cultural Foundations of Nations: Hierarchy, Covenant, and Republic*. Oxford: Blackwell, 2007.

Sommer, Doris. *Bilingual Aesthetics: A New Sentimental Education*. Durham, NC: Duke University Press, 2004.

Souriau, Étienne. *Vocabulaire d'esthétique*. Paris: Presses Universitaires de France, 1990.

Souza de, Eunice, and Lindsay Pereira, eds. *Women's Voices: Selections from Nineteenth- and Early Twentieth-Century Indian Writing in English*. Oxford: Oxford University Press, 2002.
Spivak, Gayatri. "Can the Subaltern Speak?" In *Marxism and the Interpretation of Culture*, edited by Cary Nelson and Lawrence Grossberg, 271–313. Urbana: University of Illinois Press, 1988.
Starr, Deborah A. *Remembering Cosmopolitan Egypt: Literature, Culture, and Empire*. New York: Routledge, 2009.
Tageldin, Shaden M. "One Comparative Literature? Birth of a Discipline in French-Egyptian Translation, 1810–1834." *Comparative Literature Studies* 47, no. 4 (2010): 417–45.
Tagore, Rabindranath. *Towards Universal Man*. New York: Asia, 1961.
———. *The Home and the World*. London: Penguin, 1985.
Tamalet-Talbayev, Edwige. *The Transcontinental Maghreb*. New York: Fordham University Press, 2017.
Tamzali, Wassyla. *Une femme en colère: lettre d'Alger aux Européens désabusés*. Paris: Gallimard, 2009.
Thiel, Veronika. *Assia Djebar: la polyphonie comme principe générateur de ses textes*. Vienna: Praesens Edition, 2005.
Tlatli, Soraya. "L'ambivalence linguistique dans la littérature maghébine d'expression française." *French Review* 72, no. 2 (1998): 297–307.
Tobie, Nathan. *La Folie des autres: Traité d'ethnopsychiatrie clinique*. Paris: Dunod, 1986.
Torabully, Khal. "Coolitude." *Notre librairie* 128 (1996): 59–71.
———. "Créolité, coolitude, créolisation: les imaginaires de la relation." Afrik. Accessed November 23, 2022. http://www.afrik.com/article10880.html.
Valéry, Paul. *Rhumbs: Notes et autres*. Paris: Le Divan, 1926.
Venuti, Lawrence. "Translation and National Identities." In *Nation, Language, and the Ethics of Translation*, edited by Sandra Bermann and Michael Wood, 177–202. Princeton, NJ: Princeton University Press, 2005.
Westphal, Bertrand. *La Géocritique: Réel, fiction, espace*. Paris: Éditions de Minuit, 2007.
White, Kenneth. *Petite suite géopoétique*. Mareuil-sur-Mauldre: Qui vive, 1981.
Yerasimos, Stéphane. "Cosmopolitanism: Assumed Alienation." In *Cosmopolitanism, Identity, and Authenticity in the Middle East*, edited by Roel Meijet, 35–39. Richmond: Curzon, 1999.
Zaydan, Jurgi. *tarikh al-tamaddun al-islami*. al qahira: Dar al-hilal, 1958.
Ziegler, Antje. "*Al-Harakat Baraka!* The Late Rediscovery of Mayy Ziyadah's Works." *Die Welt des Islams* 39, no. 1 (1999): 103–15.

Ziyadah, Mayy. *al-a'mal al-kamilat*, vol. 1. Beyrout: muassassat nawfal, 1982.

——. *bayna al-jazr wa al-madd*. In *al-a'mal al-kamilat*, edited by Salma al-Haffar Kuzbari. Beyrout: muassassat nawfal, 1982.

——. "fadhlu al adab." *kalimaat wa isaraat*. In *al-a'mal al-kamilat*, vol. 2, edited by Salma al-Haffar Kuzbari, 76–80. Beyrout: muassassat nawfal, 1982.

——. *ibtissamat wa dumu'*. Edited by j. 'abd allah. Beyrout: dar al-'ilm lil-malayin, 1999.

——. *Quelques fleurs de rêve: textes choisis*. Le Mans: Les Centres du monde édition, 2020.

——. "tatawur al-lughat al-'arabiya." In *nussus kharij al-majmou'a, i'dad*, edited by antun al-qawwal, 234–56. Beyrout: dar amwaj, 1993.

Zimra, Clarisse. "Mapping Memory: Architectural Metaphors in Djebar's Unfinished Quartet." *L'Esprit créateur* 43, no. 1 (2003): 58–68.

Žižek, Slavoj. "A Leftist Plea for 'Eurocentrism.'" *Critical Inquiry* 24, no. 4 (1998): 988–1009.

Zubaida, Sami. "Cosmopolitanism and the Middle East." In *Cosmopolitanism, Identity, and Authenticity in the Middle East*, edited by Roel Meijet, 15–33. Richmond: Curzon, 1999.

INDEX

Abbas, Ferhat, 97
Abbasid Caliphate, 70
'Abduh, Mohamed, 68
Ackermann, Louise Victorine, 40
aesthetics, 10, 13, 16–17, 19–20, 30, 31, 143, 147, 149–50, 151; circulation of, 37; in Devi, 132; in Djebar, 94, 104, 116; in Dutt, 41, 48–49, 55, 59, 63; multilingual, 5, 9, 12, 32; of plurality, 35; raga, 59; sounds of colonial language, 34; in Ziyadah, 72, 73
affect, 23, 53, 87, 92, 149–50
agency, 2, 6, 8, 13, 64, 147
Agrawal, Krishna Avtar, 58
Alexandria, 72, 173–74n30
Algeria, 1–2, 11, 30, 73, 98–99, 112, 116, 122, 145; Arabization in, 93; in Djebar, 85, 88, 89, 114; in Fanon, 20, 138–39; language in, 93, 96–97, 99, 103, 110, 122, 164–65n35; literature of, 95; nationalism, 97
Algerian (culture), 97
Algerian (people), 88; readers, 99; women, 11, 45, 87, 88, 96, 139, 153; writers, 2, 11, 45, 87, 88. *See also* Djebar, Assia
Algerian Arabic. See *darija*
Algerian Civil War, 112–13, 114
Algerian War, 88, 109, 112, 114, 161n24
Algiers, 11, 12, 145, 153, 155, 169n36; in Devi, 137, 139; in Djebar, 87, 88, 93, 104, 105–8, 109–10, 111–12, 114
alienation, 16, 20–22, 23–25, 27, 187n14
alterity, 16

Amazigh, 30, 93, 94, 95, 161n2, 181n37
Andalusian music, 87, 89, 93
Annunzio, D', Gabriele, 77
Antoura, 72
Appadurai, Arjun, 48
Appanah, Nathacha, 2, 118
Appiah, Kwame Anthony, 128, 130
Apter, Emily, 123–24, 171n16
Arabic: classical (see *fusha*); colloquial (see *darija*)
architecture, 11, 12, 74, 145, 148, 149, 156, 162n7, 173–74n30; of Calcutta, 63; in Djebar, 105, 109, 114–16; in Port Louis, 132. *See also* cityscape; city-walking
Aristotle, 72
assimilation, 21, 23, 48, 74
Assonne, Sydley Richard, 2
Augustine of Hippo, Saint: *Confessions*, 15, 91
aurality, 35, 89, 91, 95–95
Aurobindo (Sri), 44–45
Averroes. *See* Ibn Rushd

Bader, Clarisse, 43, 45
Badiou, Alain: *Theory of the Subject*, 15
Bartas (Guillaume de Saluste du), 40
Baudelaire, Charles, 40, 90, 113, 123, 140, 149, 153, 157, 165n42, 171n18, 184n54. *See also* Djebar, Assia
Baugmaree, 46
beauty, 31, 58, 90, 119, 120, 121, 131
Beirut, 69, 84, 173n30
Bengal, 6, 30, 37, 39, 42, 55, 59–60, 64, 65, 154

Bengali (language), 7, 11, 35, 39, 41, 44–45, 47, 143, 155, 158; in Dutt, 57–59
Bengali Renaissance, 30, 35, 38, 44–47, 69–70, 164–65n35
Bengal Sea, 10
Bengla Magazine, 41
Benhabib, Seyla, 64, 170
Benjamin, Walter, 80, 175n42, 184n54
Béranger, Pierre-Jean de, 50
Berber, 86, 91–92, 96
Bergner, Gwen, 24, 25, 29
Berman, Antoine, 81
Bertacco, Simona, 5
Bet Saïda, 72
Bhabha, Homi, 17, 19, 26, 29, 34, 153; *The Location of Culture*, 26–29, 31; Third Space, 18–19, 26–28, 31, 119, 153. *See also* oppositionality; polarity; schizophrenia, postcolonial; splitting
Bible, the, 12, 75
bi-language, 6, 9, 33–34, 35, 95, 117
Bint al-Husayn, Sukayna, 76
Blida, 87, 139
Bourdic-Viot, Henriette, 40
Braidotti, Rosi, 9
Brontë, Charlotte, 43, 153, 154
Bürger, Gottfried August, 51, 54
Bustani, Butrus al, 68
Bustani, Sulayman al, 2
Buttoo, 42
Byron, George Gordon, Lord, 42, 54, 72–73, 74, 149, 153, 172n23; *Childe Harold*, 72–73. *See also* Romanticism

Cairo, 10, 11, 12, 145, 155; in Ziyadah, 2, 66, 68, 69, 71, 72, 73, 74–75, 80–81, 84, 143. *See also* Egypt
Calcutta, 10, 11, 12, 137, 140, 153, 155; in Dutt, 38, 39, 43, 46, 50, 51, 58, 60, 62–64
Calidasa. *See* Kalidasa
Calvet, Louis-Jean, 3
cartography, 33, 51, 72–73, 135
Cascardi, Anthony: *The Subject of Modernity*, 18, 151
Catholicism, 121, 123, 125, 187n9
Césarée. *See* Cherchell
Chateaubriand, François René de, 40
Chatterjee, Bankim Chandra, 2, 38, 55; *Anandamath*, 45; *Rajmohan's Wife*, 44–45, 169n27
Chaudhuri, Amit, 38, 62, 69–70
Chenoua, 86, 87, 93, 104
Cherchell, 87, 92, 94, 104, 105, 110
Cherki, Alice, 2, 178n14
childhood, 11, 24, 25, 86–87, 91, 92, 100, 104, 107, 109–11, 125, 134
Choukri, Mohammed, 83
Christianity, 39, 43, 45, 47, 59, 70, 75, 79, 110, 143
cityscape, 11–12, 13, 144–45, 148, 149, 155–56; Algiers, 107, 111; in Devi, 132; in Djebar, 103, 108, 111, 114–16; in the Maghreb, 108. *See also* architecture; city-walking
city-walking, 10, 104, 105–6, 107–9, 111–12, 134, 137–38, 139–40. *See also* architecture; cityscape
class, social, 34, 45, 56, 63, 69, 87, 93, 101, 134, 139, 151, 169
code-switching, 177n4
Copia, Isis. *See* Ziyadah, Mayy
Corneille, Pierre, 51, 54
cosmopolitanism, 3, 10, 20, 30, 113, 143–45, 146, 148–49, 152, 155, 173–74n30; in Devi, 138; in Djebar, 104; in Dutt, 37–38, 39, 45, 47–48, 56, 60, 62–65; history of, 12–13; in Ziyadah, 66, 67–68, 69–70, 71, 74, 76, 79, 80–82, 83–84, 143, 173n30
Creole (culture), 129–30
Creole (language), 7, 11, 36, 64, 93, 117–18, 121–23, 124, 128–30, 131, 143, 144
Creole (people), 118–19, 120, 121, 123, 125, 127, 128–29

Creoleness, 117–20, 121, 122, 123, 125, 127–30, 145, 149
creolization, 12, 29–31, 62, 127, 145, 149, 151–52, 153, 155–57; in Devi, 117–19, 120, 127, 127–31, 132, 138, 139–40; in Djebar, 116; in Dutt, 42, 48, 58–62, 63, 64; process of, 33; in Ziyadah, 73, 84

darija, 7, 11, 30, 68, 75–76, 82, 86, 87, 91–96, 97, 99–101, 102–3, 122, 144
Darmesteter, James, 45, 52; *Essais de littérature anglaise*, 42, 167n9
decolonization, 1, 4–5, 7, 12–13, 25, 155, 156; in cities, 136, 137; in Devi, 138, 140–41; in Djebar, 95; in Mauritius, 129
Deleuze, Gilles, 59, 176n47
Derozio, Henry Louis Vivian, 2
Derrida, Jacques, 9; *Monolingualism of the Other*, 67–68
Desbordes-Valmore, Marceline, 40, 52–53, 54
Descartes, René, 15
Deschamps, Antoni, 50
Deschamps, Emile, 50
Devi, Ananda, 2, 10, 19, 29, 30, 118–19, 138–39, 142, 147, 148, 151, 152, 153, 157; animality in, 120; background, 119, 144; "La cathédrale," 119; *Ceux du large / Afloat*, 123; city in, 132–35, 136–38, 139–41; Creoleness in, 119, 120, 125, 127–29, 130–31; *Eve out of Her Ruins*, 29, 118, 120, 121, 122–23, 137, 138; *Les Hommes qui me parlent*, 132; homosexuality in, 120, 121, 125–26, 127–28, 131; Indian descent of, 118, 136; *Indian Tango*, 119, 133–34, 136, 137, 138, 139–40; *Moi, l'interdite*, 132–33, 137; multilingualism, 118, 119; *Rue la poudrière*, 132–33; *Le Sari vert*, 119, 120, 125–27, 132; segregation, 128; *Solstices*, 119; *La Vie de Joséphin le fou*, 132, 137. *See also* Mauritius

Dhruva, 42
dia-language, 34–36, 88, 94–95, 96, 101, 115, 142, 152, 156, 157
Dib, Mohammed, 90, 165n39, 177n8
didascaly, linguistic, 98
diglossia, 90, 178
dischronia, 73
Djebar, Assia, 2, 10, 19, 29, 142–43, 144, 147, 148, 151, 152–53, 154; Algerian identity of, 86; *Les Alouettes naïves*, 104, 108, 110; aural transmission, 94–95; background, 85; on Baudelaire, 90, 123–24, 156; *Ces voix qui m'assiègent: en marge de ma francophonie*, 85, 86, 89, 96; and cinema, 89, 94; cities in, 103–4, 105–15; *La Disparition de la langue française*, 113; education, 87–88; *Les Enfants du nouveau monde*, 104, 106; family, 88, 93; *Fantasia: An Algerian Cavalcade*, 29, 85, 86–87, 90–92, 95, 104, 105, 110–11, 154; *Far from Madina*, 103, 113; *Femmes d'Alger*, 86, 101–2, 103; and FLN, 88; *Les Impatients*, 104, 105, 107, 110, 113, 135; language of the body, 35; metaphor, use of, 102–3; multilingualism, 85, 86–89, 91–92, 93–94, 95–97; *The Nouba*, 91, 104, 161n24; *Les Nuits de Strasbourg*, 103, 112–13; *Nulle part dans la maison de mon père*, 90; reception, 88; *A Sister to Scheherazade*, 102, 103, 104, 111–12; *La Soif*, 88, 96, 106; *So Vast the Prison*, 92–93; *The Tongue's Blood Does Not Run Dry*, 98–100, 103; and women's Arabic, 89–90; *The Zerda and the Songs of Forgetting*, 85, 88, 91, 94, 104
Donadey, Anne, 86, 92, 103, 162n9, 166n47, 176n2, 178n12
Doyle, Arthur Conan, 79
Du Bellay, Joachim, 40, 51, 54
Du Bois, W. E. B.: *The Souls of Black Folk*, 17, 33
Dumas, Alexandre, 50

Dupont, Pierre, 40
Dutt, Aru, 39–40, 43. *See also* Dutt, Toru: *A Sheaf Gleaned in French Fields*
Dutt, Govin Chandra, 39
Dutt, Michael Chandra, 39
Dutt, Romesh Chandra, 2
Dutt, Toru, 2, 10, 19, 22, 29, 143, 147, 148, 151, 152–53, 154, 156, 157; *Ancient Ballads and Legends of Hindustan*, 39, 41–42, 57; "Baugmaree," 57, 58–59, 61, 155; *Bianca, or The Young Spanish Maiden*, 37, 42, 56–57; on Calcutta, 62–63; cosmopolitanism, 37, 38, 39, 60, 62–63, 64–65, 148; creolized identity, 58–59, 60; *The Diary of Mlle D'Arvers*, 29, 37, 42–43, 45, 55–56, 57; family, 2, 39, 43, 57; France, time in, 39, 49; Indian identity, 41, 45–47, 55, 56–57, 58, 59, 62; letters, 39, 43, 44, 46–47, 62–63, 147; "The Lotus," 58; nationalism, 37; reception of, 45–46; religion, 39, 42–43, 46–47, 59; *A Sheaf Gleaned in French Fields*, 39–41, 45, 48–55; social class in, 56. *See also* Hinduism
Dwivedi, A. N., 39, 41

Eden, 58, 59
education, 19, 34–35, 42, 45–46, 47, 60, 79, 87–88, 96–97, 164–65n35
Egypt, 1–2, 6, 66, 79, 145, 164–65n35; education in, 34; multilingualism, 75–76; in Ziyadah, 68, 72, 73–74, 80. *See also* Cairo
elegy, 40, 101–2
elitism, 25, 64, 84, 149
Emancipation Act of 1833, 118
English (language), 3, 4, 7, 11, 144, 151, 155; in Devi, 119, 121–22, 123, 126, 133, 144; in Djebar, 87, 97; in Dutt, 37, 39–40, 41, 42–44, 44–47, 52–53, 54, 57, 59, 68, 143, 147; language of empire, 4, 22, 34, 151, 154; in Mauritius, 117, 122; in Ziyadah, 72, 74, 76
enjoyment, 30, 145–46, 147, 148, 164. *See also* jouissance; pleasure
Escher, M. C., 115
Eurocentrism, 12, 63, 76
Even-Zohar, Itamar, 81, 82, 175n44
exile, 20, 40, 88, 109, 144, 164n32, 185–86n60

Fahmi, 'Abd al-'Aziz, 2, 173n29
Fanon, Frantz, 2, 3, 19, 24–25, 29, 31, 33, 34, 147, 149, 152, 153, 178n14; "The Black Man and Language," 27; *Black Skin, White Masks*, 17–18, 20–22, 23–24, 25, 28; *A Dying Colonialism*, 11, 138–39; "The North African Syndrome," 20–21; "Practice Log," 21
Fanon, Josie, 2
femininity, 25
feminism, 19, 29, 165, 178n12
Flax, Jane, 29
FLN (Front de Libération Nationale), 2, 26, 88
flowers, 40, 53, 57–58, 91, 154, 156
Forster, E. M.: *A Passage to India*, 26–27, 136
Foucault, Michel, 9
France, 7; colonial history, 2, 85, 97; in Djebar, 98, 144; in Dutt, 48; in Fanon, 20; in Ziyadah, 82
French (language), 7, 11, 21, 22, 23, 34, 35–36, 143–45, 146, 147, 151, 154, 155–56; in Devi, 117, 121–22, 123, 126; in Djebar, 86–88, 89–91, 92–93, 94, 95–97, 98–102, 103, 111, 113, 114, 115; in Dutt, 37, 38, 39–41, 42–43, 44, 45, 49–51, 52–53, 55–56; language of empire, 3, 4, 21, 22; Parisian, 11; toxicity of, 13; in Ziyadah, 67, 68, 70, 71–72, 74, 75–76, 77, 81–82
Freud, Sigmund, 18, 25

Front de Libération Nationale. *See* FLN
fusha, 7, 68, 74, 75–76, 82, 86, 92, 93, 95–97, 100, 122

Galilé, 72
Ganga (deity), 53
Ganges (river), 53
Gaskell, Elizabeth, 43
Gates, H. L., 25
Gautier, Théophile, 40
Gauvin, Lise, 4, 8, 35, 36, 191n2
gender, 2, 15, 24–25, 29, 30, 33, 144, 152; in Devi, 124, 125, 127, 135, 139; in Djebar, 86, 87, 90, 92–93, 96, 102, 104, 110–12, 113, 114; in Dutt, 44, 45–46, 56; in Fanon, 22, 25; in postcolonial thought, 17; in Ziyadah, 70, 73
gender studies, 4, 19–20
genocide, linguistic, 97
geopoetics, 70, 73, 149
geopolitics, 70, 83
German (language), 50, 51, 68, 74, 75, 93, 113, 114, 143
Gibran, Gibran Khalil, 67, 78, 79, 82; *The Prophet*, 67
Glissant, Édouard, 19, 32–33, 130–31, 147, 149, 160n12, 165n38, 191n2
Global South, 29
Godden, Rumer, 136, 138; *The River*, 136
Goëthe, Johann Wolfgang von, 50, 51, 54
Gosse, Edmund, 41, 45, 48–49, 167n9
Greek, 77, 82, 87, 93, 97, 113, 114
Guattari, Félix, 176n47
guilt, 3, 6, 9–10, 12, 17, 41, 46, 57, 78, 144, 155–56
Gunew, Sneja, 65

Haykal, Muhammed Husayn, 68, 76, 83
Hebrew (language), 12, 51
hegemony, 8–9, 24, 29, 66, 68, 71, 82–84, 117, 151, 169n31, 169–70nn36–37
Hind, the, 42

Hindi (language), 77
Hinduism, 2, 39, 40, 43, 44, 45, 46–47, 51, 77; in Devi, 123, 125; in Mauritius, 118, 119; mythology, 42, 45. *See also* Dutt, Toru: religion
homosexuality, 25, 67, 70, 120, 124, 125–26, 127, 131
hospitality, 38, 64, 71
Hugo, Victor, 11, 40–41, 50–51, 54, 149, 153, 167n15
Humbert, Marie-Thérèse, 2
Husayn, Taha, 70–71, 76, 83, 173n29
hybridity, 18, 26, 27–28, 29, 48, 55–57, 118, 151–52, 173

Ibn Badis, 97
Ibn Rushd, 15, 97
Imalhayène, Fatima Zohra. *See* Djebar, Assia
India, 1–2, 7, 34, 37, 136, 145; in Devi, 119, 129, 136; in Dutt, 41–42, 46, 49, 52–53, 54, 55, 147, 149; migration from, 117, 118; nationalism, 38, 45, 60; traditional literature of, 55, 56, 57, 59. *See also* Calcutta; Devi, Ananda; Dutt, Toru; Tagore, Rabindranath
Indian Ocean, 2, 10, 119
intersubjectivity, 5, 8, 34, 159
Italian (language), 68, 74, 77, 108

Jogadhy Uma, 42
jouissance, 30, 32, 146. *See also* enjoyment; pleasure
joy, 10, 12, 29, 30, 32, 73, 89, 107, 124, 130, 155, 157
Jung, Carl, 24

Kadel, Yussuf, 2
Kalidasa, 51, 149, 153
Kaya (singer), 122, 187n10
Kellman, Steven, 7
Khaldi, Boutheina, 67, 75–76, 171n19

Khatibi, Abdelkebir, 6, 9, 19, 32–34, 35–36, 161n4, 165n38, 165n42
Khoury, Raif Georges, 67, 75, 79, 81–82, 170nn6–7
Koener. *See* Körner, Carl Theodor
Körner, Carl Theodor, 51, 54
Kristeva, Julia, 30, 164n34; *The Crisis of the European Subject*, 15, 146
Kumar, Nita, 9
Kymlicka, Will, 129

La Fontaine, Jean de, 51, 54
Lakshman, 42
Lamartine, Alphonse de, 40, 41, 51, 72, 73–74, 75, 153, 172n20, 172n27
landscape, 7, 12, 13, 19, 145, 149, 153, 155–56; in Devi, 119, 132; in Djebar, 85, 91–92, 95, 104, 105–7, 108–10, 113, 115–16; in Dutt, 42, 50, 57, 59, 60, 61, 62, 64; in Ziyadah, 71–74, 80
La Rochefoucauld, François de, 72
Latin (language), 12, 15, 70, 77, 82, 87, 91, 93, 97, 113, 114, 120
Lebanon, 72, 73, 75
Leconte de Lisle, Charles Marie René, 40, 41, 149
lesbianism. *See* homosexuality
Lionnet, Françoise, 4, 29, 61, 117, 162n9, 164n32, 165n42, 176n2, 177n8, 178n12, 182n45, 191n2
Lokugé, Chandani, 57, 168n23, 169n29, 169n32
Lootens, Tricia, 54
loss, 7, 20, 26, 31, 35, 52, 53, 89, 91, 132, 153, 157
lyric, 29, 59, 73, 101–2

Madina, 104, 113
Madra, 42
Maghreb, the, 6, 33, 68, 122; in Djebar, 91–92, 95, 104, 105, 108, 112, 113; language in, 86, 89

Mahabharata, 41, 42, 50, 51
Mahjar, 67, 78
Malabou, Catherine, 8, 162n15
Malinche, La, 19
Mallarmé, Stéphane, 75
Manfaluti, Mustafa Lutfi al, 80
Manichean division, 27, 31
Martin (Miss), Mary E. R., 43, 46, 62
Martin, Nicolas, 40, 50
Mauritius, 1–2, 6, 117–19, 120, 145; Creole language in, 122, 124, 130, 131, 144; cultural identity in, 128–30; in Devi, 132, 136
Mead, Georges Herbert, 5, 159n4
Meddeb, Abdelwahab: *Talismano*, 33
Mediterranean Sea, 10, 72, 91, 108, 154
melancholia, 10, 30, 53, 106, 135–36, 138, 146, 164
Memmi, Albert, 17, 95, 152, 153
Messali, Hadj, 97
metaphor, 35, 55; in Arabic, 11; cities as, 132, 145; in Devi, 120, 132; in Djebar, 94, 96, 98, 101, 102–3, 177n4; in Dutt, 42, 55, 57, 59, 60, 64, 147; in Ziyadah, 72
Mignolo, Walter D., 63, 170n37
Milton, John, 54
minarets, 74, 156, 176n47
Mistral, Frédéric, 81
modernity, 18, 63, 68; in Devi, 138; in Djebar, 108, 114; in Ziyadah, 76, 84
Molière, 51, 54
Mongol Empire, 51
Montaigne, Michel de, 15, 40
moon, 42, 58–59
Morrison, Toni, 132, 153, 154
Muhammad, Prophet, 113
Mukherjee, Meenakshi, 44
Müller, Max, 79–80
multilingualism, 1, 3, 4–5, 5–8, 12, 148, 157, 159–60n10, 177n4; in Djebar, 85–86, 88; in Dutt, 63–64; in

Mauritius, 131; in Ziyadah, 66, 67, 75–76. See also pluralism: linguistic
murder, 121, 122, 125
Musset, Alfred de, 40, 41, 54
Mutran, Khalil, 2

Nahda (Arab renaissance), 2, 30, 66, 67, 68, 71, 73, 75, 102, 164–65n35, 166n44, 171–72n19
Nancy, Jean-Luc: *Being Singular Plural*, 15, 58
Napoléon, 40
nationalism, 2, 8, 31, 45, 55, 97, 146, 151–52, 153, 156, 157; Algerian, 97, 104; Bengali, 38; in Devi, 125, 136; Dutt's, 37, 62–63, 65; idealist, 65; Indian, 38, 45, 60, 61, 62–65; in the Nahda movement, 66, 70, 76, 79, 83; in Ziyadah, 76, 79. See also transnationalism
National Liberation Front. See FLN
Nazareth, 72
Nerval, Gérard de, 40, 51
networks, 8, 51, 52, 53–54, 60, 63, 69, 84, 105
New Delhi, 12, 133, 134, 137, 139, 140
New York, 78, 84, 113
Ngugi wa Thiong'o, 3
Nibelungen, the, 50, 51
Nile, 10
Nodier, Charles, 40, 50

Odysseus, 40
Oedipus complex, 25, 162n14
ontology, 3, 9, 15, 17, 33, 35, 85, 152
oppositionality, 19–20, 22–23, 26, 28. See also Bhabha, Homi: Third Space; polarity
orality, 20, 143, 144, 149, 181n38, 187n5; in Djebar, 89, 98, 99–100, 101, 102–3, 113
Oran, 93, 104, 112, 139, 185n60
Orientalism, 42, 69, 73–74, 80, 145, 153, 173n29

Orlando, Valérie, 88, 124, 162n9, 166n47
Orpheus, 59
Ottoman Empire, 2, 66, 68, 69, 78, 81, 114–15
Outtar, Tahar, 83
overconsciousness, linguistic, 4, 35

Padua, 113
pan-Arabism, 2, 68, 70, 71, 80, 83
pan-Islamism, 2, 68, 71, 80, 83
Paris, 51, 81, 84, 104, 105, 113, 114, 140, 145
Parry, Benita, 24
Pascal, Blaise, 72, 172n22
Patel, Shenaz, 2, 118
patriarchy, 10, 16, 44, 133, 178n17
Penman, Leigh, 12
Pereira, Lindsay, 43
plasticity, 149, 151, 155, 161n5, 168n19; of aurality, 95; brain, 60; of cinema, 94; concept of, 162n15; of culture, 19; in Devi, 119, 136; in Djebar, 94; in Dutt, 60, 64; of interpretation, 115–16; of languages, 19, 21, 23, 30, 31, 124; of literature, 146, 147; of poetry, 11, 12, 36, 147, 153, 156; of self, 29, 37, 57, 60, 64; of subjectivity, 8, 18, 28, 31, 38; of writing, 35, 114, 147
pleasure, 15, 32, 41, 56. See also enjoyment; jouissance
pluralism, 5, 8, 12, 16–17, 18, 25, 29, 32, 84, 145–46, 147–48, 151, 157, 164–65nn35–36, 166n48; Arab, 82; in cityscape, 11, 12; cultural, 1, 19, 26, 74; in Devi, 119, 120, 124, 128, 130; in Djebar, 86, 103; in Dutt, 37, 56–57, 58, 60, 63, 149; linguistic, 6, 9–10, 11, 17, 35, 56–57, 63, 124; in Mauritius, 128, 130; in self, 4, 13, 29–31, 57, 152, 156; in Ziyadah, 69, 70, 71, 74, 82, 83, 84. See also multilingualism
Poe, Edgar Allan, 72

poetics, 8, 16–17, 19, 28, 36, 147, 171n15; bilingual, 95; in Devi, 132; in Djebar, 85, 92, 95, 96; in Dutt, 44, 54, 55, 57, 60, 61, 149; ethics of, 147; of genre, 54; of relation, 33, 70, 74; of subject, 9, 10, 31, 38, 39, 57, 60, 61, 149; transcultural, 17, 61; in Ziyadah, 70, 73, 74
polarity, 27–28. *See also* Bhabha, Homi: Third Space; oppositionality
polymorphism, 38, 146
polysystems, 81, 82, 84
Port Louis, 10, 11, 121, 132–33, 134, 136, 137, 139–40, 145, 154, 155, 169n36
Prabhu, Anjali, 117, 118
Pratt, Mary Louise, 4
Prehad, 42
Prudhomme, Sully, 40
psychoanalysis, 17, 18, 19, 20, 24, 164n34
Pyamootoo, Barlen, 2, 118

Qais, Imru al, 153
Quran, the, 75, 90, 94, 122, 143, 153, 177n10
Quranic school, 35, 87

Racine, Jean, 51, 54
raga, 59
Ramayana, the, 40–41, 42, 50, 147
rape, 121. *See also* sexual assault
Ray, Satyajit, 136, 138, 148; *Mahanagar*, 136, 148
readers, 6, 7, 8, 12, 23, 54, 105, 141, 153, 157, 165n36, 166n45, 168n21, 173n28, 177n4, 191n5; Abbasid era, 70; absolute, 29; Algerian, 99; bilingual, 95; of Devi, 136; in Djebar, 113; of Djebar, 85, 86, 92, 95, 98, 99–100, 113; Dutt as a, 38, 39, 40, 41, 49, 50, 51, 54, 62, 147; of Dutt, 40, 42, 51–52, 54, 57, 59, 61; Egyptian, 80; European, 59; of Fanon, 23, 26; Francophone, 95, 133, 136; Indian, 56; multilingual, 9, 55, 60, 71, 84; Muslim, 113; North African, 87; of Tagore, 48; Ziyadah as a, 66, 70, 71
Renoir, Jean, 136, 138; *The River*, 136
Rimbaud, Arthur, 59
Romanticism, 44, 51, 72–73, 80. *See also* Byron, George Gordon, Lord
Rousseau, Jean-Jacques, 72

Sagan, Françoise, 2
Said, Edward, 17, 153, 166n1
Sakuntala, 44, 149
Sanskrit, 12, 39–42, 51, 57, 122, 147, 153, 167
Sartre, Jean-Paul, 8, 52
Savitri, 42
Sayyid, Ahmad Lutfi al-, 2, 75, 171–72n19, 173n29
Scheherezade, 102–3, 104
Schiller, Friedrich, 32, 50–51, 54, 162n16
schizophrenia, postcolonial, 32, 74, 146. *See also* Bhabha, Homi: Third Space; splitting
Scott, Walter, 50, 81–82
segregation, 12, 45, 87, 90, 118, 121, 125, 126, 127, 128
self, 1, 9, 10, 13, 18, 26–27, 28, 144, 153, 156, 160n11, 161n24; colonized, 56; creolization of, 12, 29, 48, 58–59, 60, 63, 64, 151; in Djebar, 87, 92, 104, 114; in Dutt, 37, 39, 46, 48, 56, 57, 58–59, 60, 62, 63, 64; hegemonic, 8; Indigenous, 13; multicultural, 11; multilingual, 37; plurality of, 30–31; postcolonial, 137, 152; in Ziyadah, 70
self-repair, 12
self-translation, 4, 5, 11, 12, 21, 24
semiosis, 5, 8, 152, 154
semiotics, 3, 5–7, 114–15, 138, 142–43, 152, 154, 155, 156–57, 162n7, 176n48, 191n5
sexual assault, 135
Shakespeare, William, 54, 72, 73, 149, 153, 172n23; *The Tempest*, 16

Shawqi, Ahmad, 2
Sheehi, Stephen, 69, 170n8, 173n28, 173n30
Shelley, Mary, 72
Shih, Shu-mei, 29
silence, 25, 30, 34, 84, 147; in Devi, 127, 132; in Djebar, 89, 94, 96, 97, 105, 109
Simrock, Karl, 50
Sindhu, 42
Sita, 42, 44, 149
slavery, 20, 27, 118, 169n32
Solomon, 51
Souls of Black Folk, The (DuBois), 17, 33
Souza de, Eunice, 43. *See also* Pereira, Lindsay
speech, 18, 20, 25, 34, 68, 78, 103, 131, 151
Spivak, Gayatri, 17
splitting, 17–18, 21, 26, 30, 32, 146, 156, 164n28; definition of, 27–28; in Djebar, 90, 109, 114; in Dutt, 57, 59, 60, 62, 64; in Tagore, 47, 48; in Ziyadah, 74. *See also* Bhabha, Homi: Third Space; schizophrenia, postcolonial
Starr, Deborah, 67, 170n3
Stendhal, 106–7
Strasbourg, 103, 104, 112, 114
subaltern language, 121–22, 131
subject, 9–10, 15–19, 32, 33, 142–43, 146, 149, 151, 155–56; in Bhabha, 18–19, 34; colonized, 3, 4, 5, 6, 34, 38, 47, 63, 137–38, 144, 155; creolized, 64, 73; in Devi, 121, 124, 137–38; in Djebar, 92, 96, 98–100, 103, 109, 114–16; in Dutt, 43, 46, 47, 48, 57, 60, 61, 63, 64, 65, 147; European, 18; in Fanon, 17, 18, 20–22, 24–25, 34; feminine, 34, 38, 96, 121, 144, 151; multilingual, 3, 8–9, 11, 16, 147; ontological, 3–4; plastic, 8; poetics of, 38, 39, 57, 60, 61; polymorphism of, 38; postcolonial, 9, 17, 18, 28, 29, 31, 32, 34, 145, 146, 148, 149, 152; schizophrenia of, 32, 146; split, 30, 60; white normative notion of, 18; in Ziyadah, 69, 71, 72, 73
subjectivity, 3, 5, 9–10, 13, 15–19, 23–25, 34, 35–36, 38, 48, 149, 152, 157; in Bhabha, 26; Black masculine, 17; colonized, 3, 12; in Devi, 125, 138, 140; Djebar, 85, 109, 114–15, 116; in Dutt, 60, 62, 64; feminine, 34, 151; multilingual, 10, 11, 19–20, 32; plural, 16–17; postcolonial, 16, 17, 18–19, 26, 28, 30–31, 33, 115, 138, 143, 148, 156; in Ziyadah, 68, 72, 84
Syria, 68, 72–73

Tachenwit, 86, 87, 89, 93
Tagore, Rabindranath, 2, 59, 133–34, 136, 138, 153; *Towards Universal Man*, 37, 38, 47–48
Tahtawi, Rifa'a Rafi' al, 68, 80
Tamazight, 11, 15, 36, 66, 83, 86–87, 89, 91–92, 93–95, 96, 143–44, 153, 161n2
Thackeray, William, 43, 50
Tibériade, 72
Torabully, Khal, 2, 186n3
transculturality, 17, 19, 30, 31, 38, 61, 63–64, 70, 82, 84
translation, 4–5, 6, 10, 19, 21, 28, 31, 32–33, 35–36, 75, 142, 143, 144–45, 146–47, 148, 149, 151, 155–57; in Devi, 122, 123, 124; in Djebar, 85, 86, 89, 93–94, 95, 96, 97, 100, 103, 115–16; in Dutt, 37, 39, 40, 42, 44, 48, 50–55, 61; masked, 9; process of, 5; self and, 4, 5, 11, 21, 24, 31; way of being, 32; writing as, 8; in Ziyadah, 70, 78, 79–81, 82, 83
transnationalism, 38, 71, 84. *See also* nationalism
trauma, 4, 9–10, 16, 17, 18, 20–22, 24, 25, 31, 33, 35, 62, 65, 114, 146

unheimlich (uncanny), 74, 101
universalism, 31, 37, 48, 54, 56, 59, 61, 82–83, 117–18, 170n37, 174n32, 176n49

Valéry, Paul, 10
Vigny, Alfred de, 40
Vishnu Purana, 41
Voltaire, 72

walking, 10, 104, 105–7, 108–9, 111–12, 124, 134, 137, 138, 139–40
war, 17, 88, 109, 112–13, 114, 144
weltliteratur, 70, 71, 82–83
Westernization, 47, 74
women, 10, 87, 96, 107–8, 126–27, 144, 151, 164n30; in Devi, 122–23, 124, 125, 134, 135, 136, 139, 140; in Djebar, 87, 89–90, 91, 92–93, 94, 95, 101, 110–12, 113–14; in Dutt, 43, 44–46; education, 34–35; language, use of, 45–46, 92–93, 94, 147; writers, 1, 3, 7, 8, 11, 13, 15, 17, 19, 22, 23, 30–31, 34–36, 43, 44, 71, 146, 150, 153, 155, 157. *See also* Ziyadah, Mayy: women's awakening
World War I, 69

Yazidji, Ibrahim al, 75
Young Turk Revolution, 68

Zaydan, Jurji, 68, 74, 76, 83
Ziyadah, Ilyas, 71
Ziyadah, Mayy, 2, 10, 19, 29, 66, 142, 143, 147, 148, 151, 152, 153, 156; *adab*, 70–71, 82, 84; Arabness in writing, 69; background, 67; and Byron, 72–73, 74; cosmopolitanism, 67, 69, 70, 81, 83; "fadlu al adab" ("Apology of literature"), 77–79, 83; family, 71; *Fleurs de rêve*, 70, 71–73, 74, 157; homosexuality, 67, 70; hospitalization, 67; *ibtissamat wa dumu*,' 79–80; on language, 67, 68–69, 71, 75–79; and the Mahjar, 78; multiculturalism, 70; and the Nahda, 67, 68, 72, 73; religion, 70; salon, 2, 69, 75–76, 171n19; "Speak Your Language," 67, 69, 76; translations, 79–81; "Un matin," 73; women's awakening, 69

www.ingramcontent.com/pod-product-compliance
Lightning Source LLC
Chambersburg PA
CBHW031812220426
43662CB00007B/609